IN CONCERT

ONSTAGE *and*
OFFSTAGE *with the*
BOSTON SYMPHONY
ORCHESTRA

Carl A. Vigeland

THE UNIVERSITY OF MASSACHUSETTS PRESS
AMHERST

for Bonnie

ML
1211.8
.B72
B78
1991

Originally published in 1989 by William Morrow and Company.
First paperback edition, 1991, by The University of Massachusetts Press.
All rights reserved
Printed in the United States of America
LC 91–18760
ISBN 0–87023-763-2

Library of Congress Cataloging-in-Publication Data
Vigeland, Carl A.
    In concert : onstage and offstage with the Boston Symphony
  Orchestra / Carl A. Vigeland.
        p.   cm.
    Reprint. Originally published: New York : Morrow, 1989.
    Includes bibliographical references (p.   ).
    ISBN 0–87023–763–2 (pbk. : alk. paper)
    1. Boston Symphony Orchestra.   I. Title.
ML1211.8.B72B78   1991
784.2 ' 06 ' 074461—dc20   91–18760
                                                              CIP
                                                              MN

Book design by Richard Oriolo

IN CONCERT

*L*ong before he leaves home this morning, Charlie Schlueter can feel the knot in his stomach begin to tighten. It happens every time he has to go to work. He gets up early, usually by six o'clock, and fixes breakfast, including the first of many cups of black coffee he will drink today. After nervously puttering by himself in the kitchen, putting away the dishes from the dishwasher, he glances at the *Boston Globe* the newsboy left on the porch of his simple, comfortable house in Newtonville, Massachusetts. Today is September 30, 1986, the first day of the Boston Symphony Orchestra's new season, so there are no reviews about him in the newspaper. That's a relief.

In a few hours, at 10:30 A.M., Charlie must be onstage in Symphony Hall to begin the rehearsal of Gustav Mahler's Second Symphony, the *Resurrection*. Charlie is the principal trumpet in the orchestra, a job that means more than the honor of being titular head of his section. He not only plays the most difficult trumpet solos—and any solo on the trumpet is difficult—but he also sets a tonal standard for the entire brass section, a standard that influences the way the whole orchestra sounds.

Handling the pressure of his highly vulnerable position is a constant test of his nerves, and though Charlie tries, as he puts it, "to stay a day ahead of the struggle," the nature of his profession makes tension inevitable whenever he must rehearse or perform. He says goodbye to his wife, Martha. Their two grown daughters are away at school, and Martha, an accomplished violinist, has started to spend more of her time painting in an upstairs studio at home. Charlie puts his trumpet in the passenger seat of the Toyota Corolla and backs out of the driveway onto Otis Street for the twenty-minute drive to the hall.

"Playing the trumpet is hard because it's so easy," Charlie often says. He likes aphorisms. "What I do makes no product; it's all process" is another of his favorites. He also likes analogies, which usually take the form of anecdotes that he weaves into conversation.

The pitch rising in his natural tenor voice, he recalls an incident a few seasons ago, when guest conductor Bernard Haitink led the BSO in Mahler's Seventh Symphony. At a rehearsal, the faint plaintiveness of the first chords didn't sound the way Haitink wanted them to. So Haitink stopped the orchestra and told a story about Mahler's writing this piece. Haitink said that when Mahler created the beginning of the symphony he'd been rowing a boat on the lake where he was spending the summer. Think of the sound of the oars, Haitink told the players. As soon as he heard this story, Charlie said, his sense of the music's character changed.

But this morning he is not preoccupied with the subjective qualities of Mahler's music. Guiding his car through the busy suburban traffic of Newton, Charlie tries not to think about everything that could go wrong when he gets to the hall. His part in the Mahler Second is extremely demanding, calling for endurance as well as skill, with several exposed spots of solo playing. For him, rehearsing with music director Seiji Ozawa is in many ways more unsettling than presenting a concert. No instrument stands out more in the orchestra than his, and Charlie has repeatedly gotten himself into terrible trouble for standing out too much. Yet he yearns to do just the opposite, to draw attention not to himself but to the music. In Charlie's view, he and his music director simply disagree on how. It is as though with each phrase he must prove himself. Mahler Two, as Charlie and most of his colleagues call it, will be an ordeal.

But Charlie's anxiety is mixed with anticipation. Mahler is his favorite composer. His writing for the trumpet, says Charlie, "is lyrical and refined, not just, 'Here I am a trumpet player.' "

Mahler is also unpredictable, a quality Charlie admires. He hates to do the same thing twice, and even in the most routine, pedestrian score he will look for a fresh nuance. Mahler, however, is never routine. "Just when you think he's going to be lyrical, there's a quirk. Mahler's always pushing and pulling. That's the nice thing about him, the constant shifting about. The music's schizophrenic. Each one of his symphonies is like a whole lifetime."

Charlie's life began in 1939 far from Boston in the coal-mining town of Du Quoin, Illinois. It is a community where success consists of keeping a roof over one's family and putting enough food on the table for them to survive. Music, the kind of music Charlie plays for a living, could strike most Du Quoin men and women as an anomaly in a world where the basic virtues are hard work and sacrifice. To this day, there are Schlueter relatives who don't understand what Charlie does.

If he had followed in his father's footsteps, Charlie would have entered the coal mines after finishing high school. But when Charlie was ten years old, his father introduced him to another miner, Charles Archibald, who was also a Du Quoin music teacher and an amateur trumpet player. Though Charlie had picked out an accordion in the Sears catalog, Archibald persuaded him to start with the cornet instead. Archibald's lessons were expensive for the Schlueters—seventy-five cents—but Charlie's father supported his son's interest in music, even if he did not completely understand it. Perhaps the lessons would help Charlie escape a life in the mines of Du Quoin. Charlie quickly discovered that practicing the trumpet was a way out, not of Du Quoin, but of doing household chores and, as he got older, homework.

But when Charlie was thirteen years old, his father became very sick and had to quit his job. And the Schlueters could no longer afford to pay for Charlie's trumpet lessons.

That year at school, a drawing contest was sponsored by the Egyptian Music Company (southern Illinois is known as Little Egypt, because two of the towns on the bordering Mississippi River are called Thebes and Cairo). Don Lemasters, a trumpet player and professor at nearby Southern Illinois University in Carbondale, was a partner in the Du Quoin branch of the music company, and first prize in the drawing contest was ten lessons with Lemasters on whatever instrument the winner selected.

Charlie entered the contest. Luckily, the boy's musical ability was matched by artistic talent. Charlie's winning drawing of a Christmas scene meant he could continue studying the trumpet for at least ten weeks.

Lemasters knew Charlie's family was poor, and he knew Charlie's father was sick. And before Charlie's ten lessons were over, Lemasters also knew that his young pupil was not just another boy who wanted to play the trumpet in his school's marching band. This young trumpeter was special.

Most of Don Lemasters's students showed up for their lessons armed with excuses about why they hadn't been able to practice during the past week. But Charlie practiced all the time. And he always learned what Lemasters had taught him at the last lesson.

"I can't pay for any more lessons," Charlie had to tell Lemasters after his ten weeks were up.

"I know," Lemasters said. "You don't have to. You can study with me for free."

Charlie played his first solo, *Adeste Fideles*, in fifth grade. When he was twelve, 14,000 people heard him at the Du Quoin Fair.

By the time Charlie was halfway through high school, Lemasters realized he'd taught his star pupil all he could and telephoned his friend Ed Brauer, who played trumpet in the St. Louis Symphony. He offered to pay Brauer for Charlie's lessons, if Brauer could fit him in. Brauer told Lemasters to keep his money and he found a space for Charlie in his busy schedule—Saturday mornings at 7:30.

For two years, Charlie got up each Saturday at 4 A.M. so he could make the drive to St. Louis for his lesson. His father had bought him a new trumpet, for which Mr. Schlueter had had to sign a promissory note. Charlie played in two bands, Du Quoin High's Indianairs and his own Charlie Schlueter and His Orchestra. While most of his friends planned to put away their trumpets and trombones, flutes and clarinets after high school, Charlie was determined to enter the musical world beyond Du Quoin. His next step was as easy as it was audacious.

Though he had no idea how he would pay for it, Charlie applied to the Juilliard School in New York City, probably the most prestigious music conservatory in the United States. Juilliard in the 1950s was headed by the American composer William Schuman. Some of the finest instrumentalists in the world taught there, and its string quartet, which took the name of the school, was renowned. For a high school senior from Du Quoin, Illinois, Juilliard represented not only an escape from the coal mines but also the expression of a wish to experience something new and largely unknown. And it was an early demonstration of what would become a lifelong trait, the capacity to grow.

Charlie was accepted in the class of 1961. He had a small scholarship, and earned the rest of his tuition by playing in a salsa band at a Puerto Rican nightclub in upper Manhattan. He also sang in a church choir, for which he received five dollars a week; that covered a quarter of his weekly expenses. At Juilliard, Charlie often practiced six or seven hours a day. "It kept my mind off being lonely and depressed, and having to do other work," he says.

At Juilliard, Charlie studied with William Vacchiano, beginning a relationship that he would remember affectionately as "four years of agony. I never knew what was going to happen." By virtue of his position as the New York Philharmonic's principal trumpet player as well as his teaching association with Juilliard, Vacchiano was considered the most illustrious classical trumpeter in the country. Only the best trumpet students at Juilliard studied with him, and they were required to audition before he accepted them.

Charlie had met someone who was more than his match. No matter how well he played, Vacchiano always saw room for improvement. At Charlie's first lesson, the celebrated teacher asked Charlie to turn to page 59 of Arban's *Complete Conservatory Method for Trumpet*. Since childhood, Charlie had been playing from this comprehensive 350-page manual of exercises and études by a nineteenth-century French virtuoso, Joseph Jean Baptiste Laurent Arban. The page Vacchiano requested began with one of the first things he had ever learned, a C-major scale. Somewhat befuddled by the easiness of the assignment, Charlie nevertheless did as he had been told. Had he really come all the way from Du Quoin to play this?

But Vacchiano interrupted Charlie repeatedly to correct his attack, phrasing, and breathing. Written in 2/4 time—two beats to a measure, with a quarter note getting one beat—the first exercise Vacchiano requested requires staccato tonguing. Each note must be given a clean, sharp attack, the trumpeter showing no strain as the scale ascends. The spaces between the notes that make them staccato must be even. Further sequences in the exercise present different combinations of loud and soft, and add increasingly difficult intervals between some of the notes. Intervals are tricky on the trumpet because they are often played without a change in the fingering. To get an interval right, the player must trust his ear and control the tension in his lips.

Uncountable other Arban exercises filled Charlie's lesson and practice hours, and he still uses the volume today with his own students. Mastering the trumpet's technique under Vacchiano taught Charlie something he doesn't like to remind his students: Playing the trumpet is hard because it is *hard*.

What Charlie learned or relearned from Vacchiano was to have a connection to everything he played in his professional career. There is a direct link between the staccato notes in that first Arban exercise and numerous places in the Second Symphony of Gustav Mahler. And Vacchiano was always dispensing tips. "Never keep the tuning slide in the same place," he'd remind Charlie. "No good musician accents an upbeat," he'd say. Or "A staccato eighth note followed by a sixteenth note is short." Like a father giving advice to his son, Vacchiano was getting Charlie ready to handle the musical challenges ("Carry two mutes, one for high notes and one for low") and personal challenges ahead ("Talk back to the conductor"). And, he told him, "when you're onstage and the lights go out and you're going to be broadcast, always look for security." Vacchiano meant a player shouldn't take unnecessary chances, advice that headstrong Charlie would not always follow.

Three things made a good trumpet player, according to Vacchiano. "First of all, you have to be a good bugler." Then, he continued, "you have to read." You must, in other words, know your instrument's literature and understand what different composers require of you in their scores. This, of course, is only possible if you possess a trumpet player's third quality. "You have to know what you're doing." Vacchiano liked to let that phrase dangle. He didn't want its simplicity to mask its significance.

By 1961, Charlie was a good bugler, becoming better. Completely, irrevocably, he was also on his own. His father had died when Charlie was eighteen, leaving Charlie free to make the final break from Du Quoin, but with the responsibility to go home whenever he could to see that his mother was provided for. And Charlie had met his future wife, who was studying the violin in New York and who lived in the same apartment building as he did. One night Martha heard Charlie's trumpet through her open window. A diminutive but feisty woman who acts on her thoughts, Martha wondered who was playing so beautifully and found out by ringing the doorbell of Charlie's apartment. They were an unlikely match, Charlie, from a strict Lutheran family, and Martha, a New York Jew, but they fell in love and got married the year of his graduation. Instead of taking a honeymoon, they traveled on a cross-country tour for five months as players in the American Ballet Theatre's orchestra.

Returning to his midwestern roots, Charlie in the next decade established himself as one of the country's top orchestral trumpeters. He held jobs as principal or co-principal in Kansas City, Milwaukee, and Cleveland, before taking the position of principal trumpet in Minneapolis in 1972. Then, in 1981, exactly twenty years after leaving New York, he and Martha returned east to Boston. It was a move that would shake the foundations of Charlie's career.

Winning the audition for the BSO job had been almost too easy. If he'd been a baseball pitcher, it would have been like throwing a no-hitter in his first game with a new team.

Under normal audition procedures, the BSO advertises an opening and invites candidates to send taped examples of their playing from a prescribed list of pieces. An audition committee screens these tapes and winnows the applicants. Those who survive this cut are asked to come to Boston to play for the committee behind a screen placed in the middle of the stage, hiding their identities. And the finalists from this group then play before Seiji Ozawa and the committee without the screen. For a principal position, the final candidates sometimes play with the orchestra as well. Then the audition committee makes a recommendation to Seiji on whom to select for the job. It is Seiji's decision whether to accept that recommendation.

The orchestra had actually tried to persuade Charlie to audition when Armando Ghitalla announced he was retiring after the 1978–79 season. Personnel manager Bill Moyer wanted Charlie to apply for the position being vacated by Ghitalla. Moyer, who had begun his BSO career as a trombonist in the orchestra, knew of Charlie by reputation. But when he called Charlie in Minneapolis, Charlie said he was happy where he was. Furthermore, Charlie said, he wasn't going to come to Boston and play what he called a "naked audition." At this stage in his career, he wasn't going to play unaccompanied behind a screen. Terribly unnerving, it also seemed humiliating. Having recently turned forty, Charlie thought he was too old to be treated that way.

Two years later, the job was again open. Twice more, Moyer called Charlie. The first time, with his typical bravado, Charlie suggested to Moyer that he listen to the Minneapolis orchestra on the radio. When Moyer called again, over one hundred people had been rejected in the preliminary rounds of the new audition, and Moyer said the audition committee would permit Charlie to play just with the full orchestra in the finals. Feeling he had nothing to lose, and perhaps realizing that he was trying Moyer's patience, Charlie said okay. He'd gotten his way.

All the finalists had been told in advance what works to prepare. They included the opening of the Mahler Fifth, the post horn solo from the Mahler Third, and Bartók's Concerto for Orchestra, all extremely difficult and calling for different styles. Their diversity illustrated a fact of orchestral life. But a member of the orchestra must be able to exploit his or her playing skill according to the demands of complexly varied music.

Because the audition repertoire was so mixed, Charlie brought several trumpets with him to the audition in Symphony Hall in February 1981. Walking on the stage with all his trumpets, Charlie looked like a tennis player before a big match. Certain kinds of music simply sound better on one kind of trumpet rather than another. And some music can be played only on a given type of trumpet. The extremely high notes in much of baroque music, for example, necessitate the use of a smaller, more compact trumpet, pitched several tones higher than the usual.

Playing with great confidence, Charlie quickly sensed that this orchestra was qualitatively better than the one he was used to. Though this was only an audition, the BSO players seemed to take the occasion seriously. They were more attuned to nuances in Charlie's playing, making small but important adjustments in their response to what he did. This kind of ensemble coordination, usually associated with chamber music, is possible only among the finest orchestral musicians. Charlie was very impressed.

So was the orchestra. Charlie's was the kind of performance that made being an orchestral player more exciting to a musician than anything else. The sound of his Mahler was rich and dark, the kind of trumpet sound Mahler must have had in mind when he wrote his symphonies. Charlie played *with* the orchestra, with the kind of give-and-take that defines the difference between a good trumpeter and a good orchestral trumpeter. He was being the kind of star who put the team first.

When he was finished after almost half an hour, the players did something that was almost unheard of in an audition. They applauded.

Then Charlie remained onstage to play for the audition committee alone. "How about a *Leonore?*" he asked.

For his only opera, *Fidelio*, Beethoven had composed four overtures. The first he discarded and the fourth he used for the work's 1814 revision. The middle two, taking their names from the opera's main character, Leonore, eventually became part of the orchestra repertoire. Both feature fanfares for trumpet, and one of them was on Charlie's audition list of prescribed pieces.

The committee agreed that Charlie could play the fanfare from the prescribed *Leonore*. After he did, though, no one on the committee said anything. Charlie thought perhaps he hadn't played it loudly enough. So, with the committee's permission, he repeated the overture, more loudly. Silence again greeted his last notes.

Long afterward, still mystified by the audition committee's response to his *Leonore*, Charlie asked one of the committee members about it.

Had he played the *Leonore* loudly enough? Charlie wondered.

The answer was immediate and emphatic.

"Holy shit!" Charlie, it seemed, had played it louder than they'd ever heard it, so loud he'd almost blown the audition.

Nevertheless, the committee recommended him and, to the surprise of no one present at his orchestra audition, Seiji Ozawa chose Charlie as his new principal trumpet player. His hope when he hired Charlie was that Charlie's sound would improve the character of the brass section.

Despite the comfort and security of his Minneapolis job, Charlie accepted. He knew the Boston position was more prestigious than almost any other in the world. Everything the BSO did—its regular season, the chamber group its principals played in while the rest of the orchestra played Pops, its summer Tanglewood season, its tours, its regular radio broadcasts, and its recordings—everything was bigger and better than Minneapolis. Charlie would also earn more money, though he'd spend more, too. But in Boston he'd be able to teach, not just a few private pupils but many students at the New England Conservatory of Music, a block away from Symphony Hall. That would bring in additional income and it would further his reputation. He might become a modern Vacchiano.

Arriving in Boston now, a few minutes before 9 A.M. on the last Tuesday in September, forty-seven-year-old Charlie pulls his Corolla into a garage near Symphony Hall and walks past the Stop and Shop and Amalfi's Café to the stage door. His trumpet is in a leather case over his shoulder.

A little too round in the waist, which he blames on too much gin and bourbon, Charlie has a moustache and bearded face. His dark hair, beginning to gray, is thin over his forehead but comes down over the tops of his ears. He wears glasses onstage and off, and his eyes are penetrating and inquisitive. Except when he is upset he smiles a lot, and people trust that smile, find it welcoming and friendly.

"Hey, Bill," he greets the security guard Bill McRae, then descends to the basement, quickly scans the bulletin board, checks for his mail, and stops for yet another coffee at the urn. With his free hand, he reaches for the package of Winstons that he carries in his shirt pocket. Charlie smokes cigarettes only at work, changing to a pipe at home as a concession to Martha. No one needs to tell him that cigarettes hurt him, but they seem an occupational hazard, providing a constant in a professional life filled with uncertainty. Only one of the BSO's four trumpet players doesn't smoke. And only one, Andre Côme, is older than Charlie.

Yet Charlie worries compulsively about his health. He suffers frequently from colds and seems to clear his throat and blow his nose habitually. He rides an exerciser daily in his study, and he takes a variety of vitamins, of which he keeps an ample supply in his Symphony Hall locker. He believes especially in the beneficial effects of vitamin C and vitamin B complex. He also experiments with a multitude of mental techniques to quiet his nerves. One of the simplest is avoiding unnecessary pressures, such as being rushed.

There are players in the orchestra who regularly arrive for a rehearsal or concert with barely enough time to open their instrument cases. For Charlie and the other early arrivals, finding a private place in the cramped, old building is important. Taking his coffee cup with him, Charlie walks through a hallway to a spot in the basement that is directly underneath the center of the auditorium.

Near him are a few soundproof practice rooms. Charlie calls them isolation booths and uses one for some of his teaching, but he dislikes playing in it. He can't hear himself, and despite the windows in the doors the rooms are so small that almost anyone would feel claustrophobic. Charlie claims a spot in the open basement, where he can pace as he plays and where he can glimpse other people, including members of the house crew in their repair shops.

Here, far from the brightly lit changing rooms that soon will begin to fill with his colleagues, Charlie at last takes his trumpet from its case. It is an expensive custom model, made for him in Chicago by a young man named David Monette. He fusses for a moment with its three valves. Then he holds it under his shoulder, while he puckers his lips and blows a few notes on the unattached gold-plated mouthpiece, producing funny-sounding kazoolike buzzes. He inserts the smaller end of the mouthpiece into the trumpet's unpolished leadpipe and sends a shot of hot air through four feet of tapered brass tubing. He fiddles with an apparently absentminded, automatic fingering. Finally, he is ready to warm up, except that he doesn't like to use the term. "Checking the templates" is how he describes this procedure, as though it were shrouded in a certain mystery, with Charlie wondering what will be there each day.

He begins with a series of slurred, or legato, thirds, the bottom note of each third part of an ascending scale. He plays ten such thirds consecutively: an octave's worth plus two more. This makes the last note of the last third a perfect fifth above the tonic, or note on which he began. So, for example, when he starts on C, his last third bridges the interval of E to G. From the concluding G he slurs a whole step down to F, then on down to D, B, G, and D—an arpeggio of thirds—before arriving back where he started with a final whole-step slur to C.

Such a sequence takes him less than ten seconds to play, but its difficulty does not lie in its speed. What makes this hard, though he plays it without the slightest perceptible strain, is the combination of strength and control it requires. Like much trumpet playing of this caliber, it is analogous to walking a high wire. In addition to courage, you need well-developed muscles that you apply with a light touch.

As soon as Charlie completes the figure, he breathes deeply and begins again, in a new key, usually a half step above; from C, therefore, he goes to C sharp, and so on. Charlie keeps going upward until he reaches a key whose top note, in this exercise, defines his comfortable range (D two octaves and a whole step above middle C, though he can play several notes higher). Charlie performs this exercise from a combination of memory and habit, and he improvises others that form no set pattern.

He follows with a little Mahler, playing as though he believed Mahler had composed this music just for him. Stretching the fingers of his left hand, he keeps the trumpet grasped in it, arches his eyebrows as he stretches his facial skin, and flexes the fingers of his right hand, which remain placed over the three valve keys. Attached to one of the valves is a pencil stub with which he marks his sheet music, but he uses no music now.

Splah! The sound he makes reminds him of something he's been trying to forget, the ever present possibility of failure.

He refers to his mistake self-deprecatingly as "my signature." He tries again. This time the sound is gold, something warm and dark a listener could get lost in. The sound comes from somewhere very deep inside and it fills the basement cavern while Charlie plays, waiting for the announcement over the hall's public address system that will summon the orchestra to the rehearsal.

Charlie has played Mahler Two many times before. He knows his part. But he knows, too, that the score is filled with trumpet writing that will make it necessary for him to draw on everything he has ever learned about the trumpet. And it will require something else, too. "What is best in music is not to be found in the notes," Mahler was fond of saying. For Charlie, playing this supremely nostalgic and ultimately triumphant symphony, the music is an echo of his own past, a reflection of his life.

Appearing outwardly calm, Charlie retraces his steps through the basement hallway, exchanging pleasantries with whomever he encounters. But he keeps on walking. His gimmicky digital watch tells him it's almost 10:30.

Charlie stops for a glass of water, which he carries with him to his seat at the center of the rear of the stage and places on the music stand before him. As he sits down, he can smell varnish and paint; during the orchestra's September vacation, the house crew has been painting the backstage area, and a new coat of lacquer has been applied to the stage floor. Surrounded on that stage by his fellow players, more than one hundred men and women, friends and enemies alike, Charlie feels completely, utterly alone.

TWO

andsome and chic in his white Hanae Mori shirt, white pants, and black espadrilles, Seiji Ozawa peers over his glasses, which out of vanity he will never wear during a concert, and listens to the orchestra playing Mahler Two as he keeps conducting. He's in great shape today; the people around him can sense how relaxed and fit he is after a vacation at home in Japan. A month ago at the final concert of the Tanglewood Music Festival, he led the orchestra in a stirring performance of Benjamin Britten's *War Requiem*. Buoyed by that success, feeling confident and assured, Seiji's ready this morning to pounce on the first thing he hears that he doesn't like. He's ready to pounce on his trumpets.

Seiji lets his glasses, which are on a chain, fall to his chest and stares directly at Charlie Schlueter and the five other trumpet players who sit to Charlie's right for this symphony. Without a further signal, the orchestra stops playing.

"Careful," Seiji says, referring to several sixteenth notes early in the movement. "Staccato, staccato," he continues, and then he sings what he wants, "Du, da-du, da-du," each staccato sixteenth almost a grace note. His voice is that of a schoolteacher admonishing a naughty pupil.

Charlie doesn't like this little lecture at all. *Seiji always stops me here*, he thinks, as he stares at the conductor. Charlie knows perfectly well how to play these notes. There is a "tension" to them, he believes, "something that you cannot notate." The staccatos are marked in the score with small dots above or below the notes, but the dots alone don't tell the player how short to make them. Charlie feels Mahler's staccatos must be played like Italian rhythms, like the short, sharp staccatos at the end of Respighi's *Pines of Rome*.

The Harvard Brief Dictionary of Music defines "staccato" as "the shortened performance of a note (or group of notes) so that it sounds only for a moment, the major part of its written value being replaced by a rest." Charlie believes this definition is typical of "music educators' craziness. Staccato is not a question of short but of space. It gives character."

Charlie's distinction turns on a player's sense of phrasing, on the realization from many years of experience that a staccato space between notes differs from a written rest between the same notes. In the case of this Mahler passage—which is further complicated because it also includes rests—that subtle difference defines the sound, making it alive, a little edgy, making it Mahler and not another composer. Charlie knows Seiji understands this, but he is insulted that Seiji thinks he doesn't.

The rehearsal continues. Giving the trumpets a momentary respite, Seiji speaks to the strings. "Really has to be light bow, air bow," he says in his choppy but clear English at figure 3 of the first movement. The 208-page score, divided into five movements, is marked with numerals to make it easier for the conductor and players to find their place when there is an interruption. The first movement—445 bars long—has twenty-seven such figures.

Again, at figure 3, Seiji says to the cellos, "Use more bow, but light. No crescendo." He wants their part to come out, but he doesn't want a crescendo to slip in; he doesn't want them to overdo it. This is extremely difficult to do, but Seiji never appears to wonder whether what he wants is possible. He just assumes it is, his players think, and they have to deal with the anxiety if it isn't.

Looking at his score as he speaks, Seiji almost slips from the podium, which is fourteen inches high and covered with gray carpet, except for its edges. Like the stage floor, the perimeter of the podium has been lacquered.

"Very dangerous," Seiji says, shaking his head and smiling. "Looks good, but . . ." The musicians laugh with him, relieved at this first moment of humor since Seiji began the rehearsal fifteen minutes ago by mispronouncing the names of two new violinists. They never know when he's going to make a joke, get angry, work them especially hard, or let them off easy. Fourteen years after he became their music director, they still never know whether the concert they are preparing with him is going to be a ho-hum affair or whether, once again, Seiji is going to surprise them. He's spending so much time this morning on details, on sound. But what will the performance be like? Though he doesn't let on with them, Seiji is asking himself the same question.

There is no one in the world more beautiful to watch conduct than Seiji Ozawa. His eyes express more than his words; his hands and the graceful gestures of his arms convey his feelings far better than anything he says. He wears his heart on his face and in the rhythmic movement of his short (five-foot seven-inch), trim body. Fifty-one years old, he looks his age from up close, his black hair streaked with gray, the lines to either side of his mouth and below his eyes sharply etched.

Conducting, he often seems a listener, as though he were comparing what he hears the musicians play with a version of the music he has in his head. He is.

"I'm just putting together," he says modestly. Whenever he leads an orchestra, he is searching for a kind of conductor's paradise, a sound so good that he can feel he is simply coordinating the efforts of his players. At such rare moments of complete self-effacement, Seiji becomes a very sophisticated, highly sensitive musical traffic cop. Usually, however, he must be many other things, too.

Prestigious and elite, the Boston Symphony Orchestra that Seiji took over in 1973 billed itself on recordings and in promotions as "the aristocrat of orchestras." The term referred to the orchestra's well-known sound, but it might also have applied to the haughty manner with which many of the older players viewed their new boss. Some had been playing in the orchestra since before he was born.

The orchestra Ozawa inherited had been performing since 1900 in a building considered to be among the two or three finest acoustically in the world. No doubt the superb acoustics of the McKim, Mead, and White–designed Symphony Hall had played an important role in defining the orchestra's international reputation, but so had its twelve previous music directors. Those men decided what pieces the orchestra played and hired the musicians to perform them. More than anyone else, they were responsible for the way the orchestra played and the sound for which the BSO was famous. They set the orchestra's standard, and under such music directors as Pierre Monteux, Serge Koussevitzky, and Charles Munch, that standard was high enough to compare with the finest European orchestras.

During Koussevitzky's twenty-five-year-long regime, the BSO's summer residence in Tanglewood was established, and Munch in the late 1950s took the orchestra on a tour to Japan. Both these events were to have an important meaning to Seiji Ozawa, who came from a part of the world where the music the BSO played was considered foreign.

The son of Japanese parents who had been living in Japanese-occupied Manchuria when he was born in 1935, Ozawa had grown up in Japan, to which his family had returned when he was nine. A rugby injury to his index fingers cut short a promising piano career, but at the Toho School of Music in Tokyo, Seiji was the prize conducting pupil of the school's director, Hideo Saito, who had studied in Germany.

The BSO under Munch was only the second Western symphonic ensemble Ozawa had heard in person. He was overwhelmed. The gigantic, mesmerizing, seductive sound rang in his ears. The memory of that sound, and the ambition to shape it himself, brought twenty-four-year-old Seiji to the West in 1959.

Seiji had no money then. He traveled with only a guitar and a motor scooter, and he hadn't even paid for the scooter. Its manufacturer had agreed to serve as his partial sponsor in return for publicity. In France, Seiji entered a conducting contest, and in a pattern that would persist from then on, he made an extraordinary impression with his conducting and his charm. Significantly, one of the judges was Charles Munch, who invited Seiji to study in 1960 at the BSO's summer school in Tanglewood. Seiji was deeply happy living in the lovely countryside of the Massachusetts Berkshires. There he was befriended by Koussevitzky's widow, and he met many of the musicians in the orchestra.

By the end of Seiji's two months at Tanglewood, he had stunned everyone with an extraordinary combination of talent and confidence and had won the annual Koussevitzky Prize for best conducting student. Though he was conducting pieces he had never encountered at home, his technique was already well developed, his command of the baton and of himself astonishingly mature. He learned scores quickly and easily memorized huge chunks of complicated music. And he was extremely poised on the podium, with uncommon self-assurance before the musicians. He had come a long way very quickly, but success suited him. He belonged here.

More honors and fortuitous breaks followed. Soon two of the

most formidable and influential conductors of the twentieth century gave him and his career big boosts. In rapid succession, Seiji earned a fellowship in 1960–61 with the esteemed music director of the Berlin Philharmonic Orchestra, Herbert von Karajan, and an assistant conductorship with the recently appointed music director of the New York Philharmonic, Leonard Bernstein, in 1961–62. It seemed Seiji could do no wrong.

Seiji's rise to prominence in the next decade was the kind Seiji would describe, in his typical use of hyperbole, as "fantastic!" From 1964 to 1968 he ran the Chicago Symphony Orchestra's Ravinia Festival; in 1968 he was made music adviser of the Japan Philharmonic Orchestra; meanwhile, in 1965, he became music director of the Toronto Symphony, leaving that post in 1970 for the same position in San Francisco. He continued as music director in San Francisco for several years, finally phasing out his work there with an additional season, 1976–77, as music adviser. But his formal relationship with the BSO was already deepening in 1968, when he first conducted the orchestra in Symphony Hall. In 1970, he was made artistic director of Tanglewood, and finally in 1972 music adviser of the BSO.

When he was appointed, the BSO had been searching for a permanent successor to the eminent German-born music director, William Steinberg, who was seventy-three years old and seriously ill. Speculation focused on Michael Tilson Thomas, an assistant conductor who had stepped in for Steinberg on a moment's notice, and Colin Davis, who had been guest-conducting the BSO since 1967 and was now the orchestra's principal guest conductor.

But in the end, Thomas was considered by some influential players too young, and Davis, whom the orchestra respected enormously, had indicated he didn't feel he was ready for such an assignment. Seiji's box-office charisma was second only to Bernstein's. The orchestra's trustees made what seemed the obvious choice.

In the seventies, Seiji's long hair, the beads around his neck, and his Nehru-style jackets gave him the look of a rock star. Other conductors wore a formal shirt under their tails when conducting; he put on a turtleneck. But even the conservative Brahmins forgave Seiji his dress, while audiences were attracted by what it represented.

Achievement had followed achievement, and at the age of thirty-eight, Seiji was at the top of his profession. People around the world knew his name and his reputation was still growing. He began accepting additional guest conducting assignments in Europe, he started conducting more opera, and he led the BSO on several highly acclaimed tours, including an emotional return to Japan in 1978 and an international celebration of the orchestra's centennial in 1981. Audiences in his homeland revered him, and in Europe, where French and German orchestras played magnificently under him, the plaudits of the critics continued.

But disenchantment was developing in the United States. BSO players complained he was away too often. Players and critics began to cast doubts on his musicianship; they approved of his Bartók but not his Beethoven. Some of the problems stemmed from the gap that exists between any conductor and his orchestra, between any performer and his judges; others focused on Seiji himself. For the first time in his fantastic life, Seiji had to deal with trouble that couldn't be ignored or easily resolved.

Many conductors build careers on their interpretations of certain works. Seiji had become identified with the music of Berlioz and Ravel. Their colorful and by turns splashy and subtle writing needs an extroverted baton, and Seiji had a special feel for Berlioz's *Symphonie Fantastique* and Ravel's *Daphnis et Chloé*. He was also lauded for his ability to lead large pieces written for a massive orchestra, often including soloists or chorus or both. But the longer he remained in Boston, the more often he faced a charge that he was lacking in understanding as an interpreter of nineteenth-century German music, the repertoire anchored by Beethoven and Brahms. For many orchestral players, it is the music of those two composers that inspired them to become musicians. They have proprietary feelings about Beethoven's nine symphonies, Brahms's four, and the concerti and chamber music of both men.

Mahler, who exploits the orchestra more in the manner of Berlioz and Wagner, sometimes inspired Seiji's best. But Seiji brought no sense of tradition to that music either, his critics said. To some that meant no Western hangups, while to others it spelled interpretative disaster. In what may have been a parochial criticism, his work was said to be all surface and no depth. Once this perception was formed in Boston, it became the conventional wisdom. However, Seiji's mentor, Karajan, regularly invited Seiji to guest conduct the Berlin Philharmonic in the very works for which Bostonians disparaged him. There were even persistent rumors that Karajan wanted Seiji to succeed him, while in Boston his detractors spread rumors he was going to be fired.

Furthermore, the Boston orchestra he was leading included many musicians who had known him as a student. This made it difficult for him to impose his musical will on them, and it still does today. For despite attrition, several players in important positions still hold seniority over him.

Seiji starts his fourteenth BSO season with an anticipation tempered by lingering tensions. Literally and metaphorically, he's still searching for the right sound.

Few pieces create a more massive sound than the symphony Seiji has chosen to open the 1986–87season. First performed by the BSO in 1918, Mahler Two has become a repertory piece for the orchestra, a work that appears regularly on the BSO's programs. Just two years ago, the orchestra presented the symphony at Tanglewood and again that fall on a European tour.

By the following fall, in 1985, plans for the next season focused in part on Seiji's determination to do all of Mahler's nine complete symphonies and three song cycles over a four-year period. For Seiji, this Mahler cycle would be an opportunity to show off his orchestra and, not coincidentally, himself. If Seiji could succeed with these Mahler concerts, perhaps the criticisms directed at him would cease.

So Seiji, artistic administrator Costa Pilavachi, and then general manager Thomas W. Morris, Jr., decided to open the 1986–87 season with one of the most complicated of orchestral works. In addition to a huge orchestra, part of which plays offstage, the score calls for a chorus, two soloists, and an organ. A single performance of the piece consumes nearly ninety minutes.

Once the season's opening was set, it was quickly decided to present Mahler Two twice more, given the investment in rehearsal time the orchestra would already have made. The concert would be repeated after Opening Night, and an additional performance was booked at the University of Connecticut at Storrs. And the BSO also decided this would be a fine piece to take on one of the orchestra's three annual trips to Carnegie Hall in New York City.

The sheer scope of the Mahler forces a conductor to make a host of important decisions about pace and balance. Its ambitious inclusiveness and inquisitiveness invite fundamental, profound consideration about the meaning of music, of life and death.

Mahler once wrote that he wanted his music to create not one emotion but a conflict of emotions. One of the characteristics of Mahler's music is its rapid shift of emotion, moving back and forth between lyric and almost banal. Mahler used such emotional contrast to move and color his music, which he viewed in grandiose, "Romantic" terms.

"I had long contemplated bringing in the choir in the last movement," Mahler said of his Second, "and only the fear that it would be taken as a formal imitation of Beethoven made me hesitate again and again. Then [conductor and composer Hans von] Bülow died, and I went to the memorial service. The mood in which I sat and pondered on the departed was utterly in the spirit of what I was working on at the time. Then the choir, up in the organ loft, intoned

[German poet Friedrich] Klopstock's *Resurrection* chorale. It flashed on me like lightning, and everywhere became plain and clear in my mind! It was the flash that all creative artists strive for—'conceiving by the Holy Ghost!' "

The last thing on Seiji Ozawa's mind this Tuesday morning in September is ghosts, holy or otherwise. He has just four rehearsals to get Mahler Two ready for Opening Night, which is two days away.

"Can you get this upbeat together?" Seiji asks the flutes, oboes, and clarinets, seven bars after figure 4 in the first movement. "Would you just concentrate before you play," he orders the strings, before figure 10. He's working all the players hard and they're not enjoying it one bit.

Suddenly, just before figure 11, Seiji stops the orchestra and turns to the violins on his left. He is very upset with something he has just heard.

"That arpeggio," he says. "Strings should come out more." The dynamics of the passage bother him, but so does something else. "I don't like this third bar," he continues, glaring at his young concertmaster, Malcolm Lowe.

I knew it, Lowe could reply, but he's too diplomatic to do so. An immensely talented violinist who once considered a career as a professional athlete, Lowe projects an air of complete confidence in everything he does. Of average height, he has an athlete's physique, with strong legs and arms. He sits forward on his haunches, as though he were ready to leap from his chair at any moment.

Lowe's position requires him to perform a wide range of musical and administrative duties, the least of which is shaking hands with the conductor at the beginning and end of a concert. His most important offstage task is to review the pieces the orchestra plays and mark the bowings for the strings. These bowings, indicated by a system of symbols written on the music, tell a string player how each phrase in a piece is to be played. They have an enormous impact on the way the orchestra sounds.

Earlier this month, when Seiji was in Japan, Malcolm checked the bowings for Mahler Two before he left on his own vacation. There was little reason, Malcolm felt, to fuss with the bowings that his predecessor, Joseph Silverstein, had marked two years ago, but he wished he could have questioned some of them with Seiji, including those following figure 11 of the first movement. That's a spot he would have liked to have changed. Now he regrets he didn't.

Ideally, the bowings "should serve the musical phrases as the conductor interprets them," Malcolm believes. But this is difficult to achieve when there has been no chance to discuss the piece with the conductor. Malcolm tries to anticipate Seiji's interpretation, but he finds it frustrating to play this guessing game.

In the four bars preceding figure 11—the spot at which Seiji has just questioned the sound—Silverstein apparently added to the arpeggios some slurs, curved lines over or under some notes that indicate they are to be played with no break between them. This makes the arpeggios sound like Brahms, not Mahler. Mahler is not this fancy, this Romantic, in Seiji's opinion. Instead of sharply consonant, which Mahler has marked just before with the words "non legato," the notes sound syrupy with a slur. However, Mahler has set a kind of trap for the players, since the very last, short sequence of notes in the passage is slurred, by his own direction.

Seiji confers with Malcolm, who stands, turns around, and addresses the first violins seated behind him. When the piece is performed, these few bars will take about two seconds. No one but listeners very familiar with the work will notice the difference. Nevertheless, the rest of the orchestra sits quietly now, doing nothing, the clock ticking away expensive minutes while the issue is resolved. Tomorrow, the soloists and chorus will join the orchestra, so Seiji must get through the first three movements of the symphony today. And the management doesn't want to pay the orchestra overtime on the first rehearsal of the year.

"Would you take off the slur," Malcolm tells the first violins.

"All three?" asks a voice from the rear.

"No," replies Malcolm. "Only change the bar before eleven. The last six notes are still slurred."

"Are you clear, everybody?" asks Seiji. The orchestra tries the passage again. It still isn't right. Some of the violins haven't made the requested correction.

"Take off *all* the slurs," Malcolm now says.

"If we are together, it makes much more sense," says Seiji, shaking his head with annoyance. But he adds politely, "Thank you. Sorry."

Again, the orchestra begins to play, this time without the slurs. As he continues to conduct, Seiji leans toward Malcolm and says, loudly enough for everyone to hear, "Why were these slurs in?" Malcolm doesn't reply.

The orchestra rehearses the first movement until ten minutes before noon, when Seiji calls for the twenty-minute break mandated in the musicians' contract for each two-and-a-half-hour rehearsal. Charlie Schlueter stays onstage a few minutes to practice. So do several of his colleagues, and the sound of their instruments makes a discordant music, the kind of unplanned polyphony Mahler might have reworked into one of his symphonies.

Repeatedly, Charlie plays the series of staccatos Seiji stopped him on earlier. Then he puts his trumpet down on a wooden cone specially cut for him by the stage manager and leaves the stage to relieve the tension of the rehearsal with a cigarette in the smokers' lounge, half a flight of stairs below. The hardest playing of this day is over for him, though he has a short exposed passage with three of the other trumpets coming in the third movement, assuming Seiji gets that far after the break. He tries not to think about tomorrow, when they will have two rehearsals and do the fourth and fifth movements. A trumpet player could jeopardize his job by poor playing in the fourth movement's quiet chorale, while the finale has some of the most sustained bravura writing ever composed for the brass.

In the tuning room, directly off the stage, Malcolm Lowe fidgets with a string on his violin. Frustrated at the time wasted by the discussion of the bowing at figure 11, he feels the rehearsal is not going as well as it should. Under different circumstances, he would be pleased that Seiji cared about such a small passage. It would demonstrate attention to detail within the whole work. The sum of such concerns can add up to a great performance. But the whole episode of the slur wouldn't have been necessary had Seiji been around and more accessible.

Elsewhere in the hall, preparations are being made for the black-tie dinner that will be held after the Opening Night concert. White tablecloths are spread, flowers arranged.

Shortly the musicians reassemble onstage, and at precisely 12:10 P.M., Seiji says, "Second movement." The music resumes.

The strings begin a lovely waltz marked "andante moderato." A delicate sound fills the empty hall. An underground trolley passes the corner of Huntington and Massachusetts avenues, and the rumble of the cars reverberates inside the old brick building.

"One more thing," Seiji impatiently reminds the players, shortly before a complicated sequence of changing dynamics and rhythmic patterns. "I'm taking this movement a little bit slower. Some of you are still not doing it." Then he begins conducting again, the tip of his tongue sometimes popping in and out of his mouth seemingly in time with the rhythm.

A moment later, he interjects, "This area is still a little faster. But still not fast." Seiji doesn't explain why that matters. Further on, Seiji lectures the first violins about defining an E flat that precedes an ascending scale.

Rushing to get the third movement done before one o'clock, an almost silent Seiji finally lets the musicians play for a long stretch without interruption. Perhaps in response to this release from criticism, they do so with great depth of feeling. The Scherzo pulsates with energy, the ensemble sounds whole. But there isn't time to fix more than a few spots.

"Thank you," says Seiji. The clock on the center of the stage's rear wall, hidden during performances, shows ten seconds to spare. Seiji bows. "See you tomorrow."

THREE

hree weeks before Seiji's first rehearsal with the orchestra, the BSO began to assemble its chorus for the season. On a muggy, early September evening, eighty-five nervous singers auditioned to join the Tanglewood Festival Chorus, led by John Oliver. Oliver, an energetic man and the chorus's only director since its formation in 1970, needed 150 voices for the Mahler. The amateur singers came from many walks of life and ranged in age from eighteen to sixty. About forty of them were invited back for a second, private audition. There were ten openings in the chorus.

While John Oliver's dedicated rehearsal pianist, Martin Amlin, fiddled with the knob that adjusted the height of the piano bench, John disappeared momentarily to confer with Sarah Harrington, the cheerful, superefficient chorus manager. John had spent most of that day at the Massachusetts Institute of Technology, where he teaches and heads two other choruses. He also directs a fourth chorus, the John Oliver Chorale. This leaves him almost no free time. At the age of forty-seven, he's been working long enough to have some doubts about the human cost of such commitment. There's an edge to him, but he loves singing too much to leave it. To function efficiently, he relies heavily on Sarah's administrative ability.

Seated at the registration table in the hallway, Sarah checked the cards that each of the singers had filled out earlier. The cards contained basic information about each singer, including his or her level of fluency in French and German, height ("in shoes"), and, optimistically, "name as it should appear in the [concert] program book." Sarah had arranged the cards in the order in which the singers would audition and would give them to John, who had already written notes on them about each singer's performance in the group auditions.

In a nearby darkened room, where John had led those group auditions, a woman with bare feet lay across two chairs, her eyes closed, her body motionless. Sarah would call her name in a few minutes and she would get up, put on her shoes and a nervous smile, and walk to the brightly lit chorus room, where John listened now to a Japanese tenor.

"There is a lane," the tenor sang, "which winds toward the bay/Passing a wood where the little children play."

Martin Amlin played the accompaniment to the song, written in 1902 by the American composer Charles Ives. The rhythm tricks singers. In three-quarter time, the song begins with two bars of syncopated eighth notes and quarter notes before the voice enters with a phrase of three quarter notes and a half note. Sight-reading, the tenor had to sing against the rhythm of the piano part, holding his first quarter note for its full beat. Over the course of the evening, a tendency to hurry that quarter note to keep pace with the piano would mar the sight-reading of most of the singers. But the tenor got it right.

"Thank you very much," said John, making another notation on the tenor's registration card. The tenor nodded, turned, and left the room. His private audition had lasted five minutes. He would have to wait four days before learning whether John had selected him to sing in the chorus. John gave him no hint about the decision, but if the tenor could have sat in on some of the other auditions he might have guessed that his chances were good. Some of the singers didn't even finish *There is a lane* or the other short Ives song, *Resolution,* that John sometimes substituted to break the monotony for himself and Martin.

An empty doughnut bag rested on a corner of Martin's piano. A tall young Texan who composes music and teaches part-time at Boston University, Martin felt his patience being tested that night. As singer after singer mistook the duration of the first quarter note, Martin started the song again. One woman missed the interval of a minor third that separates the notes for "a" and "lane." Almost everyone mispronounced "winds." Martin tactfully said nothing as one soprano changed key with each new phrase. Effortlessly, he changed with her, going from the song's B flat to what sounded like D, then down to an apparent C, back to B flat, and finishing in E.

"Nice transposing, kid," said John to Martin, after the soprano had been politely invited to make a quick exit.

John expressed surprise that some of the singers who had sounded so good in the group audition's octets and quartets couldn't sing alone. He had been auditioning singers for more than twenty years, ever since he'd directed a choir in the Boston suburb of Framingham. The process still intrigued him, and he sounded especially cheerful that night.

"I never get tired of auditions," he said. "The whole psychology of them, of the people, is fascinating."

But he did not add how greatly these singers differed from the musicians in the orchestra with whom they would perform, how relatively easy what they had to do was, compared to knowing how to play a Mahler staccato. An aspiring BSO player who couldn't get Ives's rhythms right would never get inside the stage door before an audition. If Malcolm Lowe or Charlie Schlueter had applied for positions with the BSO without being able to handle syncopation, they would have been ridiculed. It is John Oliver, not his singers, who, like the orchestral players, has to worry about getting everything correct.

And John was under pressure that night. Seiji, who was still in Japan, had no idea these auditions were even taking place. But John knew that when Seiji met the chorus for the first time, the night before the first orchestral rehearsal, he would expect the same perfection he demanded of his professional orchestra members. Should the chorus fail, the impact on the performance would be disastrous and John might be out of a job.

Each time Sarah opened the door to the chorus room and ushered in another singer, John always hoped for the best. When a man who introduced himself as a composer couldn't find the pitch for the first note of "There is a lane," John helped him. But he was puzzled. "What are they teaching over there at the New England Conservatory?" he wondered aloud.

"Hi, Isham," John greeted a tenor who had sung for him before. "How's life treating you?"

"The market went down eighty points today," replied Isham.

John asked him to sing some ascending arpeggios. "Okay, let's hear the bottom," John said. Isham sang several descending half scales. This was followed, at John's request, by articulated vowel sounds to consecutive whole notes and a long D beginning pianissimo, moving through a crescendo to forte, and then softening slowly through a diminuendo to piano. John asked Isham to read some German, then French.

During the group auditions, John could usually tell in a measure or two if someone had voice enough to be invited for a callback. But sometimes he had been uncertain, and so he had added the singer's name to the callback list. Now he regretted this, because it had lengthened the auditions.

"I should just trust my instincts," John said. "But it's something

I get from my grandmother: I'm always worried we're not going to have enough."

"I used to play the saxophone," replied another singer in response to a question from John about his musical training. "So did I," reported John. One woman, in response to John's greeting, started to say she was fine, then changed her mind and announced, "Actually, I'm a nervous wreck."

Few of the singers remembered to thank John afterward. "I must be losing my touch," he said to Martin. "I used to be so paternal they all thanked me."

John couldn't take his eyes off Nina Keidann when she entered the room. She was by several years the youngest of the auditioners. Pretty, with a slightly aquiline nose, high cheekbones, and reddish hair, she was dressed like a schoolgirl in a neatly pressed plaid skirt and red blouse. Her excitement was palpable and her face radiant. She seemed determined to keep her composure. Though John said only one criterion would guide his selections—"whoever's best"—it was difficult not to be influenced by Nina's wholesomeness and innocence.

A Boston University sophomore, Nina was majoring in voice. She had perfect pitch. Her voice teacher, a friend of John's, did not know she was auditioning for the chorus, which she had decided to do "on a whim." After a good night's sleep, she'd stopped herself from feeling nervous today by thinking of herself as "being excellent." And she'd remembered not to drink milk, a singer's enemy because it coats the vocal chords.

When John asked her about her age, she hesitated. "Will it affect me?" she finally asked. John smiled unthreateningly and she answered him.

"Eighteen."

She stood straight, her hands at her sides, looking directly at John. He asked her to sing some arpeggios and was startled to full attention by her clear, firm soprano voice.

"That is the way it should be," John said. "Beautifully produced."

She took a deep breath, before risking the note she had to start on as she sang, "There is a lane." She had no trouble with the rhythm, but missed a D in the third phrase.

"I have a really hard time sight-reading with words," she said. John was undisturbed at her confession. He couldn't get over Nina's self-confidence and maturity. Turning to Martin as she left, he said, "That's a talented kid."

"What's normally your top note that you're comfortable with?" John asked one of the next singers, a tenor.

"E or F," the young man answered.

"But you just sang a B above them," said John, making a notation on the tenor's card.

None of these singers had been asked to audition. The successful ones would have to commit themselves to a rehearsal and performance schedule of seventy-one dates over the course of the season. That would require most of them to rearrange their lives during peak weeks. Yet none would be paid, not even with free concert tickets to give to friends.

Between the auditions of two sopranos, John looked up from his cards and said to Martin, "I've just been reading [French composer Francis] Poulenc's diaries. They were just republished. Do you know his line, 'I prefer a pretty voice without training to the pseudo-intelligent singer, usually without voice'?"

John was clearly getting tired from all the auditions he'd been conducting. And he was certain now that he'd have enough singers. Running slightly overtime, the auditions lasted three hours, until almost eight o'clock.

"We're going to need Rudy in the Mahler," John said to Martin and Sarah as he packed the cards and a sheaf of papers in his satchel. Rudy was a Russian bass who had sung with John for many years. Normally, the range for a bass extends down to about an E, nearly two octaves below middle C. But certain basses, through endowment and training, can go several notes lower. Like many of his country-men, Rudy had such a voice.

"He's got that low B flat," John said enviously. John thinks that note, which occurs twice near the beginning and once later in the chorus of the Mahler, is "a marvelous effect."

John finished packing his papers. He had three days to review his notes and complete his selection of singers. Then Sarah would mail a letter to everyone who had auditioned and tape a message on the answering machine in her Symphony Hall office with the list of lucky names.

As he left, John stepped around the debris left by workmen who had been repairing the adjacent space backstage. A door to the auditorium was open. He could see the stage as he passed it. His chorus would stand there on Opening Night, singing Mahler. How many moments in his life John could remember here in this special hall, all the way back to his graduate student days, when he'd had a season seat in the second row and had to crane his neck to watch Erich Leinsdorf. *Music*, he sometimes thought, *music lifts us all out of our little lives*. The stage looked black. John headed home to water his plants and watch the Patriots football game on television.

"Welcome to the new season," said John to the chorus, fully assembled for the first time. It was 7:30 on a weekday evening in mid-September. Perched as usual on his stool, one foot on the floor and the other on a rung, John held his glasses in his left hand and a baton in his right. Over the hum of a fan in Boston University's Sleeper Auditorium, where the chorus would rehearse this week and the next, he chatted for a moment about the completed chorus auditions. Nina Keidann listened happily.

"It's real hard to get into this chorus," he said. "That's a great thing. Bravo to all of you for your continued interest." Though he would not make many more such pep talks, he felt this one was necessary to invigorate his singers. Both his tone and subject were different from what Seiji would use with the orchestra on its first day. Seiji's simple "Good morning" was all he usually uttered at such times; Seiji expected his players to motivate themselves. And the orchestra rarely applauded its music director, which John's chorus now did for him.

The chorus rehearsal for the Mahler Two fifth movement began with the piano. Had the orchestra been rehearsing this evening with the chorus, the notes would have been played by a few offstage instruments and a flute and piccolo onstage. Martin couldn't duplicate all this on the piano, but the sudden sound of even his poorly tuned piano in that drab room on that hot night effected the same spine-shiver that this moment of the piece invariably produces in a real performance.

With his right hand, Martin rendered the flute's part, soon joined by the piccolo's. "The bird of death," Mahler called this; "a distant nightingale, a last tremulous echo of earthly life," he wrote on another occasion. "The gentle sound of a chorus of saints and heavenly hosts is then heard."

John Oliver's chorus of doctors and lawyers, teachers, students, housewives, and one musicologist was then heard. "Aufersteh'n, ja aufersteh'n wirst du," they sang. "Rise again, yes, you will rise again." Without interruption, John conducted the entire choral conclusion of the symphony, with Martin continuing in his role as one-man orchestra. Building to an ear-piercing climax, the singers were so overwhelmed by their final glory of sound that they began laughing to break the spell.

"Well," said John. "Thank you very much." Then the real work began.

"You don't talk about the things that go well," John believes. "You rehearse the places that need attention. The spirit of the music doesn't get rehearsed."

Without a break until he dismissed them for the evening at nine o'clock, John hammered home detail upon detail. A kind of litany developed, with John speaking and the chorus responding:

"Write diminuendo from 'Staub' to 'nach.' Do you understand about diminuendo? Then you can hear the low B flat."

The chorus sang.

"Second tenors, peg it up one notch. The second bar of thirty-two is higher than you think."

The chorus sang again.

Supremely confident, John never hesitated in his directions to the chorus. He knew exactly what he wanted and expected the singers to understand him and to do as he said. He also knew that his chorus's singing in the culminating movement must contribute to each performance, not overwhelm it. But he didn't tell the chorus members this. He made them believe they were the stars of the show.

The chorus sings in the symphony's fifth movement only, a total of four different times, alone and with soloists and orchestra. But the most critical moment is the first, and John spent much of this rehearsal on getting the singers to begin with barely a murmur.

"You know, I'm listening and wondering what's wrong," he said. "What's wrong is you're all in love with this, the tune, which is very beautiful." He meant they were getting carried away. He let them try it again. "That's it. Terrific. You sound like a group who likes to sing this."

A week later, he was still stressing the same things. Most of the chorus members were singing by memory then, and the one point he reminded them about repeatedly was the soft opening. "The biggest temptation is to get louder. But don't, unless the soloist is Jessye Norman," he quipped, referring to the famous soprano.

"As far as softness is concerned, it is always a question of imagination. Don't hold back. Spend the finest kind of soft sound.

"Mentally, do a little yoga. Your neck and your shoulders should be in the coatroom. Now, once more and announcements and you can go home."

Someone wondered if the chorus would get special access to concert tickets. "I'm not aware of it," answered Sarah Harrington diplomatically.

"Will there be food at Storrs?" asked another singer.

"You will receive a dinner," replied Sarah. "But essentially there won't be any time."

On the Symphony Hall stage the evening before Seiji's first rehearsal with the orchestra, John checked his score at the podium, next to a grand piano brought in by the stage crew for a 6:30 chorus rehearsal. His evident distraction betrayed John's emotions. At seven, Seiji would arrive, and John was nervous. After working with Seiji for over fifteen years, he certainly knew who was in charge.

Behind John, a few rows of seats from the stage, a huge curtain hung from the ceiling. In an empty hall, the curtain approximates the acoustical effect of an audience. A spray can of Dust Mop Treatment, left by a member of the house crew who had been cleaning earlier, stood on a chair in the viola section, to John's right.

Worried about the little time he had before Seiji came to rehearse the chorus himself, John began this final choral rehearsal without orchestra promptly. Just as he had before, Martin played the "bird of death" motif. John asked the singers to speak several measures of their parts to get the rhythm of a certain section right. He lectured them about not separating two of the words in the passage with a breath. Then he let them sing.

"Are all the baritones here?" he inquired. At the climactic "Aufersteh'n," which comes at the very end of the symphony, John stopped everyone again and said, "Tenors, at your entrance, you're out of tune. It's not tight. Can you fix that? It shouldn't be hard."

Finally, after a few more stops and starts, they went back to the beginning. John smiled at the sound he heard, but he was worried that Seiji would not approve of it.

"That's good," he said encouragingly. "You just have to be careful to get the sound over the magic line." He was not precisely sure what he meant by that, but fortunately the metaphor conveyed to the chorus the hush he wanted.

A few minutes before seven, John stepped down from the podium. The singers took this as a signal to chat. John said Seiji would be there in a few minutes, but he actually had no idea if Seiji was even in the hall yet.

"If you want to stay in place, okay," said John. "If you want to get up and walk around, don't go far."

Martin paced nervously about the stage. He tried to think of the evening as "just another rehearsal." But he couldn't. Not with Seiji coming.

Sarah had several announcements to make. Scores for Benjamin Britten's *War Requiem*, the next piece the chorus would perform with the orchestra, could be picked up by the door, she said.

"Can I drive to the Saturday concert at Storrs instead of taking the bus?" a singer asked

"Yes," replied Sarah. "But we can't reimburse you for the mileage."

Nina was among the first to spot Seiji. She immediately began applauding with her fellow chorus members. She could not remember having been more excited. Here she was on this stage, about to sing for a major conductor.

"So," Seiji said. "I understand your German is perfect." The chorus laughed. Then there was silence. The chorus stood. Seiji's eyes closed as the chorus began singing. He carried a score, but didn't look at it.

"Maybe it's my fault," Seiji said with false modesty. He wanted to tell the chorus a story, the kind he never told his orchestra.

"The first time I heard this piece was in Vienna, with Lenny conducting." Everyone knew he meant Leonard Bernstein.

"I sat far back. I didn't know if the chorus was singing offstage." Seiji paused to be certain everyone got his point. "Much softer, if you can control it."

The chorus tried again. A siren sounded from the street. "Better," said Seiji, conducting without a baton. "Relax. This is very difficult." His voice was almost that of a hypnotist.

He conferred briefly with John. "Because I'm asking for so soft, let me do it once more," Seiji said.

Without presumption, but feeling perhaps that he needed to assert himself, John interjected something more technical: "Think, on your effort to sing softly, that you're holding back the intervals. The keener the vowel sound is, the better the pitch."

"I see," said Seiji, as though he, too, were learning something. Yet were anyone to have interrupted him like this at an orchestral rehearsal, he would have been furious. He permitted questions from his players, but never advice.

Passage by passage, even bar by bar, the rehearsal progressed. At a triplet of half notes, Seiji paused at length. Whatever upper hand John had gained a moment earlier he was about to lose now.

In the earlier rehearsals, John had always conducted this difficult bar in three beats rather than four. That was the way he thought Seiji did it. But like Malcolm Lowe, John had had no opportunity to talk with Seiji beforehand.

"Can we change that?" Seiji asked rhetorically. "In three, it sounds too simple. I always do it in four."

John looked at the score with Seiji. Seiji tapped out the rhythm and asked another rhetorical question. "Am I asking too much?"

The chorus members, who had silently watched this exchange, sang the disputed bar correctly. Seiji thanked them, his eyes closed. But then, opening them, he could not resist one more comment.

"If the conductor gives only three, it sounds artificial, plastic."

John was silent. There was nothing he could do but nod mute agreement.

At last, the chorus reached the conclusion of the symphony. Seiji stopped once more to correct another detail. "Very good," he said. "I see you Wednesday afternoon." His thanks were followed by more applause.

"It sounds fantastic," John told the singers, wanting to reassert some authority. And, though Seiji said nothing to him about this, John knew what he was responsible for.

"A wonderful sound. Brilliant at the top. Essentially, he's asking you for one hundred percent more of everything I asked." But he didn't add, to them, *Seiji needed to make the piece his.*

Nor did he seem to realize, or want to admit, that Seiji needed to make the chorus his.

FOUR

wo years after he had come to Boston, and three years before this season, Charlie Schlueter went to speak with the new orchestra manager, Anne Parsons, about a raise in his salary. He felt he had good reason to expect one. He had spent his first two seasons trying to please Seiji. And in the summer of 1983 at Tanglewood, the orchestra had performed Mahler's Third Symphony in which there is a prolonged, exposed solo that Charlie had played superbly. Seiji had said it was one of the best things Charlie had done. So Charlie was fairly confident about his playing as he began his third season. He also liked the city of Boston. He liked the size of the city, and he liked sailing on the nearby ocean.

But there were problems, too. Charlie and Martha found many of the people in the orchestra strangely distant. There was little of the after-concert socializing they were used to in other cities. And they were worried about the high cost of living in Boston. They'd had to take an expensive mortgage on their house, and the payments ate up nearly fifteen hundred dollars of Charlie's monthly income. So ever since his arrival, Charlie hadn't felt completely comfortable in his new job.

But the biggest difficulty was in figuring out Seiji. Seiji almost never spoke with Charlie. But, from what Charlie had observed, Seiji hardly spoke with anyone else in the orchestra either. Some people in the orchestra thought Seiji had been giving negative signals to Charlie. But if he had, Charlie wasn't picking them up.

During his first season, 1981–82, Charlie, like all new players in the orchestra, had been on probation. At the end of the first year, Seiji made a decision about his new players, whether to continue that probation, give them tenure, or dismiss them, depending on how they had performed in Seiji's judgment. When it was time to decide about his new principal trumpet player, Seiji gave Charlie tenure. In other words, Seiji made Charlie's appointment virtually permanent under the terms of the players' trade union agreement with the BSO.

But Seiji added a warning. He told Charlie he was dissatisfied with the way Charlie had adjusted to playing in the acoustics of Symphony Hall. Perhaps, Seiji suggested, Charlie still imagined he was back in Minnesota, where the acoustics in the Minneapolis hall were not as alive and resonant as in the rich, brilliant Boston hall. Whatever the reason, Seiji told Charlie, he played out too much. He was too loud.

Seiji also felt that in certain situations Charlie used too much vibrato. Vibrato is a technique that produces a slight variation in the pitch of a note. Properly applied, it gives added emotion to the music. But it is a controversial issue in trumpet playing, akin to a singer's addition of vibrato to make a passage more expressive. Too much can sound affected and, worse, change what a composer wrote. The consequences are not unlike a lovely poem ruined by the addition of italics.

"You hear a sound you like and you try to imitate it," says Charlie's old Juilliard teacher, Bill Vacchiano, of his vibrato. "I got mine from Max Schlossberg and Charlie got his from me. It's very tricky to teach, but if you know how to use it, it's gorgeous." To Vacchiano, his vibrato is like an heirloom, a prized family watch passed on from father to son. But the sound of that vibrato is something he can't put precisely into words. He can only talk around it, tell stories about it, give tips on how to employ it. And he can use words to describe the feeling of the sound. He calls the vibrato he believes he and Charlie share "melancholy."

Actually, for Seiji, the problem of Charlie's alleged volume was more chronic than his use of too much vibrato. And he felt the problem had less to do with the quality of Charlie's playing than with the way Charlie fit in with the rest of the orchestra. He believed Charlie was a fine musician, but he was concerned about how his playing affected the sound of the entire orchestra. If, indeed, Charlie did play too loudly, then the rest of the trumpets would follow, and so would the entire brass section. The orchestra's balance would be thrown off.

"In this orchestra," Seiji believed, "what we need is color, blend, harmony." Not one man—or one section—stealing the show.

Though he did not articulate this to Charlie, Seiji also assumed that his players, particularly his principals, would come to a rehearsal with their concept of how to play a particular piece based in part on how they assumed Seiji would want it. Then, in a sense, Seiji could shape the sound within the ensemble. This was how he worked with John Oliver, never telling John beforehand exactly how to do something, but always assuming that John would know.

As he did with the chorus, Seiji needed to make the sound of his principal trumpet his sound, not Charlie's. Then Seiji could make the necessary adjustments. As personnel manager Bill Moyer explains it, "Seiji expects his principal players to divine his musical ideas." Seiji didn't feel Charlie was doing that. But Charlie didn't feel he should be playing guessing games about what Seiji wanted. And, like most trumpet players, he thought his instrument should be prominent.

As a premier orchestral musician for over two decades, Charlie was hurt by what Seiji told him. It was a blow to his considerable pride. What he didn't understand, or was only beginning to discover, was that Seiji had another agenda as well. Most simply, he needed to assert his leadership, which was under attack at this time. And it was difficult for Seiji to criticize the older players who had been in the orchestra when Seiji was a student in Japan. As one of the first principals Seiji had hired himself, Charlie made a better target. Seiji, however, soon learned that he could hit the target easily enough, but that knocking it down was much harder.

Charlie had experienced his share of run-ins during his career. Once, in Cleveland, he'd confronted George Szell, the music director there, and asked why he wasn't being given as many solos as he thought he should, since he was co-principal. Not used to such questions, Szell had testily told Charlie he needn't worry, he'd still be paid what he'd been promised. Charlie had had the audacity to reply that he hadn't come to Cleveland for the money.

When in Boston in his third season Charlie *was* asking for money, he wasn't talking to the music director.

Away from the podium, Seiji is remote. He tries never to get into unpleasant confrontations. He delegates such work to others. "Seiji speaks with a player if there's a particular problem he wants to discuss," explains Anne Parsons. "But if Seiji doesn't want that player in the orchestra anymore, then it's my problem."

Parsons was then a recent graduate of Smith College, where she had played the flute and managed the college orchestra. Attractive and intelligent, she was also ambitious. Though large numbers of women now play in symphony orchestras, few have had successful careers in administering them.

She had completed a yearlong management internship with the American Symphony Orchestra League, then worked with the National Symphony Orchestra for two years before assuming her duties with the BSO.

Despite her title of orchestra manager, she was hardly the head of the organization, but she handled a host of administrative duties in the production of concerts. Soon after she started, she was given a new assignment by manager Tom Morris (who has since left the BSO) to take over contract matters involving the players.

Though her flute playing might have given her some empathy with Charlie's position as a player, she no longer considered herself a performing musician. "It's just a hobby now, a part of my past," she says without emotion. She explains her work very seriously: "You have to understand the possibilities so you can react when things happen," instead of simply, "You need a sixth sense in this job."

And she can be clinical in discussing her association with an organization that usually conjures up images of beauty. "I sit through every concert I work," she says matter-of-factly. "I want to; I feel I should." She is certainly not the kind of person to enjoy an after-concert bourbon with Charlie Schlueter.

When he met with her, he was old enough to be Anne's father, but if he thought that fact was going to make speaking with her easier, he quickly found out otherwise. Charlie had to plead his case with a newcomer who had been handed a responsibility that put her on the spot. Face to face with this somewhat burly, utterly engaging man, she had to be tough. She couldn't let sentiment dictate what she said.

She didn't. But instead of replying directly with a no to Charlie's request for a raise, Anne spoke about Seiji's view of Charlie's sound. And what she told him was that Seiji was not happy with Charlie's playing. Though this conversation was not the formal procedure necessary to initiate such proceedings, she made it clear that Seiji planned to dismiss Charlie.

Charlie was devastated. After moving his family halfway across the country from Minnesota to Massachusetts, after getting tenure despite the music director's reservations about him, after making what he thought were the adjustments the music director desired, how could it have come to this? After everything he had done, all he had worked so hard to achieve, how could he be informed that he was finished, as if he were just like someone in the coal mines?

The 1983–84 season, when Charlie met with Anne Parsons, was the beginning of the worst period of Charlie's life. It is extremely rare for a music director to dismiss a player of Charlie's experience and rank in any orchestra. Not to renew Charlie's contract meant the BSO would have to make a case against him. Seiji would have to state why he no longer wanted Charlie in the orchestra, when only two years earlier the orchestra had all but begged him to come. He had to make the fault seem Charlie's.

Charlie had always struck others as a player who liked to take risks, who never would be happy without the built-in edge of excitement that came with the conspicuous position of principal. He had a very strong musical personality and he had never been afraid to show it off. But now he was in a situation not even a risk-taker would want. Many players in similar circumstances would have looked for a way out.

But Charlie wanted to stay in Boston. And he also wanted to prove that Seiji was wrong. That meant the beginning of a long, and personally painful, fight for his job. Exercising his union rights after he received his official termination at the end of the 1983–84 season, Charlie appealed his case and eventually filed for arbitration to reverse Seiji's decision. But the appeals process was a lengthy one, and throughout the whole period of waiting for a hearing to be convened he had to keep performing.

Playing the trumpet is difficult enough without the added pressure of doing it before someone who wants to get rid of you. Each instrument in the orchestra presents a player with its own peculiar, inherent problems. The tubing of a French horn is so long that a player can produce almost any note with any valve combination, making a clean attack very hard. Reed instruments are notoriously sensitive to the slightest imperfection in a player's embouchure. A violinist must constantly combat fatigue in the arms.

The terror of the trumpet lies mainly in the terrible consequences of a mistaken tone, particularly in a prominent passage of a piece. Many of the notes on the instrument are produced simply by varying the volume and rate of air blown through the mouthpiece. A slight miscalculation will result in a note that may sound several tones higher or lower than the correct one. Like an opera singer, the trumpeter must hear the note in his head beforehand, often while the rest of the orchestra is playing other notes, sometimes when no other instrument is playing. Even slight tension in the player can cause a mistake; so, in certain circumstances, can an unresponsive trumpet. Charlie calls the awful moments when this happens "train wrecks," and like all trumpet players he lives in mortal dread of them.

After Charlie learned that Seiji didn't want him in the orchestra, the tension became almost unbearable. He was often too tense even to play all the right notes, let alone to play as he thought Seiji wanted him to. And Charlie's fear fed on itself, so that one mistake inevitably led to another. Sometimes, then, he did play too loudly or with too much vibrato, a reflex reaction to the tension. The harder Charlie tried to play well, the more tense he felt; the more tense he felt, the more poorly he played; the more poorly he played, the harder he tried to play well. Charlie smoked a lot of Winstons, and he'd have a drink before a concert.

He needed emotional strength. He'd always had an interest in how other performers handled the anxieties of their work, and around this time he read a book by a psychologist and writer, Eloise Ristad, that helped him greatly. A dynamic older woman, Ristad had adapted the ideas of such writers as Timothy Gallwey, author of *The Inner Game of Tennis*, to the situations faced by musicians. In print she was a proselytizer and in person she was charismatic. Charlie came under her spell and believed in her.

He could respond very directly to what Ristad described in her book as the "sudden panic" of performance. "We beg for release from our destiny and at the same time court the very experience that terrifies us," she wrote. "When the crucial moment to perform arrives, we try to talk ourselves into a calm state, and get even more tense. We try to convince ourselves that this much adrenaline is outrageous, but our knees only get shakier. We walk onstage and pretend the audience isn't there at all, but someone coughs and the game is up. A well-meaning friend says, 'There's nothing to get nervous about,' and it almost helps, because the desire to strangle distracts us for the moment."

Charlie, of course, had plenty to be nervous about. His job was in jeopardy. His reputation was on the line. And his sense of himself, his belief that he was good at what he did, was under attack each day he came to the hall. A passport picture taken during the time before his arbitration shows a gaunt, worried man.

When his two-day arbitration hearing was finally held in New York City in December 1984, Charlie felt so assailed that the original issues prompting his dismissal seemed almost academic. It was as though he were on trial, but the jury had already concluded he was guilty. He had a last chance to prove he was innocent, but in the cold, bleak atmosphere of a roomful of legal representatives and other antagonists, he felt more naked than he would have at a blind audition.

All his adult life, Charlie had communicated through his trumpet. Now, at this critical juncture, he had to do so through a lawyer.

He had a very good one. Rather than responding to the musical issues on which Seiji himself testified, Charlie's lawyer argued that the music director had not followed proper procedures. Seiji hadn't correctly conveyed to Charlie the reasons for his dissatisfaction.

Some of Charlie's colleagues defended him, but others were afraid to. And many players, wondering what had happened to the man who had played such a magnificent audition three years earlier, agreed with Seiji's assessment. They habitually thought any trumpet player was too loud, and they were secretly happy to think Charlie would be leaving. They resented the attention the principal trumpet player always got, and they believed Charlie had been obstinate in his role as a leader in the orchestra. They felt that instead of playing with them, as he had at his audition, he now compelled them to play with him. They didn't like that.

But the outcome of Charlie's hearing did not turn on artistic questions. The quality of Charlie's playing was finally not the issue on which the arbitrator made his decision in April 1985.

The trade agreement, under the terms of which Charlie and the other members of the orchestra work, is designed in part to protect players from being treated capriciously by conductors. No longer is it possible, as it was in Toscanini's era, for a musician to be fired simply because the conductor doesn't like him.

No one had accused Seiji of dismissing Charlie on a whim. But, agreeing with Charlie's lawyer, the arbitrator decided that Seiji hadn't obeyed the rules spelled out in the trade agreement. Charlie could keep his job, the arbitrator decreed, but on technical grounds, not artistic ones.

Charlie had achieved a hollow vindication. And Seiji had lost face in the eyes of his other players. Nothing had been resolved. The conflict between the two men remained, and so did much bitterness.

Attempting to salvage something positive from the incident, Seiji approached Charlie afterward. He did not take back what he'd said, but he proposed that they put this episode behind them and start over.

Deeply wounded by the entire affair, Charlie nevertheless agreed. But he knew that all he'd really won was the continuation of a regular paycheck, and he hadn't come to Boston for the money any more than he had to Cleveland.

Eloise Ristad visited Charlie in Boston in the fall of 1985, six months after his arbitration victory. She'd been teaching some workshops in New Hampshire, and Charlie had arranged for them to have lunch one day, after the orchestra had rehearsed excerpts from Prokofiev's *Romeo and Juliet* ballet music. That music is full of radiant writing for the trumpet and cornet, but Charlie hadn't been playing it at all well. He confessed this to Ristad when she arrived at the hall. They talked in one of the basement "isolation booths," where Charlie had been practicing after the rehearsal.

"How are you and Seiji getting along?" Eloise asked Charlie. Charlie looked at the floor and mumbled something incoherent.

Then, startling Charlie, Eloise said, "I want you to tell me all the reasons Seiji's such a great conductor. It's okay. You can lie," she added.

Charlie could not understand why she was making him say this. But he did what she asked him to. He lamely told her what a fine musician the conductor was, how profoundly he interpreted the scores the orchestra performed, how incisively and inspiringly he led the players. Gradually, as he spoke, his head came up, and Eloise said to him, "Now, I want you to repeat after me, 'I will be strong in Seiji's presence.' "

Charlie wondered what talking about the conductor like this had to do with how he played Prokofiev. But Eloise seemed very certain of what she was doing. She was not threatening, but she was insistent. It occurred to Charlie later that it was almost as if she were hypnotizing him.

"I will be strong in Seiji's presence," he said.

The performance of the Prokofiev went very well. Charlie was a different player from the one he had been in the rehearsals.

Whatever Eloise had done—and it did seem a little mysterious—it helped for the moment. And Charlie believed completely that she was the one who had helped.

Charlie never saw Ristad again. While staying in the Midwest at the home of a friend, where she was working on another book, Eloise went canoeing one day. The canoe capsized and she died of hypothermia. Her death left Charlie with a great sense of loss, but he has never forgotten their friendship. Charlie is not a sentimental man, but he is certain, he says, that "Eloise is up there looking down at me."

FIVE

"Good morning," Seiji says curtly to his musicians.

It is Wednesday, October 1, and the time is 10:30 A.M. It is an extraordinarily busy day for everyone at Symphony Hall. The orchestra has two rehearsals today and one more tomorrow before the Opening Night concert tomorrow evening. Seiji knows these final preparations will be much more difficult than the actual performance. He has a tremendous number of things on his mind. In two hours, the soloists for the Mahler symphony will arrive onstage, and both the chorus and the soloists will join the orchestra this afternoon. Seiji must have the orchestra ready before that.

"Last movement," orders Seiji.

During these next five and a half hours, and again at the final rehearsal tomorrow, one overriding purpose will focus everything Seiji does and says: imposing his vision of the music on the performers. He assumes everyone knows the music; getting the notes right isn't the purpose of these rehearsals. But getting the performers to do what he wants won't be easy. They all have their own ideas about the symphony, and some of those ideas clash with Seiji's. While John Oliver's chorus of amateurs will acquiesce to whatever he asks them, the orchestra won't be cowed. Most of the members of the orchestra are certain they know more about Mahler than their conductor does.

Seiji's awareness of this fact determines much of what happens during a rehearsal. It sharpens his keen sense of when to stop and speak and when to let something go. And his goal of artistic perfection may also conflict with the rehearsal's limited length. In the production of an art that aspires to a timeless ideal of beauty, Seiji must constantly watch the clock.

Strict union regulations govern the duration of a rehearsal, the timing of a break, the scheduling of a second rehearsal on a day there are two, and so on. Additionally, the weekly number of rehearsals or concerts—called services—is regulated: There are eight services in a normal week. The twenty-minute break must come no later than ninety minutes into the rehearsal, unless the conductor has otherwise advised the orchestra's five-member Players Committee. The Players Committee, which represents the players' interests in these and many other matters, can agree or disagree with a later beginning of the break. But past another half hour without a break and the rehearsal is considered done or in overtime.

So Seiji must be pragmatic. Not surprisingly, his pithy instructions burst forth in rapid, terse speech.

Nor is it a surprise that one of his first comments is directed at the trumpets. "Don't pace it," Seiji says sharply to Charlie at an early juncture in the finale, when the first trumpet plays a kind of antiphonal response to the first trombone. "Just stay in tempo."

Even more than most of his fellow principals, Charlie has to go along. In the year and a half since his arbitration victory, Charlie has worked hard to reestablish his standing in the orchestra. There have been some good moments, such as a memorable Mahler Three performance when the orchestra toured Japan last winter. Seiji complimented him for his playing then. But the going has also been rough. Many of the other players have ostracized Charlie, making him a scapegoat for anything that goes wrong. And Richard Dyer, music critic for the city's largest newspaper, *The Boston Globe,* has begun a campaign to complete the firing that the arbitration so narrowly voided. Repeatedly and viciously, *Globe* reviews of BSO concerts ignore Charlie and the trumpets when they play well and zero in on the slightest mistake.

Seiji hasn't been having an easy time of it either, with the critics or with his players. "There is not enough leadership coming from the very top, from the music director himself," charged the *Globe* critic in a long article published last spring.

But there are other, intimately related matters that worry Seiji Ozawa more than any criticism. Since last summer, the BSO and the Philips recording company have been discussing the possibility of a Mahler Two recording in December, when the piece will be performed again. Such an important recording would be an international showcase for Seiji and his orchestra. Usually, if Seiji and the orchestra are going to make a recording, the dates are planned well in advance. But this symphony is long—about an hour and a half—and complicated, with its huge cast of large orchestra, chorus, and soloists. So the negotiations for its recording have been mired in a series of questions about time, money, soloists, score royalties— every conceivable contingency.

And Seiji's concerns about the recording are compounded by a bigger headache, which could also affect the recording. Since September 1, the orchestra has been playing without a contract. At the end of this month, if the players and BSO management have not negotiated a new three-year trade agreement, the players, for the first time in the history of the BSO, may vote to strike.

Negotiations have been stalled since summer. The most recent agreement, which ended on the last day of the Tanglewood season, paid a first-year player $45,760 (almost twice the starting salary only six years earlier). An additional $1,040 was guaranteed as payment from radio broadcasts of BSO concerts. The $46,800 total, under the terms of which the players have started the current season, does not include fringe benefits. Most of the musicians earn more than the base, but the range for senior and principal members of the orchestra rarely exceeds $75,000, except for the concertmaster, who earns about $100,000.

The highest-paid performers, whose salaries are not covered under the trade agreement, are Seiji Ozawa, at a recent average of $400,000 per year, and Boston Pops conductor John Williams, over $300,000. Next in line, though he is not a performer, is the general manager of the orchestra—at about $140,000. The discrepancies between these amounts and the typical player's salary are galling to the orchestra, particularly since neither conductor works the entire year in Boston and the general manager is not a musician.

Because the orchestra's total budget of $24 million is the biggest orchestral budget in the world, the players believe the institution is well off. But the BSO is always seeking new funds to meet its many expenses. Player salaries plus fees for conductors and soloists compose the largest general item in the orchestra's budget. The total figure for concert expenses, which also includes promotion, is over $17 million and rising. Concert revenue is the single greatest line item in the general breakdown of income, with ticket sales accounting for most of the $14.1 million amount. At a top price of $38.50, the BSO charges more for a seat than any other orchestra in the country. Additional salary increases will almost certainly cause ticket prices to go up, and management is worried that there is a limit to what the public will pay.

These numbers mean little to Seiji. He cares about the impact of salary discussions on his instrumentalists. He fears they may be distracted by a trade agreement meeting they are holding today. Somehow, he must block this out of his mind and hope that he can convince his orchestra to do the same.

*   *   *

Within the orchestra, the worst complaining comes from string players, whose numbers comprise nearly two thirds of the players. Some of them scorn Seiji's penchant for memorizing scores, as though he did it by rote. And though they admire his technical strengths, including his ability to give the beat, they mock his grasp of their talent. "He's not a musician; he doesn't play an instrument," says one.

Unlike their colleagues in the woodwinds and brass, most of the string players rarely get a solo. But they, too, spent years learning to become musicians, dreaming of the day they'd be the new Jascha Heifetz or Isaac Stern. Now, instead, they play the accompaniment to the solos of others, or they play passages together that are called tutti. Technically, this music can be very challenging, but it gives the players no chance to shine on their own.

Marylou Speaker Churchill, principal second violin, seems resigned to the strings' role, which she describes somewhat disdainfully as being a "scrubber." She contrasts the strings' main function to the orchestral playing of the principals. While she may be a little jealous, she's careful not to sound critical of her colleagues and to allow certain principals some latitude.

In her seventeenth BSO season and tenth as a section head, Marylou is no "second fiddle," despite her title of principal second violin. What she and her section play usually differs from the part of the first violinists and can sometimes exceed it in importance. But she's not a soloist either. "We, who are so many individuals, have to play together," she says. "If we don't, it doesn't sound good. That's the orchestra routine for violinists. To keep alive musically within that structure, we play concertos outside."

A striking woman with a wide smile and a large, enveloping presence, Marylou might star in a Wagner opera were she a singer. She observes Seiji intently while she plays the violin in the orchestra, her chair just a few feet from the conductor's podium. Seiji must meet that gaze and try to ignore the criticism it sometimes conveys.

For a string player to be excited by a tutti assignment, the conductor must be utterly convincing in his interpretation of the music. He must make his orders to the players inspirational. In the long discussion of the violin slurs at figure eleven of the first movement during yesterday's opening rehearsal, Seiji did not take time to explain his motives. He couldn't, or the rehearsal would have gone on too long. He would have been obliged to continue a running commentary on the entire piece. Therefore, he must trust that his players understand the grander purpose of their mutual endeavor. Otherwise, their work degenerates into indifference.

Instead, they contend in a war of wills. "Six bars after eight, second violins have a decrescendo," Seiji says. Sometimes he halts the orchestra, other times not. But the requests continue, one after another. "Already, the syncopation is very strange," Seiji says. He sings what he wants, the musical line picked up by the violas, the cellos, and some woodwinds. "Three bars after seven, flutes. Same story, six bars after seven." An oboist asks if he should slur two notes there. "Yes," replies Seiji immediately. Then, very quickly as the orchestra keeps playing, the spot these passages have been pointing toward arrives, a thunderstorm of full orchestra.

The hall reverberates with the stirring sound. A stranger wandering into the auditorium at this moment might conclude that the heavens were opening. During a performance of the symphony, when Mahler lets the orchestra explode like this, the audience is usually overwhelmed with an emotion that few other works arouse. Yet in the eye of this musical storm, Seiji appears unaffected by what he is hearing. In fact, he is really conserving his energy. His concentration precludes theatrics. As soon as the orchestra moves on, Seiji turns his attention to the problems the next passage presents. His absorption in the music is so total that he seems not to notice when Marylou Speaker Churchill stands and leaves the stage to replace a broken violin string.

Before she returns to the stage, Seiji stops the orchestra and asks, "Is everyone using maximum bow at figure fourteen?" This passage is a harsh transitional sequence leading eventually to a march. Seiji reminds the players he's conducting here in 4/4 time, four beats to a measure, as he has most of the movement. He gives this reminder because he just conducted several passages in two beats to a measure. That had the result of accelerating the motion of the music, the quarter notes getting only half a beat instead of a full one, and half notes a single beat rather than two. Here, switching to four signals a sudden slowing-down.

The players adjust to this change automatically, but Seiji takes the beginning of the passage several times to be certain they are playing together each of the staccato eighth notes, which are preceded by triplet grace notes. If one instrument comes in late or early here, the grace notes will stand out instead of disappearing into the notes that follow.

Any player may decide for reasons of phrasing or emphasis to play a certain note longer than the conductor may want. "There's a tendency to hold on too long to a beautiful note," explains Marylou. But she knows when that happens the result can be the disintegration of ensemble: "The piece can fall apart." She gives Seiji credit for working on this.

The notes that the strings play at figure 14 are not beautiful in a lyric sense. But Seiji thinks the strings are playing them that way, instead of with the raw quality he wants. Now, as if to remind Charlie that he needn't feel singled out for criticism, Seiji chastises the strings. However, he addresses them collectively.

"It's too nice," he says.

They try it again.

"I still don't like it," he interrupts impatiently. "Would you be more together."

Finally, nodding, he hears the sound he wants. "That's it," he says, and they move on until Seiji dismisses most of them for an early break.

* * *

It is 11:30, an hour after the rehearsal's beginning, and the orchestra has reached the musical bridge to the entrance of the chorus (though the chorus is not yet onstage because this portion of the rehearsal is for orchestra only). In his manuscript, Mahler called this place "Der grosse Apell," or "The Great Call," misspelling *Appell*. The music in this section, which employs only three onstage players and several off, is at times almost inaudible, but nothing in the score taxes a conductor more than this passage because it requires such careful coordination of the various parts—the four trumpets, four French horns, and kettledrum offstage, and the flute, piccolo, and (briefly) bass drum onstage.

In his copy of the score, Seiji has more markings for "Der grosse Apell" than he has anywhere else. He has blocked out the two complicated pages in color-coded shorthand, much of it in Japanese. In bold letters, he has written an English *L* for left, indicating the direction from which one of the four offstage trumpets first sounds. Later, he has used the same mark, *L*, for the entrance of the French horns. With a triangle, he has reminded himself to conduct a measure of trumpet triplets in three. In his rushed, almost scrawled hand, he has added several pianissimo symbols—just as Mahler did in his own manuscript—to the measures that immediately follow the section, when the chorus enters with its hushed "Aufersteh'n."

"There's no secret to conducting this passage," Seiji says modestly. "It's very simple. The main problem is the piccolo and flute play onstage."

But additionally, there is the problem of getting the offstage players to sound far away but distinct, and of getting them to play together with the two onstage instruments.

Doriot Anthony Dwyer, who plays the flute part, thinks the music here "is hanging by a thread." She knows how easily a tiny mistake by someone can throw off the whole passage, which she refers to as "The Big A."

Doriot, who when she joined the BSO in 1952 became the first woman in a principal's position in an American orchestra, is quirky and eccentric. She tends to forget things, including her flute, which she has sometimes lost when the orchestra was on tour. But she is a keenly intelligent participant in the music performed by her orchestra, and she certainly never forgets an important entrance for the flute. Besides, she is a fabulous flutist.

Offstage, her conversation is filled with startling observations rather than conventional opinions. She likes the way Mahler switches from one emotion to another in his symphonies, but she makes an important point about those emotions. In her view, they do not juxtapose obvious dualities. "The opposite of love isn't hate," she says. "Love and hate are both so passionate, they cross over. The opposite of love is indifference." Mahler's music, she is saying, works in part because his jumps from a soaring lyric melody to a brutal march vary the kind of passion, not the degree. He never slips to the indifferent or humdrum.

"And Mahler wrote so beautifully for my instrument. The music lies well." It is also very difficult, especially her part in "Der grosse Apell." But she says she doesn't worry about it. Once the logistics get worked out, "it doesn't cause that much stress."

Part of those logistics involves getting the offstage players offstage, and then back on again afterward. To save money, the BSO has not hired extra musicians to play the offstage parts here or in two other places in the fifth movement. Instead, an assistant of Bill Moyer's has mapped out a diagram for the exit and entrance of these players, with the vain hope that their comings and goings will not distract from the rest of the performance. Once, though, in a performance in London, the percussionist came back onstage through the wrong door.

The players try to avoid such confusion now, but they can't help it. Perhaps Seiji feels he could not entrust such an important passage to outside players, but the orchestra's decision not to hire extras is already costing rehearsal time as the musicians figure out the paths onstage and offstage they are to take. And later this "savings" will be jarring to audiences, who will have to watch the musicians moving around.

Seiji summons one of his two recently appointed assistant conductors, Pascal Verrot. A diminutive Frenchman, Verrot does whatever Seiji tells him to in this role. It is not for him to interpret this section of the piece. But he will conduct offstage. The offstage players will see him as well as a closed-circuit television picture of Seiji on the podium.

Seiji tries the passage with everyone who plays it onstage. Then he sends the offstage players out and tests the sound of one of the trumpets with its end, or bell, pointed toward the stage-right door.

He thinks the sound is too loud, so he asks the player, Charles Daval, to point his bell away from the door. Seiji sings the part as he wants it, and Daval tries to duplicate what the conductor has done.

A young man who has played in the orchestra for three years, Daval feels under extreme pressure today. Like Charlie Schlueter, Daval was on probation his first season, but unlike Charlie he wasn't given tenure. Instead, his probation was continued for the next season and then another. Now he has learned that Seiji has not only refused him tenure again but will not renew the probation. Daval will play out this year and then must look for another job. But he does not slack off here. He knows that how he plays may affect his chances for a good recommendation, and it will certainly affect how his Boston colleagues view him.

Mahler, who was the premier conductor of his generation, fretted about "Der grosse Apell" so much that he used to require a separate rehearsal just for this passage. But the Boston orchestra can't afford that. The cost would be too great and there isn't time anyway. Seiji must let the players who've been rehearsing "The Big A" go now, so they can have a break in the rehearsal like their colleagues. And Seiji needs one, too. In a very short time the soloists will be onstage, and Seiji will need to be refreshed for that.

*   *   *

Backstage is bustling. A kettledrum has to be moved and the stagehand can't be found, even after being paged. Finally, though he's not supposed to, someone in the orchestra moves it. Seiji confers with Pascal once more about "Der grosse Apell" and then disappears up the narrow stairs to his dressing room, where the usual entourage of administrators awaits him.

The flowers for the tables at tonight's postconcert dinner have arrived.

Behind closed doors, soprano soloist Edith Wiens completes her vocalizing, while in another dressing room a few feet away, contralto Maureen Forrester finishes hers. Wiens is a young Canadian soprano, living now in West Germany, who made her debut with Boston singing Mahler Two at Tanglewood two years ago. Forrester is a veteran whose long, brilliant career has been distinguished by her Mahler interpretations. Each for different reasons has broken other commitments to appear in these BSO performances.

For both of them, this symphony and these performances have special significance. Maureen Forrester last sang Mahler Two with the BSO in the 1970s, when her career was already well established. But her first performance of it was twenty-nine years ago, when her career took off with this symphony. The conductor then was Bruno Walter, whose own career had begun as an assistant of Mahler's. She made a famous recording of it under Walter with the New York Philharmonic, and like Walter, Forrester has been associated with Mahler ever since. Nevertheless, some people in the music business wonder if she is too old to be singing still.

For Edith Wiens, the *Resurrection* Symphony has a very personal meaning. While performing the piece several years ago in Switzerland, Edith was staying with friends, one of whose children went hiking on a glacier. The child fell through a crevasse in the ice, and he was dead by the time rescuers found him. That night, in his room, his parents saw his open diary on his desk. For the date of the

Mahler concert, he had written two words, "Resurrection/Edith." She is unable to forget this tragedy whenever she sings the piece.

Edith waits in the wings with Maureen as Seiji and the orchestra skip through several spots in the finale. Neither betrays nervousness. At 12:25 P.M. they take their places, sitting in the center of the chorus space, behind the orchestra. The playing continues as they come in. In the actual performance, they will come onstage after the second movement (but the chorus members will file in before the piece begins and remain seated until they sing).

Mahler was always troubled about where to situate the soloists, and the question has vexed conductors ever since. Instrumental soloists typically place themselves next to the podium, and vocal soloists in most works do the same. But to do that in this symphony would mean having the soloists front and center for much of the piece long before they begin to sing—in the soprano's case, for nearly an hour. Seating them with the chorus permits the two women to sneak onstage after the first two movements of the symphony and also enables the soloists to blend in their voices with the chorus when the score tells them to.

Nevertheless, the distance between these seats and the podium puts additional pressure on the conductor and soloists. Because they are so far apart, it is more difficult for them to stay together during subtle tempo changes in phrases. But Seiji believes this arrangement works better, and Maureen agrees. After the third movement, the Scherzo, the audience is still focused on the orchestra. Forrester's sudden standing in the back to sing "Urlicht," the fourth movement, forces the audience to look up at her dramatic, surprising entrance.

Edith sits down now but Maureen remains standing. In her black skirt and black and gray blouse, Maureen seems regal, her hair golden, her hands cupped together below her broad chest. "O glaube," she sings emotionally. "Mein Herz, o glaube." "Oh believe, my heart, believe."

Sitting in the first balcony, John Oliver is overcome by the beauty of Maureen's voice. To him, she sounds thirty-five years old. Onstage, the orchestra members also sense they are participating in something extraordinary. The deep, mysterious voice captures the spirit of the lyrics, and in its conviction and expression embodies the music.

Shortly, Edith also stands. She is wearing a blue dress with red sash, and her glowing presence is in bright contrast to that of the players in the orchestra. (Comfort governs their rehearsal apparel, which ranges from T-shirts and jeans to an occasional dress or sports jacket.) But there is a charged, almost anguished look on Edith's face, appropriate to the spirit of Mahler's subject. Mentally, she has prepared herself for this moment by remembering the death of her friends' child.

Seiji leads the orchestra and the two singers through the end of the finale. The music sounds odd without the chorus. But the chorus will not convene until one o'clock to prepare for this afternoon's rehearsal. The playing nevertheless taxes the players. Red-faced from exertion, Charlie looks relieved when he and the other five trumpets play their last E-flat-major chord.

Seiji wipes his brow and finally introduces the soloists to the orchestra. Then he directs the orchestra back to the end of the Scherzo, after which the contralto part begins. Maureen waits as he conducts the enigmatic five-bar close of that third movement, following which Mahler has written an order to proceed without a break to "Urlicht." Maureen must be ready to sing as soon as the Scherzo ends.

Twice Seiji starts and stops the playing of the music at the juncture of the two movements. Twice he starts and stops the orchestra's first notes after Maureen begins singing. Usually, a soloist must measure up in the ears of the orchestra. But she is so confident and has such an aura about her that her presence seems to put the players and Seiji on the spot. Finally, Seiji lets the music take its course, not stopping again until the beginning of the finale. There

Mahler has again ordered no break during a performance, but Seiji calls for one now. Immediately and spontaneously, the orchestra applauds Maureen, who beams in response.

Seiji spends five minutes fixing a few dynamics. He asks the strings to play more slowly at the end. They repeat the final six bars of "Urlicht." The entire movement takes up only six pages in the score and lasts less than five minutes, but everything that follows hinges on the song's transcendence.

"That was more together," Seiji says. Then he gives the musicians a real compliment. "Perfect," he says. This is the closest he ever comes to expressing his feelings verbally to the musicians.

Seiji looks at the clock, which shows five minutes before one. "I guess we have no time for another movement," he announces. "Thank you." With these words, the players realize they can leave for lunch.

Charlie Schlueter and a few players remain onstage, practicing places they have just rehearsed. The mood is suddenly quiet, a brief respite before the music—and the tension—resume in full force in an hour.

Seiji also lingers for a few minutes to talk with concertmaster Malcolm Lowe. It is almost a ritual for these two men to have a conversation after a break has been called. Seiji may be hard to get hold of away from the hall, but he's always available at these moments. Talking with Malcolm seems to relax him after the highly charged exertion of the rehearsal. Usually, the two men confer about a bowing here, a phrase there, but the purpose of the chats is also to convey a kind of camaraderie, a sense of mutual need for each other.

"Ten times they played it. Ten! Seiji's working on lots of details, which was a great relief to me. I was glad to know it wasn't just us he was after."

John Oliver is in the chorus room, where only a few weeks ago he held the auditions for his chorus. His singers are now packed into rows of chairs there, awaiting their two o'clock rehearsal and listening to his description of yesterday's orchestra rehearsal. By exaggerating the number of times Seiji stopped the orchestra in the first movement to correct the slurs at figure 11, he is preparing the chorus psychologically for the kind of picky detail work it may face in a few minutes.

Martin Amlin plays the familiar "bird of death" motif from "Der grosse Apell," the chorus begins singing, but John stops it immediately.

"If you could convince yourselves that singing is unnecessary here, except the low bass," he pleads, to explain anew the softness of the beginning. He uses the word "murmur" to describe the sound he is looking for. "Don't feel obliged to sing," he continues. "If you feel the note is not there, don't start."

As they go through their final preparations, they sing as a group for one reason: to please John.

And John concentrates on the sound he hears. Drawing on his long experience with Seiji, he listens for anything he thinks may displease the music director. Many of the chorus members sang the symphony two years ago at Tanglewood, and ten of them were with John sixteen years ago, also at Tanglewood, when John first prepared a chorus for a BSO performance. That concert, conducted by Leonard Bernstein, was also a Mahler Two. He tells today's chorus about his feelings then.

"That was the very first time I felt my life was on the line," he says. "I couldn't get this opening soft enough." He steers his narrative toward its intended goal, an almost jargonistic description of how he accomplished the challenge.

"I didn't know how to combine the pitch. Lenny smoked his thousandth cigarette. But finally we got it right: To make the upper intervals right, you have to think pitch, not voice. That's a great moment when the 'ja' is louder than the 'auf.' "

He means that the "aufersteh'n" following "ja" must be just as insubstantial as the "Aufersteh'n" that precedes "ja," to be certain the musical phrasing makes sense with the words.

Seiji would never have this kind of pedagogic discussion with the orchestra, partly because it is of a nature that a professionally trained musician would already understand, and partly because there are too many instruments in the orchestra for Seiji to know them all well enough to discuss each one this technically.

When Seiji worked with the violins on figure 11 of the first movement yesterday, he repeatedly stressed the kind of sound he wanted, just as John has with his singers. But Seiji didn't try to explain how the violinists should actually play. He would not presume to be a violin teacher. Nor would he tell Charlie how to play a certain passage softer, because he is not a trumpeter. He must trust that his musicians can translate his requests into execution on their particular instruments.

"I really don't mind if some of you don't sing," John again reminds the chorus. Then, after a series of further stops and starts, he gives them one final thought about the beginning to keep with them when they face Seiji. "It's all imagination, not singing."

Nina Keidann listens as though *her* life were on the line. She has never sung before in a chorus whose director took what the singers were doing this seriously.

Sarah Harrington distributes a revised seating plan, with the different parts mixed. Instead of grouping the tenors in one section, the sopranos in another, John believes they blend better if they are scattered somewhat at random. Nina finds her name in the fourth row, near the center, where she will have a good view of the soloists and be on an almost direct sightline with Seiji.

With a brief break to use the bathrooms and get themselves a last cup of coffee or tea, Nina and the other singers form a long line from the hallway outside the chorus room into the basement of Symphony Hall. Soon, they are seated between the orchestra and the back wall. Seiji appears, and the chorus applauds.

*   *   *

For the first time since the rehearsal began, all the part-icipants—over 250 people—are assembled together. Although Seiji shows no more excitement over this than he would reveal were he rehearsing one singer with piano in a small room, this is an important moment for him. He conveys his authority by the simple fact of his presence, by his total control of himself. Using his score, Seiji begins the rehearsal at an orchestral climax at which he and John have decided to have the chorus stand.

Like the question of where to seat the soloists, the issue of when the chorus should stand bothered Mahler, as it has every conductor of the symphony since its premier in 1895. The chorus's first notes invariably surprise an audience. But Seiji seems to have forgotten now just how surprised he was by the chorus's opening notes when Bernstein conducted the piece in Vienna many years ago. As he himself should have recalled, if the chorus had stood up conspicuously several pages in the score before it began singing, obviously he wouldn't have been so fooled.

Having the chorus stand beforehand makes it easier to sing, but this tells the audience what is going to happen. Nevertheless, Seiji decides this is the "safest" course to take, and John acquiesces. "I'd speak with Seiji if I thought it mattered," reacts John with prickliness when he's asked about this. Clearly it does matter, but this only raises another question: When would he have spoken to Seiji? They have both been too busy to sit down and discuss such a problem calmly.

Sitting himself in the first balcony, next to Sarah Harrington and Seiji's other assistant conductor, Carl St. Clair, John leans over the railing when Seiji conducts the chorus's first "Aufersteh'n." Will Seiji be pleased? John has to wait to find out, because Seiji lets the music continue.

Edith Wiens sings her first notes with the chorus. Twice she soars piercingly above the chorus soprano line; the second time this happens, Charlie is also playing, very softly. After Edith sings, Maureen Forrester gives her a maternal pat. Then it is Maureen's turn. Holding a handkerchief, she sings while the entire chorus rivets its attention on her. Mezzo-soprano Donna Hewitt-Didham, a large, outgoing woman, wipes tears from her eyes as she listens to Maureen. Soon everyone in the chorus is singing and the entire orchestra is playing. At the end, the volume assumes an almost physical form.

Seiji looks at his score and claps for attention. "Chorus," he says. John again leans over the railing to hear.

"Chorus. The beginning was excellent."

"But," pipes up a voice from within the orchestra. Many onstage laugh.

"The first 'Aufersteh'n' was good," continues Seiji. But he didn't like the second one. He asks them to do it again, watching his downbeat. The orchestra members take this moment to chat among themselves. John sits back more comfortably, relieved that things are going relatively well.

A trumpet player who has been offstage just before the chorus's entrance asks Seiji when he is supposed to return. Seiji thinks it over before deciding on the upbeat before the bar that concludes the first choral section.

"I'm glad you asked this now," Seiji says. "Tomorrow is too late." Either most of the players are too busy talking to hear Seiji or they think this humor unbecoming, because few of them laugh. They prefer jokes about the music director, not themselves. And they're tired of these constant details.

Seiji seems unaware of their feelings; he speaks now as if he has forgotten these are people he is addressing. Repeating the final "Aufersteh'n" section once more, mouthing the words as he conducts, Seiji stops the orchestra and chorus just before they finish. To the men and women of the chorus, most of whom have taken time off from their work or, in Nina's case, cut a class to be here today, he says only, "Go out quietly." Most of them sit for another minute before they realize they have been dismissed. Seiji has heard what he wants to and now he doesn't need them until tomorrow. Before they have finished leaving the stage, he tells the orchestra to turn to a spot in the third movement he wants to check. He is like a general in battle here. Having observed his troops on the left flank, he turns to the right, without a thought or care for the individual emotions of his soldiers. But music isn't war.

Maureen Forrester and Edith Wiens, who have lived through this experience many times and are being paid well to do so again, are happy to leave with the chorus. It's a beautiful, warm day in Boston and they decide to walk back to their hotel rooms at the nearby Copley Plaza. Along the way, they stop at Saks Fifth Avenue to window-shop.

Nina Keidann returns to her campus to study for an exam she has to take tomorrow. That will mean missing the final rehearsal, but she's been given permission by Sarah. She's too awed by her participation in these concerts to see the irony in the situation. Her choral singing is voluntary, but being excused from a rehearsal is more difficult than skipping school.

Much to its displeasure, the orchestra is detained by Seiji to read through *Drala*, a new work by Boston composer Peter Lieberson that the BSO will premiere a week from now. Though the players are professionals, accustomed to such jarring jumps from one composer to another, they're tired after their long day. And many of them dislike the new work. But Seiji, of course, has his way.

Elsewhere in the building, a painter touches up the ceiling in the second-floor men's room. Peppino Natale, Seiji's chauffeur, waits at the stage door, near the security guard's desk, to drive an exhausted Seiji home in the BSO's black Lincoln Continental.

Today's music making has gone well, but many of the people are still at cross-purposes with one another. Charlie Schlueter is still insecure about his standing with Seiji. John Oliver feels pushed to the sidelines. Many of the others in the orchestra are disgruntled about having to play so much Mahler, about the possibility of a strike, about their musical lot in life. Nina and many in the chorus have no idea what else has been going on in the preparations for tomorrow night's concert, but they've been around the hall long enough today to realize now they are not the entire show. Only Maureen and Edith seem relatively happy, but they're visitors.

Early the next morning, Peppino reverses his routine, getting a refreshed Seiji back to the hall on time for the last Mahler rehearsal. On the podium, Seiji by habit begins by shaking hands with Malcolm Lowe and uttering his usual brief greeting to the other players: "Good Morning." Leonard Bernstein, notes one of the BSO librarians, talks to an orchestra "as if he just got off the phone with the composer." Seiji instead plunges immediately into more details. But there is a sprightliness to his talk today, and an urgency that is not marred by anxiety. He conveys confidence to his orchestra by the example he sets, and they seem glad to get to work. Because these exhausting rehearsals are almost over, everyone is in a much better mood now.

"Cellos, basses, open up four in first movement," he says. By "open up" in this instance he means "turn to" (in another context, the direction would indicate an opening-up of the sound). They play the unison passage, which is a variation of the opening, and then at their conductor's command they play it again.

"Yes, thank you," says Seiji. "It's getting better, but still not together. Some are still not tight with fingers."

They do it once more, this time starting on the third beat of the second bar of the same passage. Seiji looks, listens, lets them continue. Then he stops and directs them to another passage that still needs attention, then another. The corners of the pages in his score are folded to remind him of these spots, but he needs no other prompting to remember what he wants to say. In not quite half an hour, he fixes a dozen such details. The result, when the orchestra goes back to the beginning, is sharper, crisper sounding. Seiji and the orchestra are on a kind of roll.

The music making gathers momentum. Seiji interrupts less frequently and he stops looking at his score. He often asks for help to get the precise bar count preceding or following a place he's discussing, but he has the entire symphony in his head.

Rarely does he refer to Mahler by name when he's talking. Instead, when he wants to invoke a higher authority, he just says "composer," which makes that word seem a synonym for "God." To Seiji, who scrupulously follows Mahler's many notations in the margins, it is.

Sensing that his players need some explanation for the direction in which this morning's work is taking them, he finally pauses after an hour to make a major point. "I don't know why, but after holiday, to find the missing contact, you push," he says. He means they have been pressing, instead of playing with one another in a relatively relaxed, responsive manner. "And this is not the usual stage setup," he continues, with reference to the enlarged space on which they are performing. The stage has grown with a five-foot extension installed earlier, but this often happens for Mahler. His Eighth Symphony necessitates the use of an eleven-foot extension. Front rows of seats in the auditorium are removed and the stage crew carries large pieces of wood, including risers, from the basement via a freight elevator hidden in the center of the auditorium's floor.

"We have a little problem in hearing each other," Seiji concludes. The only way someone sitting in the rear of the second-violin section can know for certain that he or she is together with someone in the rear of the viola section, all the way across the stage, is to watch Seiji. Just to listen won't work since, as Marylou Speaker Churchill points out, "the stage is wide and sound travels slower than light."

None of the players talks back to Seiji when he makes his remarks. They mutter a lot, but it isn't their place to debate with their conductor. Moreover, they understand and in some ways agree with what he is saying here. But the high energy with which they began the rehearsal is ebbing. It is all somehow antithetical to the spirit of the music, even if it is necessary.

The principal French horn, Charles Kavalovski, has a question that he believes must be addressed, even if it tries his colleagues' patience. They're tired and want to take a break.

"I'm sorry to bring this up now," he apologizes. But with the cramped seating on stage, he explains, the trombones' slides are hitting the horns' bells during passages that call for the bells to be pointed up. Usually, the bell stays in the player's lap, with one of his hands inside it to lessen the volume of sound. But Mahler sometimes asks for the fuller bells-up sound.

"There must be some solution," responds an amused Seiji. The players in the vicinity of the horns and trombones move their chairs forward, giving the trombones more space. But this doesn't really solve the problem. An annoyed Seiji turns his head and indicates the problem will have to be solved later. There's no time for this now. He looks at Malcolm Lowe, makes a funny face, then barks out, "Movement two." Back to the music.

Seiji stops the players three times before cutting from the movement's middle to the Scherzo. This rapid shift catches the veteran principal timpanist, Everett Firth, by surprise and he misses his entrance. But Seiji says nothing. Vic, as Seiji calls him, is one of his favorite players in the orchestra and he rarely criticizes him.

Pressed for time, Seiji quickly cuts again, this time to a later passage in the Scherzo. "Careful," he warns at some delicate staccatos. Two more quick checks later in the movement and the time is 11:45. Before going to his dressing room after the break he has called, Seiji sits down on the podium and chats again with Malcolm. Then he devotes a precious minute to the horn-trombone seating problem, as though to avoid having to deal with whatever bureaucratic problem may await him when he's greeted by the usual retinue of administrators in his dressing room. He tries out Kavalovski's chair, but he hasn't a solution. The stage manager, Al Robison, will have to handle it. The tired look on Seiji's face makes it seem he'd be happy to sit here in this chair for the rest of the day with absolutely nothing to do. But he manages a laugh and a shake of his head as he gets up and smiles at Robison. He treats Robison with the same respect and politeness with which he treats the most famous soloist.

Almost immediately, the chorus starts filing in, followed by the orchestra and soloists. They're still finding their seats when Seiji returns from the break and begins at the Scherzo's end, twice checking the transition to "Urlicht." No further interruption follows until the first offstage playing in the fifth movement. Then Charles Daval hits a wrong note in the next offstage passage, and there is much laughter onstage.

But the incident isn't funny to Daval. Nor is the laughter of his colleagues directed personally at him. What he's just done is what they all fear.

Continuing to the end, Seiji makes a fist with a raised arm as the music reaches its triumphant conclusion. During the final bars, his whole body shudders as he moves up and down and then extends his fist again. In the frightening silence that follows this charged moment, he looks at the clock. It says two minutes past one, which means the orchestra is now on overtime.

Seiji keeps them only another five minutes, even though the players will be paid for a full extra quarter hour. Incredibly, he spends this time fixing three more tiny details. He is sweating profusely and is clearly moved by the experience of conducting this performance attended by no one. Surely now, with this huge group of people having just completed music that addresses the most profound of questions, that articulates a range of emotions from overwhelming sadness to the utter joy of the conclusion—surely now he will say something about what he has just heard, about the concert tonight, about Mahler.

But Seiji passes up this opportunity for praise or eloquence. At

Symphony Hall this midday, no one talks about life or death, no one speaks of love. Seiji dismisses everyone for the afternoon with an anticlimactic thank-you. The endurance test of the past three rehearsals is finally over. Now, with very little time to rest, Seiji and the other performers must get themselves ready for the concert.

SIX

*C*harlie never goes home after a rehearsal on a day when there's also a concert that night. Instead, at a fee of seventy-five dollars for a one-hour lesson, he teaches on many of these free afternoons. With two daughters in college, he needs all the extra income he can earn. More important, he likes teaching, likes the contact with his young students, many of whom become his friends. He gets back far more thanks and affection from his students than he ever does from Seiji. Charlie's students revere him. They visit him at home, where he throws an annual barbecue for them. They practice hard because they want to please him and because they know he will help them find jobs after their studies. They stay in touch with him after they leave Boston, and some of his graduates fly in when they can for a lesson or arrange to study again with him during the summer at Tanglewood.

But Charlie wouldn't go home before a concert even if he weren't teaching. Though he's an inveterate putterer-around-the-house and loves gadgets of all kinds, he wouldn't know how to pass the time calmly with a performance on his mind. He has too much pent-up energy now and needs something as focused as teaching to keep him from becoming preoccupied with how he'll play, how Seiji will react, what the critics will say. His near dismissal was such a terrible blow to his confidence that he is still recovering. His students remind him of how much he has to give others. They restore his confidence and make him happy to be playing the trumpet. With a desire that is evident to those around him, he dreams of better times. He has better reason than almost anyone else in the orchestra to hate Seiji, but he never disparages the music director in public. Privately he mentions things about Seiji's conducting he dislikes, as any intelligent player will. But he admits admiration, too, and is determined to make Seiji respect him. He cares deeply about this.

By late afternoon on a typical Thursday before a concert, Charlie would be going to dinner at Amalfi's or at his favorite Thai restaurant. If he were in a rush, he'd grab a slice of pizza at the place across from the New England Conservatory of Music, where he does some of his teaching.

But today isn't typical. The Opening Night concert is officially scheduled to begin at 6:30, instead of the usual 8 o'clock. Management has chosen the earlier time because some of the concertgoers will stay for the "gala dinner" afterward. These people have paid $250 to enjoy what one of the co-chairwomen of the evening has described as "the glories of music and the glories of food."

And an hour before the concert begins, something unheard of in the orchestra's history is going to happen. Charlie and his colleagues are planning to demonstrate over the trade agreement.

Shortly before 5:30, Charlie stops at his basement locker. He has on a turtleneck and a tweed blazer. With the necklace of beads he wears when he's not performing, his beard, and longish hair, he looks like a college professor of the sixties. But now, changing into his tails, his appearance is transformed into that of a diplomat or a ballroom dancer, elegant and proper.

Soon, like Charlie, most of the other BSO players are standing outside in the rain. In their formal concert clothes, they are stationed at every door of Symphony Hall. In one hour the orchestra has to be onstage to perform Mahler Two, this time before a full house. But now, when most of them should be downstairs warming up and preparing themselves mentally for the concert, they are instead passing out leaflets to the arriving concertgoers. Only the most ardent union members among them take this new duty seriously. For many it's a lark, but the mood could easily turn ugly if their commitment was made fun of.

The men in tuxedoes and the women in long gowns accept the leaflets, and then they sip champagne at a reception inside.

For once, violist Ron Wilkison is early for a concert. Though he hasn't been a faithful attendee at the players' discussions of the trade agreement, he thinks it's important to participate now in this little demonstration. He stands with several other players near the box office canopy at the main entrance on Massachusetts Avenue, amiably enjoying the fresh air and the company of some friends in the orchestra. He lights one of the British cigarettes he rations to himself—ten a day, which he keeps in a fancy metal cigarette case.

Near him, a limousine pulls up alongside the curb and several wealthy patrons of the orchestra get out. With an embarrassed smile, Ron hands one of them a leaflet. "The Boston Symphony Orchestra will not continue to attract the world's best musicians unless it maintains artistic parity in salary and benefits with other great orchestras in the world," the leaflet states. Typed single-spaced, the one-page document has been duplicated on tan paper with the polite heading "A Message from the Players of the Boston Symphony Orchestra." Ron and the other players are certainly polite as they pass them out.

But the scene outside the hall is too bizarre to be described simply as polite. Normally, after the intense push to prepare a difficult work in rehearsal, the players feel up before a concert, like athletes before a big game. It is the players' responsibility as professionals and Seiji's as their music director to pace themselves so that their mood remains high despite the distractions of the rest of their lives. But tonight they are thrown off the rhythm of their accustomed routine. As they begin to drift inside to get their instruments, they see TV reporters interviewing their head negoti-ator, Ron Barron, who is also the principal trombonist. They wonder what he's saying on camera instead of thinking about what they're going to play. Their attention has been diverted, making Mahler seem an afterthought.

About ten minutes before he has to be onstage, Charlie Schlueter leaves his leafleting post and in his basement spot begins his familiar prerehearsal, preconcert workout, which he refuses to call warming-up. "Warming-up is a euphemism, a cliché," he says. "I need to see that everything is working as it should." On a normal Opening Night he would have been doing this for nearly an hour by now. Yet he doesn't believe the demonstration has been a distraction. "It's nothing different from the past four months," he says defen-sively, referring to the long period of stalled contract negotiations.

Though he felt on the spot several times during the rehearsals this week, Charlie thinks he played well. And the muscles in his lips have survived the ordeal of Mahler so far. Still, to rehearse this difficult piece four times in three days is a lot of trumpet playing, especially with the performance coming on the same day as the final rehearsal. But Seiji doesn't seem to realize this. While Seiji is careful to guard a singer's strength, he doesn't seem to understand the physical demands he puts on some of his instrumentalists.

Charlie isn't the only trumpeter who feels this way tonight. Andre Côme, who plays second trumpet, is outgoing and warm-hearted, and he lets very little bother him. He has a good time performing and he never pontificates about his work. But he shakes his head when he thinks about all the notes he's already played this week. The sustained upper-register music for trumpet in the Mahler symphony has taken a toll on his lips, and Andre wishes he could have let off a little during parts of the rehearsals. But the music director would have none of that.

"In my next life," kids Andre, "I want to be Seiji's trumpet teacher." If only Seiji played the trumpet, Andre thinks, the conductor might appreciate better what the trumpets do. Near him another trumpeter, Peter Chapman, practices a place in the fifth movement. He holds his trumpet in one hand and a cigarette in the other. The pose makes him look like a jazz player in a nightclub. Though no more than a dozen people in the orchestra smoke, this is still a high number for such an overeducated group. But there is little moralizing about personal habits. A player could stand on his head before a concert and no one would say anything if it was clear this helped calm his nerves.

Charlie calms his at these times by thinking of his friend Eloise. "Our minds are tricky and complex and full of surprises," she wrote in her book, *A Soprano on Her Head.* "I'm a great advocate for approaching life with a strong positive attitude, but a positive attitude by itself never produced a fine performer. There is a whole choreography leading to that fine performance, and it involves a lot of plain old hard work. Somewhere along with the hard work must be the permission to blow it. With that permission, we can afford to be a little more reckless in what we dare. As we become more reckless, we also become more committed, for we know we are stretching ourselves."

Once when they were talking with each other, Charlie told Eloise that he'd given himself permission to blow a passage but he still felt tight about it. "Yes," she replied. "But you didn't believe it." She meant Charlie hadn't really given himself permission to make a mistake. He'd only told himself he could, while still feeling he had to play the passage perfectly.

He tries now not to feel tight about the difficult symphony he is about to play. But it's very hard to convince himself that it's okay if he blows a passage in it. As a musician, he knows that the success or failure of a performance is not a simple result of how many notes are played correctly. If that were true, rather than attend live performances people would just listen to recordings, in which multiple takes are merged to create the illusion of perfection. But as a person who has lived through the near loss of his livelihood, Charlie worries about too many mistakes.

There are days when Charlie still can't believe what happened to him, and then there are moments when he remembers it only too well. He sometimes seems to be willing himself to think, *Now, from now on, everything's going to be fine.* Then Seiji stops the orchestra to address the trumpets or keeps going but glares at him and Charlie will think, *Oh, no, here we go again.*

The tension he feels then grips him terribly, but he remembers something Eloise told him to do. Looking into the hall's vast space, he picks out a color or shape and focuses on it before playing again. That has worked often enough for him to believe in it.

The unpolished brass of Charlie's trumpet is warm now. Moisture from his mouth collects less quickly on the inside of the metal than it did earlier, but he still has to stop frequently to depress the trumpet's "spittoon" to rid the tubing of saliva. Every brass player must cope with this fact of musical life. By the end of a performance, the floor by Charlie's feet is splotched with wet saliva marks.

Now that the trumpet is completely warm, the pitch has come up. Before, "it was five or ten cents flat." Charlie's templates have checked out pretty well, but he lingers another moment before leaving for the stage. He tries a few places in the Mahler, including a soft, subtle series of small arpeggios from the end of the first movement.

Mahler long thought of this first movement as a funeral march, although he eventually disavowed any programmatic explanation for it. Charlie certainly doesn't care about any "story" the music may tell. "I make a point about not getting the background," he says.

Despite his love of analogies, he thinks here in very pure terms about sound, about phrasing. If this is a contradiction, it hasn't occurred to him.

Because this arpeggio passage is so quiet and lasts only nine measures, many trumpeters—and their conductors—pay little attention to it. Certainly there is far more dramatic trumpet music in the piece, and the trumpet part in this passage often gets buried by the other instruments playing at the same time. The notes never take the instrument higher than G an octave and a half above middle C. The G is notated as D in the score, since the part is written for a trumpet pitched in F. That means that Charlie must transpose the passage a fourth higher than notated, since his C trumpet is pitched a fourth lower than an F trumpet.

He makes the transposition by second nature, transposing by mentally changing the clef in which the music is notated, a skill he learned at Juilliard.

Charlie takes such skill for granted. He never brags. His technical grasp of his instrument and its literature he mentions casually. That isn't what makes his art. But a passage such as this one in Mahler defines him as an artist. Without overasserting his role, he uses this tiny place in the piece to convey a large emotion, in much the same way as a great painter will add a subtle shade of coloring or variation of brushstroke that brings part of a painting to life.

Charlie believes you never should play the same phrase exactly the same way twice. "It's like sunsets," he'll explain. The little arpeggios suddenly become a part of Charlie's life, not a string of notes. It's a sunset in Du Quoin or the way the wind rustled in the leaves outside his bedroom window last night.

But Charlie doesn't dwell on his possession of the music's possibilities. This most loquacious of musicians is suddenly silent. He has a concert to play, an expectant audience and skeptical conductor to face.

*   *   *

Upstairs, around the corner from the box office, the glow of the chandelier in Seiji's spacious dressing room contrasts sharply with the bright lights for the TV cameras outside. Now that the news crews have plenty of footage about the demonstration for tonight's eleven o'clock news, they are hoping to get a shot of Seiji when he emerges from his sanctum. Seiji paces past the lone window from one side of the room to the other and then stands still for a moment under the chandelier. The light reveals streaks of gray in his long black hair.

If he had chosen to, he could essentially have stopped the demonstration simply by making an appearance at it. The concert-goers and reporters would have ignored the players just to rub elbows with the famous, glamorous maestro. But Seiji has to distance himself from the strife. His players are not hurting financially, but they are not wealthy like many in the Opening Night audience. Professionally, Seiji belongs more with his players; economically, with his patrons. He doesn't really fall into either group, however. He respects the traditions of the organization too much to get involved directly. He thinks it is out of his hands.

Seiji has changed into his formal wear and is paging through the Mahler score and chatting with a few of the aides who are permitted entrance before a performance. His aides scurry, dodging around the grand piano in the room's center, but he remains calm. He has no more idea than the people waiting in line at the box office if this performance will take off or go flat. He knows he has made a good start this week with the rigorous rehearsals, but now he must try to make all that hard, detailed work pay off. And the only thing he can do now before it begins is to think about Mahler, not money. He wishes more of his players were doing that, too. He would never walk onto the concert stage having consciously been thinking about something else, no matter what the cause. He has too much respect for the music.

Knowing the piece as well as he does, Seiji must guard against the danger of routine. He must make the symphony sound fresh. That was the purpose of much of what he did during the rehearsals, because many of the musicians were playing the piece as they had the last time it had been performed.

But what draws him to the symphony and what compels him to conduct it now is not necessarily what attracts his players to it—or what draws an audience, for that matter. Like *Symphonie Fantastique,* the famous Berlioz work that Seiji often conducted earlier in his career, Mahler Two is a conductor's piece. It demands that the conductor be completely in charge or its performance will fall apart.

Seiji doesn't believe Mahler's meaning can be put into words. It's in the music, and his responsibility is to make this clear in his conducting. That he can talk about.

"It takes time," says Seiji, explaining how he does this. "It's like book reading. First, you have to know the words." He pauses, as if pleased with the elegant simplicity of the analogy he is making. He continues.

"In music, you have to know technique. *Then,* you ask: What is this about?" He mentions different schools, by which he means general kinds of music, such as Impressionist, German Romantic, and so on. He calls this "background." Again, knowing this "takes time." Coming from a man whose understanding of the "background" and ability to translate this knowledge places him in an exclusive group of a dozen or so such conductors in the entire world, this is an extraordinary understatement.

Working on a piece, Seiji takes it apart. In the much-rehearsed Mahler measures just before figure 11 of the first movement, for example, he had to have thought through the whole piece before he could assign an importance to that spot. Seiji's word for such a place is a "buildup," and he goes through the entire symphony looking for such places, which he also calls "characters." Between the "buildups" there are "meltdowns," such as the chords that eventually follow figure 11 a few pages later in the score—to be precise, just before figure 13.

As he talks about this, Seiji refers to these places from memory, and he can cite the tiniest marking, even recalling exactly where on the page Mahler has written the words "non legato" before figure 11. He is akin to an actor who has learned a monologue from Joyce's *Ulysses* and not only knows the lines but can tell you where the page breaks are. But he's not the same as the freak who memorizes the phone book: There, names and numbers represent facts; here, in a musical score, symbols stand for sounds that trigger emotions.

When he opens up his multilined score, Seiji sees what every single instrument is doing at every moment, with all the parts written one under another. Adding to the complexity, the keys for the instruments are not all the same, because many of those instruments, like the trumpet, are pitched differently.

But Seiji doesn't block out the score simply according to what instruments are playing at a given moment or the direction the melodic line or development is taking. When he reads and studies a score, he sees it through what he calls the composer's "technique," a word that in this context has a huge meaning for him. It stands for everything the composer is doing musically—the harmony, the counterpoint, the rhythm.

The technique comprises the details of a piece, as opposed to its overall architecture. But Seiji doesn't use conventional architectural terminology. He speaks instead of "life starts." Several pages after figure 13 of the first movement, which a musicologist would describe as part of the first movement's second development, there is such a life start. When Seiji knows all the life starts, plus the underlying technique, he knows the piece.

"I become Mahler's life," he says then. He is not boasting, just stating in his idiomatic speech an incredible fact. By a feat of musical reincarnation, he knows Mahler Two as if he himself had composed it.

*   *   *

100

But the symphony is also a players' piece. Despite the complaints of the string players, there is far less plain accompaniment in
this symphony than in many others. And for the other instruments,
whose separate parts Seiji must keep together, Mahler has created
highly individualistic passages.

From the very first measures, in fact, Mahler pushes the
musicians to a kind of virtuosity they will encounter over and over
in the symphony. The quickly changing dynamic and rhythmic
patterns of the opening immediately test the orchestra's cello and
bass players, who have to play loudly and clearly—"an extremely
difficult combination," says principal bass Edwin Barker.

He first played Mahler Two as a member of the Chicago
Symphony under Sir Georg Solti. That was in 1976–77, Ed's first
season after graduating from the New England Conservatory of
Music as the top student in his class. A year later he returned to
Boston and joined the BSO. Young, confident, and very talented,
he's a player Seiji depends on. He never seems to make a mistake and
he never criticizes his boss.

He plays the Mahler Two opening more "on the string" than he
used to, by which he means that he draws the bow back and forth
instead of letting it up. But the stroke must still be "very heavy,
hammered, almost percussive." To achieve this, Barker has put extra
rosin on his bow. Instead of the usual three rubs of rosin, he has
given the bow nine. He needs to make the opening sound "rough,
very masculine, emphatic, heavy—anything but fleet. That's why it's
so hard."

Mahler is capable of the most delicate solo writing for every
instrument in the orchestra, but he never holds back. He expands
the expressive and technical range of each instrument. In a typical
Haydn symphony, for example, Charlie might play four or five notes
at a time and then nothing for a long stretch. Here, in Mahler, there
is more challenging, interesting material for the trumpet than in
most concerti for the instrument. That is why Charlie likes playing

Mahler so much. It is also why he and so many of the other players also find him intimidating. There is no letup in the piece.

The instrumentalists aren't the only performers trying to handle their preperformance jitters. Everyone is a little on edge.

"Be ready," says John Oliver to his singers in the chorus room. "If the ending is slower tonight, it's nothing to be excited about. Seiji was pressed for time in the last rehearsal."

In the adjacent hallway, a throng of waiters and waitresses try to keep from bumping into one another. The Cohen Annex is one of several rooms that will be used for the dinner after the concert. Now water glasses are being filled, baskets of rolls placed on the tables. Soon the chorus emerges to line up for its walk onto the stage before the beginning of the performance. The waiters and waitresses have to stop what they are doing until the singers have gotten out of the way.

Passing the basement "isolation booths," the singers can see Malcolm Lowe emerge from his hiding place in one of them. A perquisite of his position of concertmaster is his own dressing room. But backstage space in Symphony Hall is cramped, and for these concerts Edith Wiens is using Malcolm's dressing room. So Malcolm has had to cloister himself here to focus on the music.

Wherever he is before a performance, no one bothers Malcolm without good reason. He describes this time as "agitated anticipation." Tonight it is mixed with a deep personal attachment to the music he and the orchestra are about to perform. Ten years ago, as the young concertmaster of the Orchestre Symphonique de Québec, Malcolm listened to a favorite recording of Mahler Two every night to relax from the tension of his work.

Like Seiji, Malcolm seems unaffected personally by the leafleting, but as concertmaster he is concerned about its effect on the other players. Malcolm has to walk a tightrope here. His loyalty as a player is to his colleagues in the orchestra. But as concertmaster he must remain supportive of Seiji, give him his complete attention and best playing. Though no one's life depends on how he handles the precarious balance, Malcolm sometimes feels his does. But he has nothing to guide him except his own best instincts. They've worked so far. "You don't change what got you to where you are," he says. However, he internalizes conflict, and the people closest to him worry about the impact on his physical health. Anyone who knew him would notice how quickly this week Malcolm has lost his summer tan.

"First call." Assistant personnel manager Harry Shapiro's familiar voice over the backstage p.a. startles the players not yet onstage to attention. The time is 6:35 P.M. and the concert is about to begin.

"I have just been passing through the glorious country which sent Gustav Mahler into similar raptures so shortly before his death," Alban Berg wrote to his wife in 1911. Berg was en route to Prague, where he planned to attend concerts featuring music by Mahler, who had died a few months before. "The mountains completely under snow show right down to the foothills, then green meadows, brown fields, and that sky: almost unbearably beautiful, I wish you could have seen it, you'd have forgotten all the trials of the journey. But now I must watch all this magnificence sad and alone, and . . . the sadness won't leave me until tomorrow. The right mood, really, for . . . the Second Symphony."

Despite the demonstration, the elegant, softly lit hall buzzes with the murmurs of the waiting crowd, who seem in the mood for music if not Mahler. The hall smells of cooked food being kept warm for the dinner. A blue curtain hangs below the front of the stage extension. Though muted, the color jars with the burnished gold along the balustrades and over the proscenium. The players thumb through their music or fidget with their instruments, all except a few bass players whose heavy instruments rest against cabinets next to the players' tall stools.

A planned fifteen minutes late, at 6:45 P.M., Malcolm Lowe stands onstage, signaling the principal oboist, Ralph Gomberg, for the Boston A—441 vibrations per second. Gomberg activates an electronic box, kept onstage, that accurately gives him the A, which he then plays. Repeated chords and arpeggios follow until everyone has the pitch.

Personnel manager Bill Moyer takes a last peek through a knothole in the stage door to make certain everyone is ready. Behind him, Edith Wiens looks out from her dressing room. Except for the organist, who plays only forty-eight measures at the very end, she has the longest wait of all the performers before her first entrance. But she's used to such vocalist's vigils. She has learned to pace her emotions as well as her physical preparations, so that more than an hour after the piece has started she will sound in full voice.

Seiji's score has already been placed on the podium by one of the librarians, Marty Burlingame. "His security blanket," Marty calls the score, because Seiji will not look at it. It will remain on the podium during the performance, unopened.

At last, Seiji emerges from his dressing room. He stops at the door to the stage, which stage manager Al Robison will open for him. Though he doesn't play in the orchestra, Robison is considered an official member, and for the concert he has changed into his tux. "I used to play a good Gramophone," he jokes. "Now I play first trunk." His beaming face is a perfect foil for Seiji's look of utter gravity.

Seiji takes a deep breath and knocks on the door's wood for good luck. He always does this before he conducts a concert. When the orchestra is on tour, if the hall it's visiting doesn't have a wooden door, Robison holds a small wooden saké cup for Seiji to strike.

The house lights have dimmed; the audience is hushed, the musicians mute. Seiji makes his entrance to warm applause. He has never lost his following among the public. He shakes hands with Malcolm Lowe. He bows. He ascends the podium and looks around at his "group." He touches his score with the fingers of his left hand, as if to reassure himself it is there. Then, moving his shoulders up and down a few times to relax the muscles there, he contorts his body into a kind of coil, from which he appears to untwist as he gives a most emphatic downbeat. For the first time this week, the orchestra will play the piece from beginning to end.

Music usually has a way of blocking out external events for the performers. What lingers now, hard as it is for the players to define precisely, is the sense of oddity that the protest demonstration has given the concert. The initial mood of this evening is wrong, and it takes some time, takes some music, before everyone in the orchestra has settled in again to Mahler's world of sound and emotion.

Nothing is wrong, with the exception of a few missed notes, and much is right. The ensemble work that Seiji insisted on has resulted in numerous small instances of coordinated playing and felicitous phrasing. But there is not enough spark, no tingling edge.

Because of the tremendous contrast between the first and second movements, Mahler asks in a note printed on the last page of the first movement for a five-minute pause there. Like most conductors of the piece, Seiji meets Mahler literally halfway. He takes a break, actually sitting down in a chair next to the podium, but the primary purpose of this is to seat latecomers. Instead of in silence, the orchestra spends these two and a half minutes in the kind of nervous warmup that preceded the beginning of the piece. Malcolm watches the audience so he can give Seiji the signal to continue. Finally, he nods toward Seiji, who starts the second movement.

Another pause follows the second movement, so the soloists can take their places in the middle of the chorus's front row.

After Maureen Forrester has started singing "Urlicht," a different interruption occurs. It certainly isn't in Mahler's score, and it doesn't stop the music, but a blond-haired woman in a white dress and white hat unabashedly takes her seat in the second balcony.

Nothing can disturb Maureen, however. She has listened, transfixed, to the third movement, weeping to herself during an especially beautiful waltz Charlie and three other trumpets played. Now, the rapt attention of the audience attests to a sense they are hearing what they came for tonight.

After the Scherzo's enigmatic close, her first notes are sudden and dramatic. "O Röschen roth!" she sings. "Oh little red rose!" After only four notes, she has changed the entire atmosphere of this performance. With mutes, the strings enter. But not until the chorale that follows, with Charlie's trumpet quietly picking up the pitch of Maureen's part, does the presence of the orchestra shyly assert itself here. So quietly does "Urlicht" start that the stage and all the other people on it seem simply a backdrop to frame the almost motionless, riveting figure whose voice is so mysterious and moving.

Twenty-nine years before, when Maureen first performed this piece, Charlie's teacher, Bill Vacchiano, played the first-trumpet part. Now, seated beside her, to her left, Vacchiano's pupil waits for Maureen to complete the first phrase. Moved by the sound of her voice, he feels an identification with Maureen. She sings, he thinks, like he plays.

Seiji takes the chorale slowly, at what Maureen feels is a "holy tempo." She believes the chorale "represents one's destiny. I never think about dying," she says. "I'm not formally religious. I live each day as if it were the last; I live it double time. But at a certain point you realize, 'One day it will be over.' "

After "Urlicht," again at Mahler's insistence, there is no break before the finale. Seiji begins the last movement with a measured urgency, and the performers finally catch his emotion and make it theirs. The sound of the full orchestra reverberates to the very last row in the rear of the second balcony.

Seiji can sense this, and his job now is to keep a lid on the music's emotion so it doesn't reach a climax too soon. This is hard in Mahler Two, because there are so many moments in the finale when the music peaks, only to quiet and build again. Many less-experienced conductors bring the piece to an early emotional resolution, robbing the magnificent finish of its grandeur and power.

The musicians, meanwhile, must continue to concentrate on their individual roles. Assistant timpanist Arthur Press keeps an ear close to his kettledrums, which he makes certain are in tune for a prominent low E (which Mahler mistakenly wrote in his manuscript as F and mysteriously never corrected). Buddy Wright is happy that the hall is warm, because that makes changing clarinets easier; a cold clarinet will sound flat. As tired as he is from the contract negotiations, trombonist Ron Barron plays with great élan, changing mouthpieces before a chorale to help his endurance. Enthusiastic and voluble first violinist Amnon Levy finds his part a "bottomless wealth of endless material—like the universe!" But that doesn't keep his bowing arm from feeling exhausted.

Despite the disconcerting comings and goings of the offstage players, the hall is hushed for the chorus's first notes, almost as though John Oliver had coached the audience as well. There is of course a difference between liking a sound and being overcome by it. The whole performance has integrity, but in the last fifteen minutes the audience hears superb playing and singing, expertly paced and balanced, building to a triumphant close.

A standing ovation follows the final chords, and Seiji and the chorus are called back for repeated bows. John Oliver joins them at center stage, and both the orchestra and chorus take turns clapping for each other. A girl in a kimono presents flowers, still in their plastic wrap, to Seiji. Following the final bow, as the orchestra leaves the stage, the chorus applauds the trumpets. Charlie is happy with the praise.

But on this night mingling money and music, when the orchestra has insulted its most generous donors by demonstrating before the concert, there can be no real rejoicing after the final "aufersteh'n." Instead, following the excitement of the finale, there is an empty feeling, a hollowness that no normal postconcert letdown can explain. It is as if Mahler Two were a decoration or diversion, a musical ornament to placate the well-heeled crowd, many of whom are furious at the management and players for letting their dispute become so public. They feel the demonstration should never have been allowed to happen, that it should have been unnecessary.

The musicians, on the other hand, remain resentful. They feel underappreciated. As professionals, they've played competently tonight, even spectacularly at times, but their hearts haven't been completely in it.

A passion was missing from their playing, a conviction that nothing matters more than the music. Were he on a more solid footing with the conductor, Charlie might have been able to take more risks in this performance, to provide the kind of leadership the other players could follow. But an incredible distance still exists between him and Seiji, undermining the efforts of both and contributing to a malaise that others can feel. The two men do not even see each other afterward. Charlie heads home, while Seiji remains to make an appearance at the dinner.

Seiji misses the first course. He's trapped in his dressing room, where he must exchange greetings with several board members while his palace guard of assistants looks on. The room is very crowded, with another TV crew taping footage and everyone jockeying for the conductor's attention.

Though he appears on camera with the ease of a movie star, Seiji doesn't like these public occasions. And he remains perplexed at the excitement his personal presence generates. The music should do that, he feels, not the music director. But it is Seiji Ozawa's name that sells tickets, not Mahler's. When he enters Cohen Annex for the dinner, Seiji receives another round of applause from the guests. He makes some brief remarks. "Tonight's piece not relaxing," he jokes.

With an almost mystic serenity, Seiji seems untroubled by the effect of the demonstration on the music and the evening. One has the sense that had this night's concert been the best he'd ever conducted, he would be acting no differently. This has been a grueling week for him, but he knows what he and the orchestra accomplished. If the contract issue can just get settled or put aside, the orchestra is ready to forget its other problems and play well. Like the manager of a baseball team that loses its first game after spring training, Seiji knows there will be another game. He knows there are people in the orchestra who think the problem tonight was the conductor, not the contract, but he heard what the orchestra did this week. The important thing now is to keep going.

Dinner tables have also been placed in two other rooms that usually serve as hall lounges, and tonight's soloists, Edith and Maureen, have been strategically seated in them to make up for Seiji's being in the annex. Among the more conspicuously missing from the dinner are most members of the orchestra, or "the help," as Charlie refers to himself and his colleagues in this context. On a rotating basis, some of them are invited each time such an occasion is held, but most are physically and emotionally separated from the people for whom they have just played. What they have done is taken for granted, as though the only thanks they needed was the paycheck that this dinner's revenues will help underwrite.

Seated at the center table in the Hatch Room, Edith Wiens is ebullient after her soprano solo. She is also very hungry. Like most of the other performers, she didn't eat before the concert. Now she devours her dinner, listening politely as one of the orchestra's longtime patronesses, seated across from Edith, vents her anger over the preconcert demonstration.

"I didn't think these people were the class who'd do such a thing," the woman says with displeasure. She also directs her criticism at the BSO management for scheduling another performance of Mahler Two tomorrow afternoon. That is when she is supposed to come to the first concert on her subscription series, but she feels she's heard all the Mahler she wants to tonight. "Tomorrow's ticket cost me thirty-five dollars," she adds indignantly. And for another $35— actually $35.70, at the subscription price of $714 for the full season of twenty Friday afternoon concerts—she will have to sit through another Mahler symphony, his Fifth, in November.

When he was younger, Seiji might have charmed this woman and others like her merely by being around. She would have forgiven the BSO anything, simply because of its captivating, dynamic conductor. And Seiji would have turned an evening such as this into a night on the town with his musicians and friends. But Seiji is older now and busier. His responsibilities—to himself and the institution—are much greater. He doesn't have time for socializing and he isn't interested in sharing his life with lots of other people. Tomorrow he must conduct Mahler Two again. Not surprisingly, he flees from the dinner as soon as he can.

he trumpets were shocking at the end of the first movement and in the ill-tuned, imprecise chorale accompanying [Maureen] Forrester (in which there was also a false percussion entrance)." Reading this morning's *Boston Globe* at home, Charlie is shocked. He ignores the reference to the percussion and the rest of the review that precedes critic Richard Dyer's attack on the trumpets. Though Richard has referred to all the trumpets, Charlie is certain the critic is talking about him alone. Charlie is, after all, the principal trumpet player. He tries to shrug it off. "If I believed everything Richard wrote, I'd have quit five years ago," he says. But he is deeply hurt by the criticism and also by the absence of any word about what he did right last night, any word about the arpeggios at the end of the first movement, the waltz in the Scherzo, the soft accompaniment to Edith in the finale.

Nor does Charlie agree with the substance of Richard's specific criticism. He thinks the chorale went beautifully. Granted that only one of the trumpets would have to be slightly out of tune at the entrance for all of them to sound out of tune. But that doesn't ruin the chorale, let alone the piece. Nor does a "train wreck" at the end of the first movement. Lots of players made lots of individual, specific mistakes last night. There isn't a performance in which that doesn't happen, and Richard knows this. *Why*, Charlie wonders, *does he pick on me?* And why is the tone always so personal, as though Richard felt put upon by having to hear Charlie play? Charlie thinks Richard doesn't know what he's talking about. Either that, or he's a very cruel person.

He scans the review again. "The individual soloists of the BSO are great artists, and they sounded like it again last night." Then a list: Malcolm Lowe, Doriot Anthony Dwyer, Harold Wright, Ronald Barron, Everett Firth. Not Charlie Schlueter.

Charlie knows what some of the other players in the orchestra will think when they read this. They will disagree with most of what Dyer has written, but when they get to the line about the trumpets, many of them will nod yes. To them, Charlie, since his fall from grace, is a convenient person to blame for their own mistakes. They can use what happened to him to cover for themselves. "The brass were too loud," they can say. Even some of the other brass players say this, and the statement has a way of becoming a self-fulfilling prophecy. And Charlie doesn't help his cause. He hardly knows some of the people in the orchestra. He had to develop a thick skin after what happened to him, but he's still very touchy. Around the hall, he's enormously popular with most of the people who work backstage. But he watches himself with his colleagues. He remembers who stood up for him at his arbitration and who was afraid to.

Charlie leaves the paper on the kitchen counter, knowing Martha probably won't want to read it. If she does, nothing in the review will surprise her. More than anyone else, more even than her husband, she has taken to heart what happened three years ago. She no longer goes to Symphony Hall for concerts. And she's stopped playing the violin.

Martha remembers the raves Charlie used to get in Minnesota. She remembers the fun they all had there, the good times with others in the orchestra. She remembers that first time she heard Charlie play, before she even knew his name, that sound in the night in New York many years ago, a tone so beautiful she fell in love with the man who made it. Has anyone here heard that sound? Would Richard know it if he did?

Usually after a concert, Richard Dyer returns to the newspaper's office on Morrissey Boulevard to write his review. The orchestra's program schedule is blocked out in weeks that begin on Thursday, and Richard's review is supposed to appear in the late edition of the Friday morning paper. An eight o'clock concert normally ends around ten o'clock, and Richard's drive from the hall along Massachusetts Avenue takes about half an hour. That means he has about forty-five minutes to write his review by his 11:15 deadline. To do that, he composes part of it in his head beforehand, but he also prides himself on being able to write quickly. When he gets to the office, his editor tells him how much space he has, and Richard writes his review to fit, stopping a line or two short of the required length. That way he knows the whole review will run.

A fifteen-year veteran of the *Globe*, Richard studied English as a Harvard graduate student and taught at the University of Iowa before beginning his newspaper career. In addition to his reviews, he writes a weekly reporting piece that appears in the Sunday edition of his newspaper. He also reports musical news during the week. In today's paper, for example, he also has a short piece on the demonstration.

That assignment and the dinner after the Opening Night concert kept him at the hall late, and he wrote his review there on a portable word processor that connects to the *Globe*'s computer with a telephone modem. He likes writing under the time pressure of such a tight deadline. "It's something a newspaper person can do," he says. His recall of concerts and recordings is wide. His greatest field of expertise is opera, and he is a devoted supporter of new music.

When Richard first mentioned Charlie, five years ago, he described the new principal trumpet player as "a superb instrumentalist of forceful musical personality." For a time after that, there were fine reviews, but lately the only good one Richard has given Charlie was for a Tanglewood performance of Handel's *Messiah* a year ago. "In 'The Trumpet Shall Sound' ... Charles Schlueter shone," Richard wrote then. In the year since, he has ignored Charlie, while complaining habitually about the brass or just the trumpets. Though he hasn't said anything quite this damaging in print, Richard has voiced his opinion that the brass either go along with Charlie or let him hang himself. In other words, Richard thinks Charlie plays too loud. The rest of the brass either follow Charlie's lead and play out or they let Charlie stand out by himself. Either way, the result displeases Richard.

"Tricky Dicky," Charlie calls Richard to himself. Actually, they never see one another. Richard never goes backstage. The only time he and Charlie ever met was on a train in Japan, when the orchestra was on tour and Charlie asked the person sitting in his assigned seat to move. Though he didn't know it, the person was Richard. In his search for an explanation of Richard's animosity toward him, Charlie has even wondered if this incident had anything to do with the bad reviews he's been getting. But Richard was still saying basically positive things about him back then. Charlie remains puzzled.

Luckily for Charlie, Richard seems to dislike Seiji's conducting even more than Charlie's playing. The trumpets aren't the only performers singled out for blame in today's review. In fact, what Richard says about the trumpets is no more damaging than what he regularly says about the music director.

While crediting Seiji with a good Scherzo and finale, Richard takes a major swipe at him for the overall performance. "The ensemble playing was not often at the BSO's highest standard, as far from the way it sounded in this music under Claudio Abbado in 1979 as Ozawa's overall interpretation was from the precise and deeply felt one by his Italian colleague. . . . Not all the problems that beset the BSO can be solved at the negotiating table," he concludes.

Ellen Pfeifer, the critic for the *Boston Herald*, the city's other major newspaper, is just as negative as Richard in some of her comments about Seiji. She thought the Scherzo was "disastrous." And of the finale, she says, "The tempo too often seemed slow, the phrasing square and pedestrian. Ozawa wanted to make the most of the stunning climaxes, but he neglected to grade them, to save some of the thunder for the end. Not only did he undercut some of Mahler's fastidiously calculated effects, but he made some of the thunderous passages so opaque and sludgy that one couldn't differentiate the musical lines." Happily for Charlie, Pfeifer doesn't mention the trumpets.

The *Herald* is rarely discussed when a review appears, perhaps on the assumption that most of the people who attend BSO concerts don't read that paper. The *Herald* is known as a working-class tabloid, while the *Globe* is considered to have a more educated readership. But the negative criticism that Pfeifer pens for the *Herald* is of a piece with what Dyer says in the *Globe*. In Europe, Seiji generally gets excellent reviews. But in Boston he has alienated the critics who listen to him most often. Even a superb Opening Night performance probably wouldn't have changed the tone of what the critics have said.

Back at the hall on Friday, where there is another concert in the afternoon, the players discuss their own reactions to the concert and Dyer's review. "Mahler isn't Debussy," grumbles violinist Fredy Ostrovsky, referring to Richard's use of the word "coarseness" in his critique. Beginning his thirty-fourth season, Ostrovsky is almost always the first member of the orchestra to arrive for a concert.

Today is no exception. Fredy is there by late morning, long before the 2 P.M. curtain.

Others, as they come in singly and in small groups, seem unperturbed by the harsh judgment of their work last night. Some even agree with it. A violinist complains about Seiji's dynamics, which he, too, compares unfavorably with those of Abbado in 1979. Abbado is one of several conductors who exaggerate Mahler's dynamics to add a further tension to the music. Seiji's interpretation is much cleaner, much closer to the score's markings. There are no theatrics in Seiji's interpretation, no flashy touches that catch a critic's ear.

The chorus members, who came in for praise from both newspaper critics—as they usually do—are naturally pleased. Pfeifer commended their "virile tone and enthusiasm," while Dyer called their singing "thrilling." Neither critic gave Seiji any of the credit for this. "Did you see Dyer this morning?" the chorus members ask one another with raised eyebrows and high-pitched voices, as they arrive after lunch. They are somewhat bemused by the attacks on their paid partners.

At 1:10 P.M., Peppino announces to the people who happen to be standing near the stage door, "I go get maestro. Be back in ten minutes." Instead, it is nearly forty minutes before he returns. He gets Seiji to the hall with just enough time for the maestro to change his clothes for the concert.

Seiji's late arrival is a clue to how busy he is this fall. Charlie and most of the other orchestral players have lots to do, but Seiji has a truly daunting calendar, a mass of dates and times and engagements that never end. He has much music to study this fall and cannot afford the luxury of dwelling on yesterday. There is another Mahler Two performance tomorrow in Connecticut. Then, next week, there are six orchestra rehearsals and three new concerts. The Berlin Philharmonic Orchestra gives a concert here soon, and its director, Herbert von Karajan, is ill. Seiji may take his place here in Boston and on part of the rest of its tour if Karajan can't come. In two weeks he and the BSO have a recording date for Prokofiev's complete *Romeo and Juliet*, which they will also present in concert. In a month, he will make a trip home to visit his family in Japan, and will conduct an anniversary concert in San Francisco on the way back to Boston for more concerts and three more recording sessions, before he goes to Berlin to guest-conduct. Mahler Five in Boston will follow, and then more Mahler Two in December, with a Mahler Two recording still possible.

On this Friday afternoon, Seiji blocks out the prospect of this huge array of coming events by conducting a solid performance of Mahler. He seems oblivious to the criticism of last night's performance, as though the reviews were a very small part of his very large world. And he says he doesn't read what the critics write. In any event, he wills himself to focus on the music with extraordinary self-control. With less at stake because Opening Night is behind it, and without the distraction of another demonstration, the orchestra is much more relaxed. It sounds like it wants to play, perhaps to prove it can do better than it did last night. The playing today is splendid.

Friday afternoon concerts in Boston are a long-standing tradition, an idyllic feature of the city's cultural and social life enjoyed by generations of people. The doors to the hall open two hours before the concert, and early arrivals can loll away the time in one of the lounges, eating sandwiches and sipping on drinks while reading the informative program notes. The hall has a resonant, radiant quality to it then, with a palpable sense of the past. Fridays are tranquil.

Elderly concertgoers, many of them women who have been coming for over fifty years, arrive by limousine. Some of them leave early, standing up and walking out of the hall while the music is still being performed, in order to avoid the traffic on their return to Back Bay townhouses or Chestnut Hill estates. No one puts a stop to this rather boorish behavior because the ladies are also very generous donors to the BSO.

Many students also attend these afternoon concerts, buying

inexpensive seats that are sold only on the day of the performance. Consequently, the Friday audience is an intriguing mix of young and old, and includes many who are quite knowledgeable about the music and many who come only because their mothers and grandmothers did.

Seiji does not relax afterward, nor does he fraternize with his musicians, even though there is no family at home to have dinner with. But he has many administrative responsibilities as music director. For example, Seiji is intimately involved with the selection of the soloists for the proposed Mahler Two recording. The Philips recording company wants a soprano with a bigger box office name than Edith Wiens, and Seiji has agreed to telephone Kiri Te Kanawa to ask her.

Because Seiji is away so often, his schedule for these offstage working periods gets backed up. He'll put off what he can, and he's notorious for canceling appointments with reporters and board chairmen alike at the last minute. But when he decides to devote some of his precious time to meetings and discussions, he does so with the same concentration with which he studies a score. Woe to the person who comes to see Seiji unprepared.

Being with Seiji is an intense experience for most people, even those who work with him regularly. Late that Friday afternoon, he meets with Peter Lieberson, the composer of *Drala*, which the orchestra will premier next week. Lieberson finds the Japanese music director's manner a refreshing change from the easy familiarity of most Americans. Peter senses a space around Seiji, an inscrutability Americans aren't used to. "It's hard to know what to expect when you're with him," he says. "It makes you mean what you say."

Lieberson is the envy of many Boston composers because he is the son of the former head of Columbia Records. Intense and articulate, he knew so many famous performers as a boy that their company is second nature to him. For this meeting with the music director, he is well prepared.

His new piece was written on a BSO commission for which

Seiji is responsible. Three years ago, the orchestra performed another commission, Lieberson's Piano Concerto. Following the final performance, Lieberson, Seiji, soloist Peter Serkin, and friends went out to dinner, where Seiji impulsively asked Lieberson to write another piece. The result was *Drala*, inspired by his Buddhist thinking.

Seiji now reviews Peter's score with him, suggesting small changes that will make its performance work better. Peter is impressed by how well Seiji already knows *Drala*. It is almost as if Seiji is guiding him through his composition.

As soon as they are finished, Seiji busies himself with more administrative work while he awaits the arrival of the former BSO artistic administrator, his old friend Bill Bernell. Better than anyone here in Boston, Bernell can talk with him freely, can even tell Seiji to do something he doesn't want to do. Calm, personable, and devoted to Seiji, Bernell is not in awe of him.

Eight years older than Seiji, Bernell has recently been engaged as his "personal representative." He knows the music business so thoroughly he is a kind of walking encyclopedia of composers, soloists, and other halls and conductors. But perhaps more importantly, he knows Seiji as almost no other American does. (He is also among the few people who refer to the conductor by his last name.) Their relationship goes back many years.

After service in World War II, Bernell bypassed college and got jobs with the San Francisco Opera and San Francisco Symphony. He worked there until 1979, and then followed Seiji to Boston, where he stayed out of the spotlight, planning programs. He left Boston a year ago, returning to San Francisco, where Seiji still owns a home. Seiji now frequently visits him en route to or from Japan.

Seiji depends on Bernell to be honest with him about his program choices and questions about guest conducting and recordings. In a city where he really has no close relationships with anyone, it is a lift to his spirits for Bernell to be around for a few days.

*   *   *

The buses leave Symphony Hall the next evening at 5:30 for the two-hour trip to the University of Connecticut at Storrs, where the orchestra is again performing Mahler Two. The orchestra and staff grumble about having to make this "run-out," in part because the bus ride takes longer than the concert. Neither Seiji nor the soloists are on the buses. They travel by limousine and Peppino makes the drive twice, first with Maureen and Edith and then with Seiji and Bernell.

Both Seiji and Bill are cheerful this rainy evening. Bernell's looking forward to hearing Maureen sing. She's a friend, and he visits with her before the concert in the dressing room she shares with Edith. They swap stories, and Bernell sips on her grapefruit juice while she changes into her dress behind a locker. Edith is warming up, singing the line from "Aufersteh'n" where her part soars above the soprano line of the chorus. Bernell tells them both about the party he's having for his sixtieth birthday in two months in San Francisco. Seiji has promised to fly over with his family from Japan. Bill's very proud of this.

The nondescript auditorium at Storrs has poor acoustics. And those players who haven't come in their formal clothes have to change in the backstage hallway, improvising a dressing area by using a few storage lockers. But as professionals the players rise to the occasion, and they play well. The audience is enthusiastic and the players sense this, with the performance getting better as it progresses. Everyone is in a hurry to leave afterward, except Seiji, whose exhaustion finally catches up with him.

He slumps in his dressing room, with only Peppino, Bernell, and Bernell's Boston successor, Costa Pilavachi, for company. In a few minutes, they will go out for pizza on their way to Seiji's home in Tanglewood, where he hasn't been since summer. They'll stay overnight there, and Seiji will finally be able to put this long, first week behind him. He lingers now, wearing a kimono after the concert.

Counting back to the chorus rehearsal he led on Monday, this is the sixth day in a row he's conducted Mahler Two. After so much time at center stage, he seems relieved just to be sitting here, doing nothing, with people to whom he has nothing to prove. The buses with the players have already left and no one else knows his exact whereabouts. His family is halfway around the world. He says little. His hair, always perfectly groomed before he goes onstage, is disheveled. The heavy perspiration that covered his face during the concert has almost dried. Maybe in the morning the weather will clear and he and Costa can play tennis on the court near his mountainside home, with its beautiful view of the Berkshires. The three men will discuss future program possibilities in Seiji's three-continent career, looking for links between what he conducts in Japan and Boston, Boston and Europe. Then it will be back to Boston. Even when he's taking time off, Seiji is always on the way to someplace else.

EIGHT

About the only person in the orchestra who never looks at a newspaper review when he gets up in the morning is the concertmaster, Malcolm Lowe. This intense man lives a life removed from the daily concerns of most of his colleagues. The most visible player onstage, he is the most elusive off. Few of his colleagues know him well, but he is not eccentric. His life and his work are inseparable. If the strings are the soul of the orchestra, he is its heart. It is a role he was born for.

Like Charlie, Malcolm rises at dawn. He leaves his apartment in the Greenhouse, two blocks up Huntington Avenue from Symphony Hall, to get some exercise. He can see the hall from the quiet lobby when he opens the door. He walks briskly for half an hour, making a loop on the neighborhood's sidewalks. When he returns to his apartment, his wife-to-be, Colleen, and their young son, Brenden, are up. Brenden is playing with his toys, but he ignores his miniature violin until his father is practicing.

No critic's comment bothers Malcolm on such a morning. Malcolm is aware that Seiji and the orchestra serve as frequent targets of criticism, but he seems not to care what anyone writes about his own playing. His reviews are invariably favorable, but he is much harder on himself.

The apartment is small. Malcolm and Colleen have been house hunting, but they haven't found anything yet. And Malcolm is beginning to be concerned about buying something when there is a possibility the orchestra will go on strike. His violin is the centerpiece of the living room, kept in its case on the table as though it were the focal object in a shrine. The inside of the case is decorated with family memorabilia, such as little drawings by Brenden. Brenden knows he isn't supposed to play in the living room while his father practices, but this is a hard rule to enforce because the small room is near the dining alcove and next to the kitchen. And Malcolm doesn't like to be stern with him. Firmly but gently, Colleen reminds Brenden, "Daddy's working." Brenden leaves the room as his father takes out his violin.

Almost three years ago, when Seiji selected Malcolm as the tenth concertmaster in the BSO's history, he made what was probably his single most significant decision since becoming music director. Malcolm's predecessor, Joseph Silverstein, had been concertmaster since 1961, when he was only twenty-nine. In addition to being a violinist of great skill and feeling, Silverstein had an outgoing personality and was a musician with a considerable presence in Boston. During his last twelve years with Boston he was also an assistant conductor of the orchestra. This gave him a unique forum with the BSO. Seiji constantly had to assert himself as both Silverstein's conductor and, in a sense, his colleague. This situation led to thinly veiled disagreements between the men over matters of interpretation. And in the view of many, it contributed to poor morale among the players, who were unwitting partners in the conflict.

At the time of his audition with the BSO, Malcolm was still virtually unknown in the United States. But in Canada, where he had grown up, Malcolm had already made a name for himself as a prizewinning violinist, soloist, and orchestral concertmaster.

He had been born in the tiny town of Hamiota, Manitoba, where his parents ran a farm. Both his parents were musicians, and like his two brothers and one sister, Malcolm began his music lessons with his mother and father. Malcolm eventually studied with some of the world's most famous violinists, but his most formative musical experience was hearing his father play the violin when he was very young.

His ability to remember that and make what he heard his was more important than his sheer virtuosity when he auditioned for the BSO. Like Charlie, Malcolm had mastered the ability to convey the emotions of his life through those of the music. Everyone who tried out for his position could play extremely well, but Malcolm also possessed in his playing a sound no one could put precisely into words, but that "absolutely appealed," as one of the people present at his audition recalls. It was the perfect sound for Symphony Hall, a rich, full sound that was also capable of great delicacy and clarity.

"I've known my sound since I was a child, listening during naps on our farm to the wonderful violin sound of my father," Malcolm says. "In my ear, that's where my sound comes from." Malcolm would lie quietly as his father practiced, finally falling asleep to that sound. It was a gift he would never forget, the beginning of "something inside that adores music." It is a gift he is already passing on to his own son, who keeps coming into the room while his father practices.

Brenden plays with some blocks while Malcolm checks the instrument's four strings, which are tuned in fifths: G, D, A, E. Fussing automatically with the pegs that adjust the strings' tension, he tunes the instrument. He plucks a few notes and rapidly plays some chords.

Outside the two windows in his living room, the sun has just climbed past the ridge of rooftops in Boston's South End. Traffic, light now shortly after seven o'clock, will soon get busier. But the traffic sounds don't bother Malcolm. He is soon so lost in his music that he doesn't seem to hear them.

Brenden comes into the room again. This time he carries with him his small Suzuki violin. Malcolm smiles at him. "Play the alphabet," he says in a gentle, humoring voice. Brenden knows this means to play a few notes, which he's learned have the names of letters in the alphabet.

Brenden then leaves and Malcolm closes his eyes and begins playing. The fingers of his left hand now move very fast, shifting position as an arpeggio jumps an octave. Malcolm frowns, the pale skin of his forehead furrowed. Each press of a finger on the violin's fingerboard makes a rat-tat-tat sound independent of the bow on the strings. In the concert hall when the orchestra is playing together, no one hears this sound, but it is unmistakable here. The sound of those fingers moving is the only hint of the physical exertion involved in what Malcolm seems to be doing so effortlessly. Then, when he takes the violin away from his chin, there is another hint: a red mark on his neck where the bout of the violin hits his Adam's apple.

For Malcolm, this first playing of the day is like saying a rosary or meditating. It is a habit and a necessity that calms him and prepares him for his day. Were he to break this routine, his whole day would go out of sync. He has been living like this so many years that an alternative is inconceivable. But he fantasizes about one. He is not only a world-class violinist but a fine athlete. He sometimes wonders if he would have been happier becoming a professional golfer as a young man, rather than a violinist. He thinks he was good enough to have done that or to have tried out for professional baseball. In fact, he plays golf so well that he daydreams about joining the PGA Senior Tour when he turns fifty, but that's seventeen years away.

"I have to practice the violin," he says ruefully. But the time he devotes to that orders his world and gives meaning to each day.

Practicing is a given, like sleeping and eating. Malcolm could undoubtedly get away with doing less, and on many occasions when he's had no choice, he has. But he wouldn't feel right about himself if he regularly cut corners.

Colleen sets the table for breakfast. Malcolm, in his slippers and favorite dark-blue cardigan, doesn't seem to notice. He studies a score on the music stand, which is placed between his stereo and ultrasonic humidifier. The humidifier is necessary to keep the air moist for both Malcolm and his violin. Excessively dry air is not good for his instrument's wood or for Malcolm, who suffers from a chronic series of colds and other ailments. Everything in the room is very tidy and clean. The morning sun shines brightly through the windows. Malcolm must stop soon or he won't have time to eat before he walks to the hall.

Searching his memory for a sound, he closes his eyes again and draws the bow across the taut strings. The sound has great strength, but a lyric quality as well—"like a two-hundred-and-fifty-yard chip shot," he says.

Before he could develop his sound, he had to learn how to play the violin. His father first taught him that, too. He can remember his father taking him onto his lap when he was just Brenden's age. Malcolm grasped the bow and his father helped him, more than thirty years ago in Hamiota. That now-mythic place on the Canadian plains was so far from Boston, so far from where Malcolm would one day make his living. Malcolm remembers the farm, remembers his father's John Deere tractor. He remembers playing baseball, pitching to his father, who stood behind an imaginary plate.

Malcolm becomes very sentimental when he talks about his father. "He could have done so much if he had pushed," says Malcolm, as though he were forgetting how hard his father pushed his son. For Malcolm, becoming a musician was an inevitability. When he was a child, his mother spoiled him, but his father instilled in him a regimen of practice he still remembers with a kind of dread and awe.

"Ten to twelve hours a day, all winter," he recalls, clearly overstating the amount. But his meaning is clear: All his free time, except for sports, was spent playing the violin. "Every day, I had to practice the Galamian scale book three times a day." The violinist and teacher Ivan Galamian also ran a music school called Meadowmount, where Malcolm went for four summers in his teens. His sister and two brothers were also always practicing, and today they are all professional musicians like Malcolm. For Charlie, music was a way out of Du Quoin; for Malcolm, it was the continuation of a way of life that began when he learned to talk.

Now that the season has started, Malcolm keeps up with his work by blocking out his practice time with careful planning. In addition to his morning sessions, he practices again when he gets home. He has to stay several weeks ahead of the orchestra's programs, so he can mark the bowings in advance. And he has his own solo work to prepare as well. Early this winter he's going to be the soloist with the BSO in Vieuxtemps's Violin Concerto no. 4. And he has other engagements in the spring.

Malcolm also has some contractual duties to fulfill as concertmaster, including participation on all audition committees. He takes this part of his job as seriously as he does his playing, because as concertmaster he is concerned with the overall quality of the orchestra, and he knows that one poor player can make those around him sound badly, too. Malcolm looks for more than technical proficiency in new players, however. He wants musicians who will give something extra, who won't sit rigidly as some of the other violinists do, barely moving their bodies as they play. He wants players who care.

No one in the orchestra cares more about what he does than Charlie, but, ironically, Malcolm remains remarkably silent on the subject of the orchestra's principal trumpet player. After he became concertmaster, Malcolm had a perfect opportunity to intervene in the long-standing conflict between Charlie and Seiji, but he is too politically astute to have started out by making that mistake. For someone to question Seiji's judgment about Charlie would be tantamount to criticizing not only his authority as music director but his musicianship as a conductor. And as a string player, Malcolm knows very little about playing the trumpet. During Malcolm's first season, Charlie was under extreme pressure, and his playing sometimes suffered. So it was easier and safer for Malcolm to confront other, less volatile issues. And it was less upsetting to the equilibrium he needs to function as a violinist.

Malcolm is determined to have some kind of life beyond the orchestra. Colleen, whom he will marry next year, is a physical therapist from Vermont, where she and Malcolm take Brenden when they can. In the winter, she's hoping to teach Malcolm how to cross-country ski, in return for the golfing lessons he's been giving her. They travel when they can, taking long weekends in Vermont or sometimes jetting south for a few days. Occasionally they have dinner with someone else in the orchestra, but in general there is little socializing away from the hall among most of the musicians.

Malcolm was married to a violinist who had started playing in the BSO before Malcolm became concertmaster. Malcolm never mentions his former wife, who now lives in Chicago and plays in the orchestra there, having narrowly missed selection as the Boston orchestra's associate concertmaster this past summer. But if someone brings up her name, he asks pleasantly how she is. Malcolm's that way. His hazel eyes might intimidate a stranger, so intense is their focus, but his naturally good disposition deflects that feeling. His first instinct on meeting a person is to trust the other and assume the best.

He rarely raises his voice. Very little upsets him, except being interrupted when he's practicing or napping. (He takes frequent naps, and Colleen covers for him on the phone.) He doesn't often get angry, except at colleagues who aren't loyal, or musicians who slack off in rehearsal and then complain later about Seiji. But he makes no spectacle of his criticism. He smiles. He says something indirect, not to be misunderstood, but to be polite. He easily weaves words such as "transcendence" and "essence" and "values" into his conversation. He believes in basic virtues, and his conversation reflects that. But too much talk at one time makes him self-conscious.

Like Seiji, Malcolm is deliberate, even methodical, in his habits. Neither man is happy with mistakes. When he's practicing, Malcolm won't quit until he's got a passage right. With the orchestra, of course, Seiji can't afford that luxury. But he assumes Malcolm's playing will be flawless, an expectation that Malcolm has helped create, even though it puts additional pressure on him.

Malcolm desperately looks for order wherever he can find it. He dresses neatly and combs his black hair neatly. He keeps his moustache trimmed. Nothing, not a dish or paper or one of Brenden's toys, is out of place in his apartment.

What Colleen cares about matters deeply to Malcolm. They're like children together, devotedly happy in each other's company. "That reminds me of *The Tao of Pooh*," Colleen will say to someone, referring to a small volume by Benjamin Hoff that uses A. A. Milne's Pooh books to explain Taoism. And Malcolm will nod in recognition, as though at that moment Pooh were as important a part of his life as Beethoven.

He has the ability to take everything seriously, sometimes with maddening results. Once, playing a recreational round of golf, he became upset when his opponent conceded a six-inch putt to Malcolm and picked up Malcolm's ball.

"Please put the ball back," he said. "This might be a record round." He didn't want it marred by what golfers call a "gimme." Malcolm promptly double-bogeyed the next hole, his potential record round ruined.

The moral dimension to his self-image is ingrained. He never hesitates to categorize actions as right or wrong. Nothing he does comes casually, not golf, not conversation, certainly not music. He keeps redefining his goal, making it forever impossible to reach:

perfection. But the happiness he feels when he attains a momentary triumph is incalculable.

One such momentary triumph was his audition in February 1984. He knew he was competing against the best orchestral violinists in the world. Some had flown to Boston from Europe at the BSO's invitation. Half a dozen were violinists already in the BSO, some of whom would later leave the orchestra for prestigious positions elsewhere. (One became a member of the eminent Juilliard String Quartet).

During the first, live round of the auditions, Malcolm felt he had not been on top of his playing. So before the finals that followed, he was nervous. "But I was eager to show Seiji and the committee what I could do," he recalls.

As he played parts of a Mozart violin concerto and another by Shostakovich, he felt comfortable. "It was a direct situation," he says. "Seiji sat only twenty feet away. I felt very good when I finished. I felt that my performance had been convincing."

But it had been much more than that. From the moment he walked onto the stage, Malcolm had been impressive. His manner was confident without being overbearing. Though he obviously took this occasion seriously, he managed to smile. To be a good concertmaster, you need to be able to relate directly with people, and it was easy to see that Malcolm had that quality in abundance. At this terribly nerve-racking time, he was nevertheless at ease. He made you want to be in his company. And how magnificently he played!

Seiji and the audition committee were convinced they'd found their man. The committee members included Charlie Schlueter, whose own stunning audition had taken place exactly three years before. The committee made up its mind right away, and Seiji announced Malcolm's appointment the next day.

Malcolm wishes he and Seiji were closer and had more time to discuss the pieces the orchestra plays. But this is one of his few criticisms of Seiji. He doesn't think people give Seiji enough credit for his accomplishments. One of the most important is the hiring of good musicians, but this is difficult for Malcolm to talk about without his sounding immodest. Seiji, after all, hired him, and Malcolm has been consulted on all appointments since.

The two men don't quarrel, and onstage they often understand each other without having to speak. Malcolm's tact keeps him from disagreeing with Seiji in front of the orchestra, and Seiji's respect for his concertmaster's musicianship encourages a free exchange of ideas when they do have the chance to meet. The very first time Malcolm met Seiji, after his audition, he thought of the conductor as "very gentle, very down to earth." Now, in his third season as concert-master, Malcolm still thinks of Seiji in a straightforward manner. "Seiji is who he is," he says, as though questions about the music director as a person were a trespass. "I'm mystified when I hear from others that he's elusive."

But Malcolm sounds like he is making a brief when he says this, perhaps aware that many of his colleagues think he, Malcolm, is elusive. Both men want their own way without having to explain why to others. Both guard their time away from the hall. They share themselves through their art, but they prefer to do it on their own terms.

If Malcolm had been writing a review of Opening Night, he would probably have mentioned many tiny flaws in his playing that no one else noticed, and talked about the privilege of performing Mahler. But he'd rather not talk about it at all, which is one reason Seiji made such a good choice for concertmaster. Seiji and the orchestra need that attitude now, that single-minded determination to get on with it. They need it to look beyond a potentially damaging labor situation, and the truly damaging conflict between Seiji and Charlie, to concentrate on the real business of making music.

"But it's not a business," Malcolm protests, with a passionate force of conviction that years of practice and performing have earned him. "Maybe I'm naïve," he continues, not for a second believing he is. "But music can't work that way, can't flourish without the idea that it is a gift."

No one in the orchestra began his career without such a belief, but the pressure to produce, the daily grind of season after season, and the vicissitudes of life work against the finest aspirations. Many players lose sight of their original ambition. They watch the clock at rehearsals. They show up for a concert with barely enough time to warm up. They don't realize what that does to them, Malcolm believes. Quietly, he reminds his colleagues by the example he sets why they are playing. He has no cross to bear except his own rigorous, lofty criterion of excellence.

But the stress that puts on him has taken a toll. His health has bothered him since before he arrived in Boston. In fact, it had something to do with his coming to Boston in the first place.

Four years ago, when Malcolm was concertmaster of the Orchestre Symphonique de Québec, he woke up one morning and couldn't move his right hand. That is the hand with which he holds his bow, and without its mobility he couldn't play the violin. To relax, Malcolm often meditates and practices yoga. Several days before his hand injury, while doing a yoga headstand, he had twisted his right wrist. When he couldn't move his hand, he assumed the twist had caused the problem and was confident it would clear up quickly.

But the hand did not get better. Malcolm saw a series of doctors and specialists, but no one could diagnose the problem. Finally, he had to give up his position in Québec, where he had played since 1977, and look for medical help elsewhere. He traveled to Boston and found a doctor at Massachusetts General Hospital who prescribed a new treatment. For an entire year, Malcolm did not play the violin. His career was threatened. But at last physical therapy worked, and in June 1983 he performed for the first time since the injury. Under Andrew Davis, with the Toronto Symphony, he played Mozart's Violin Concerto in G Major, the same piece that less than a year later was on the repertoire list for his audition as BSO concertmaster.

Since assuming his Boston post two years ago, in September 1984, poor health has continued to plague Malcolm. During his second BSO season, he was out for an extended period with mononucleosis. The illness sapped his energy and caused a strain between him and some of his new colleagues. Those who did not know him well began to whisper backstage about his constitution. His few close friends shook their heads in a different kind of collective disbelief. How could someone so physically fit, with an athlete's body, be somehow so frail?

Malcolm seems to accept his medical problems as the price he must pay for success. In an old-fashioned way, he manifests the belief that nothing worth doing is easy. It is no accident that the game he loves best, golf, is maddeningly difficult to play and impossible to master completely. Great golfers are heroes to Malcolm, because they contend with an adversity that is built into the sport, just as Malcolm must in music.

Malcolm's musical heroes form a pantheon of greats, men who, at the top of their profession, draw others to hear them because when they perform "something is happening." He mentions a few names: Vladimir Horowitz, Nathan Milstein, Isaac Stern. The respect he has for these artists knows no bounds, because he feels that, in a very real sense, they have confronted the hardest questions life poses and made them into their art.

"To stand on one's own takes courage," Malcolm believes very deeply. Though he does not mention Seiji Ozawa when he says this, he could be explaining another of the reasons he respects the conductor.

Were Malcolm to step outside the political ramifications of his role as concertmaster for a moment, he could be describing Charlie. But Malcolm is too circumspect to admit more than, simply, "Charlie is playing softer now than he did before the incident." Malcolm is also too busy, has too many other responsibilities, to help Charlie now even if he wanted to, much as he must know that Charlie desperately needs all the encouragement he can get.

NINE

Charlie Schlueter takes on the Boston traffic with gusto and heads out of the city. He weaves in and out of the highway lanes with the same abandon and skill that characterize his best trumpet playing. He shifts gears with the ease of a race car driver, keeping his eyes focused for potential trouble ahead. He's finished a night concert and left his trumpet and the knot in his stomach at the hall. Now he's on his way to Plum Island, on Boston's North Shore, where he and Martha own a cottage with another couple. Despite his speed, he doesn't arrive until around midnight.

Charlie likes Plum Island especially when the wind blows in off the Atlantic and clouds hang in an overcast gray sky. Busy and honky-tonky in summer, it assumes a different atmosphere after the vacationers leave, its small deserted streets smelling of salt water, its clam shacks closed, its bathhouses boarded up, the empty space and quiet making it a good place to forget critics and conductors.

After the painful critical reception to the beginning of this season, Charlie takes off for Plum Island whenever he can—usually right after each Saturday night concert—though Martha often stays behind in Boston to paint.

He sleeps a little late the next morning and waits until after breakfast to call Martha, who he thinks "still looks like she did when we were in school." Their conversation is brief, almost businesslike, but they seem comfortable with the evolution of their relationship into somewhat separate lives. Charlie is enormously proud of Martha's painting, Martha of her husband's valor. Though she rarely goes to Symphony Hall because of her bitterness after Charlie's near loss of his job, she retains her excitement about music in general and her husband's playing in particular. Someone once said to her, that you could trace a line from Mahler and one of his symphonies to Charlie and his trumpet, to the whole orchestra and the conductor, to the audience and—

"—and," she interrupted, "to God."

Charlie putters around the cottage. He loves home improvement projects, and he'll make new bed frames this Christmas, when he has some extended time off. At some point in the day, he heads outside to the beach. As he walks just below the tide line, where the water has wet the sand enough to give a firm footing, he thinks about his father in the coal mines and remembers his own early battles with conductors.

But he thinks also about Eloise, whom he holds in reverential esteem. "The familiarity of our problems can be dangerously seductive," she wrote. "Although success beckons with one hand, it signals caution with the other. While we think we are responding to the hand that beckons, another part of us heeds only the caution. The part of us that holds back knows that change involves challenges—losses as well as gains. Change always means a little dying, a leaving behind of something old and tattered and no longer useful to us even though comfortably familiar."

Charlie understands very well the meaning of that passage. He knows it would be possible for him to step down voluntarily or to look for a job elsewhere, but he also knows that isn't the kind of change that would suit him, nor is it the kind Eloise meant. His identity is too closely associated with the idea of his being the Boston principal to give it up. Still, he is weary of the constant pressure to please others. It would be nice to be rid of that, to have a little respect. But how?

Before the day ends, Charlie will make some phone calls. He has a kind of support group of friends in Boston and around the country with whom he stays in touch, not so much to report news as to relieve the anxiety he feels performing. He's too old now to practice eight or nine hours a day, so he talks on the telephone instead. Charlie turns these exchanges into extraordinarily personal confessionals. His confidence in himself and in his playing is still shaky, and when something goes wrong, or he thinks something might go wrong, he needs to talk it out.

"I ate dinner at a new Thai restaurant," he'll begin. Or, "I was coming over a crest in the road and I got nailed by the police. Had the radar detector on, too. Zap! So, fifty bucks." Then he mentions an incident in a rehearsal or concert, always alluding to Seiji. He wants to hear from others that whatever has happened most recently with the music director is normal, that he doesn't need to worry. His friends, a diverse group of players in other orchestras, former students, teachers, are uniformly reassuring. Charlie occupies a unique niche in all their lives. They're happy when he calls. He always asks about their lives. And he gives them the sense that they are a part of the adventure of his. They want things to work out for him.

Charlie doesn't usually practice the trumpet when he's at Plum Island. He believes in regular breaks, and his lip usually needs a rest.

But the pace of the season picks up after September, and Charlie has to take his practice time when he can get it. He is busy with his teaching, too. Weekday mornings find him in his upstairs studio at the rear of the New England Conservatory of Music, a few blocks from Symphony Hall.

Waiting one day for a student who is late for his lesson, Charlie fools around for a few minutes on his trumpet. When the student doesn't show up, Charlie turns the time into practice. First he plays a little Mahler Two, which the orchestra will perform again in December.

Perfectly, with a sound that is thrilling even in the dead acoustics of the small room, he hits the high C from the last movement. Charlie is always relieved after that note, perhaps remembering something his old teacher Vacchiano used to say to his students. "You don't want to miss the high C's. No one cares if you miss the lows." Like those of professional sopranos and tenors, trumpeters' careers rest in part on their ability to produce high, exposed notes cleanly and without apparent effort.

Charlie cuts to a passage near the end. "I never had an instrument I could start and keep the sound so soft," he says of his Monette trumpet. The Monette is unusually responsive to a player of Charlie's caliber, enabling him to play certain notes with very little air pressure. Twice he plays the passage, and each time the sound is soft and sure. Then he jumps to a passage from Mahler Four in which there is a difficult interval. "You can get a lot of cackles on that one," he says, meaning it's a notoriously easy interval to miss. In another sudden switch, he begins the opening measures of Mahler Five, which the orchestra will play next month, in November. The first movement of that symphony, which he has played many times during auditions but never performed, is almost a concerto for trumpet.

Even when he plays alone like this, with no one to judge him, Charlie pays strict attention to the sound he is making. It is as certain a part of himself as his bearded face. Charlie's sound evokes the loneliness of a childhood spent learning how to do something no one in his family understood. It is an elegant sound, but full of expression and emotion. There is a little Harry James in the sound, a good measure of Vacchiano, a lot of metamorphosed Du Quoin. A Juilliard classmate of Charlie's remembers walking by the practice rooms at Juilliard thirty years ago. "You could always tell without opening the door which room Charlie was practicing in," he recalls. "He had his sound even then."

"I think about the concept of sound, not how I'm going to do it," Charlie says. "When your mind is involved in *how*, it sets up all sorts of hurdles." Instead of thinking about fingering or tonguing, he concentrates on "sound connecting to sound."

Now, as Charlie frets about his November date with Mahler's Fifth Symphony, he practices its opening phrase "with enough confidence to sound boring." He experiments, "trying to see how many things I can do with nuance and color." As with any experiment, some results are better than others. Some are outright mistakes, but Charlie says that doesn't matter. "Once you make a mistake it's gone," he maintains, in one of his oddly defensive comments about "train wrecks." Sometimes he seems to have taken Eloise's advice about "permission to blow it" too much to heart, as though he'd forgotten there must also be something called "permission to succeed."

But Charlie says he is after something more important than rote proficiency, something that he calls texture. "If you play everything with the same nice beautiful sound, it becomes soporific," he says. "There are a jillion ways to play, within the confines." The confines include the instrument's limits and the parameters set by the composer. Charlie wants to stretch the confines, to play, he says, "at the edge." He wants to live dangerously when he's playing, to take risks, because he believes that the result will be a sound that is interesting to hear and that communicates the emotion of the music.

When he does so here, in the privacy of his studio, the consequences are harmless to Charlie's reputation. When he makes a mistake, he simply tries again. But he doesn't define a mistake as a missed note. To him, it would be a mistake to play the same way over and over. Thinking like this, however, may militate against the more accepted norm of striving for Malcolm's kind of perfection.

Yet Malcolm would argue that he, too, is after something more important than technical perfection. And there are musicians within the orchestra and others in Symphony Hall who wish Charlie didn't play so close to the edge. They wish Charlie would take fewer chances sometimes, because the consequence of a missed note during a concert can mar the performance for everyone. But Charlie doesn't know how to play any other way. Taking chances drives the way he approaches music. "And Charlie couldn't live as a fourth trumpet," says Randy Croley, a freelance trumpet player who was hired as an extra for Mahler Two.

Randy, on the other hand, is more comfortable with his substitute status than he would be as a permanent orchestral member. He never knows where the next paycheck is coming from, but he likes the freedom of not having to go to the same job every day. He admires the way Charlie keeps control of himself when Seiji picks on him during a rehearsal, in part because Randy isn't sure he could handle such stress himself. He worries about the effect of that stress on Charlie. Knowing from his own experience how difficult playing in a major orchestra is, he can't quite believe that Charlie does it under the constant additional pressure of a running feud with the music director.

Bill Moyer was the person who officially engaged Randy for his Mahler Two work, but he owes the assignment to Charlie, whose advice Moyer solicits when the orchestra needs additional trumpet players. Though Randy has never studied with Charlie, he has played with him often enough to think of Charlie as "one of the top two or three trumpeters in the world."

Violinist Jenny Shames, who has never forgotten Charlie's magnificent playing at his audition, wonders if Charlie gets himself into risky situations because in a strange way he likes to be in them.

When the orchestra doesn't go along with Charlie, Jenny feels onstage as if Charlie were saying to everyone, "Okay, guys, why aren't you with me?" Such an attitude, she thinks, makes the other players feel Charlie believes he's right and they're wrong. When he plays well, however, she says, "it picks everyone up."

Oddly, for someone who feels the way he does about risk taking, Charlie has no interest in a career as a soloist. For one thing, it's a very difficult way to make a living. Only a handful of trumpet players, like Wynton Marsalis and Maurice André, are able to survive on recitals and recordings. And a soloist must have an altogether different kind of personality, able to thrive on the pressure of being on the spot and not for a minute believing in the possibility of failure. Charlie, on the other hand, seems to accept trouble as the inevitable result of playing on the edge.

But Charlie wouldn't want a soloist's career even if he could have it. He likes playing in the orchestra because symphonic music is much richer than the limited solo trumpet repertoire. Instead of the standard Bach, Purcell, and Handel works that a soloist plays, along with a handful of more recent compositions and a few concerti, Charlie prefers the great symphonies that form the nucleus of an orchestra's programs. And he enjoys the musical company of other orchestral musicians, though not all his colleagues in Boston enjoy his.

Some seem convinced like Richard Dyer that he'll never change, or they are unable to acknowledge that in fact he has tried, that he has slowly been making some adjustments in his playing. Charlie's relationship with his colleagues is complicated by their memory of his hearing. Some perceive that the battle between Charlie and Seiji is in part a political one, having at least as much to do with Seiji's authority as music director as with Charlie's ability as a player. But Charlie has a hard time remembering that, or understanding the politics of newspaper reviews. He courts some of his troubles, forgetting that there are times when Seiji wants dependability, not risk taking, whatever the liabilities of the former and the rewards of the latter.

Charlie seems never to have learned how to talk with Seiji. Once, about two years ago, not long before Charlie's arbitration hearing, Seiji took Charlie aside after a concert on tour in Berlin.

"I know you're trying hard," Charlie remembers Seiji's saying. "But it's still not good."

"In what?" asked Charlie.

"Mahler," Seiji replied.

"What's the problem?"

"Intonation."

"You mean I'm the only one who isn't in tune?" Charlie asked rhetorically, knowing that he wasn't the only one. But the others weren't on such bad terms with their music director.

While Charlie vividly remembers the effect of Seiji's criticism on him, he will never understand what his contentious retort could have meant to Seiji. His words could have easily been construed as belligerent or insubordinate. He should probably have turned the other cheek, but that is the kind of risk Charlie doesn't take. It goes against the grain of his training and career. As his teacher used to say, "Talk back to the conductor."

And Charlie takes the wrong things personally. He once gave Seiji a copy of Eloise's book, *A Soprano on Her Head*. He's still mystified that Seiji has never said anything to him about it. He feels hurt, when he ought to realize that Seiji has no time—or need—to read the book. And Charlie continues to read Richard's reviews the moment they appear, forgetting that this is a battle he can never win—nor, for that matter, should care about winning. Moreover, since both Seiji and the BSO brass are typically well received elsewhere, he ought to realize how capricious criticism can be. Charlie used to get fine reviews in Minnesota, and still does in Boston when Richard sends a substitute.

The week after the orchestra's premiere of the intricate, metaphorical work *Drala*—a critical success that bolsters the orchestra's commitment to new music—Seiji and the players plunge into Prokofiev's three-hour ballet music based on *Romeo and Juliet.* Charlie plays part of the Prokofiev on the cornet.

The orchestra plays a portion of the full piece at each of three concerts and records the entire work for Deutsche Grammophon. On the recording, Charlie gives one of the best performances of his BSO career. But during the first concert he makes a mistake in a small but important section and Richard Dyer, reviewing the concert for the *Globe,* pounces on him. "The trumpet went awry in 'Masks,' " Richard reports. But Richard won't leave it at that. "Some of the brass playing was so raw that string players stuffed their fingers in their ears." Dyer is apparently unaware that several players sometimes place cotton in their ears because the volume of sound in certain works can hurt their hearing. Even Malcolm has to do this on occasion, while principal horn Charles Kavalovski routinely wears earplugs.

Naturally, Charlie takes personally Richard's comment about the "raw" brass. And it isn't any easier for him the next week when Charlie and the orchestra give three memorable performances of Benjamin Britten's *War Requiem,* and Richard focuses his review on Seiji and the singers, without mention of Charlie. As the principal trumpet player of one of the world's great orchestras, he ought to find any such well-received performance a satisfaction. But he worries when no one recognizes his own contribution. After what he went through, he thinks he has a right to that anxiety. And when he has played well, as he did in the Britten, he believes he should get some credit.

Following an afternoon concert or rehearsal, Charlie seeks solace in the warmth of the company and the alcohol in Amalfi's bar. Some orchestra members drink too much, but Charlie limits himself to one martini before dinner and one glass of red wine with his food. He calls the barmaid by her first name. He trades stories with a few friends from the orchestra who eat and drink with him here, with the light fading outside and the evening air in Boston cold now. But something is missing from his life.

*   *   *

For Seiji, this month is one long continuation of the endurance test with which the season began. He has little time to dwell on his relationship with Charlie, or with anyone else in the orchestra, for that matter.

Between rehearsals for the Prokofiev and just after a final performance of *Drala,* he takes the place of an ailing Herbert von Karajan in a Symphony Hall concert by the Berlin Philharmonic Orchestra.

Despite little rehearsal time, and before an audience that is initially disappointed not to be seeing Karajan, Seiji conducts with confidence and passion. There is no hint that he has just been conducting vastly different music with a completely different orchestra, and he leads both of the concert's symphonies from memory. Particularly in the Brahms First Symphony, which comes last on the program, he draws an emotional intensity from the visiting players that grows with the performance. The large crowd responds enthusiastically, but Richard Dyer puts it down in his review as "localized excitement."

Unlike Charlie, Seiji pays scant attention to such remarks. Later in the week, Richard jumps on Seiji again, this time for the Prokofiev. "Between the 'Prince's Command' and the 'Interlude,' the entire performance collapsed," Dyer concludes. "Ozawa gestured, and nothing was there."

Seiji can relax even when he makes a mistake during the second *Romeo and Juliet* performance. The Prokofiev employs several extra musicians who play mandolin in two sections. "The seven dwarfs," stage manager Al Robison nicknames the mandolin players, one of whom is assistant concertmaster Max Hobart. Before he plays, Hobart must leave his violinist's seat behind Malcolm, go backstage for his mandolin, and come back onstage with the other mandolin players. Then, during a pause in the piece after the mandolins have played, he goes back out, gets his violin, and rejoins the violin section. But Seiji, with so much music on his mind this week, forgets to give Hobart enough time to do this. Seiji starts the next section too early, and Hobart is left holding his violin backstage.

Many conductors would blame such a mistake on someone else or pretend it didn't happen. And Seiji would glare at Charlie for a similar infraction. But Seiji is amused at his momentary, uncharacteristic lapse in concentration. Coming offstage after the performance, before returning to the podium for a bow, he smiles mischievously. "Sorry," he says, looking for Hobart. Then, still breathing hard from the exertion of conducting, and oblivious to the applause that can be heard even with the stage door temporarily closed, he asks Robison where the other mandolin players are. He wants to take them back onstage with him, but they have already left for home.

Contract negotiations are still stalled, and musicians away from Boston have been taking sides. Players from many other orchestras write their BSO colleagues, wishing them success, because what happens here will influence trade agreements elsewhere. But the most eminent musician to write doesn't cast his support with either the players or the management. Leonard Bernstein addresses Ron Barron, head of the Players Committee, urging the men and women of the orchestra to remember, "The art you care for is precious; treat it with care, gently." It is the kind of apolitical, inspirational message that Seiji never remembers to give. Seiji, in fact, is sufficiently distanced from the issue to keep his commitments in Japan, where he flies after the last performance of the *War Requiem*. He leaves his phone number on the basement bulletin board, but with little expectation that any of the "rank-and-file" players will call him.

All month long, the two sides have been inching toward an agreement, despite posturing to the contrary. The day of the Berlin Philharmonic concert, when the BSO players hosted a luncheon for their German counterparts, strike committees were formed. Later, the Players Committee sent a letter to the players in which the committee used the actual word "strike." The tone of the letter was more ominous than that of the leaflet the players had passed out on Opening Night. But the labor situation has not been a distraction to the players when they were onstage, as it was on Opening Night, because there have been no public demonstrations since then.

By a margin of not quite two to one, the players approve the new contract on the next-to-last day of the month. The guaranteed minimum salary under the offer is $48,360, with additional increases during the second and third years of the proposed three-year agreement. The figures are in line with what players in other major American orchestras earn.

The Players Committee declines to drink a champagne toast with the negotiating team for the corporation, but there is little bitterness among the majority of the players, whose attitude is typified by the comment of one of the strings. "The contract settlement is basically a good one," he says. "Fifteen percent over three years is better than the projected inflation rate," he adds with satisfaction. None of the musicians will starve.

But despite the signing of the contract, all is not well backstage with the BSO, literally or figuratively. The concertmaster is absent today, the thirty-first of October, and none of the players seem to know why. In fact, Malcolm is at his doctor's, complaining of a painful ear problem that hinders his ability to play the violin. Once again, illness has kept him away from the orchestra, which especially needs his presence now.

The November issue of *Boston Magazine* has just hit the newsstands, with its lead story a profile of Seiji called "Confessions of a Conductor." The tone of the piece is far worse than anything the critics said after Opening Night or since. And a quotation in the story attributed to Seiji on the subject of his controversial principal trumpet player confirms Charlie's worst fears about his tense relationship with the music director. Whatever has healed since Charlie almost lost his job is reopened again.

"I'm shocked at what my colleagues said about each other," confesses another of the strings. What disturbs many of the players is that some of those quoted didn't confine the subject of their interviews to themselves or Seiji. They vented their anger over a long list of grievances, balanced in the story with very little that is positive.

Jenny Shames and another of the finalists for the associate concertmaster's position are reported to be upset with Seiji for the way he handled their audition. Principal second violin Marylou Speaker Churchill is quoted directly on Seiji's "lack of understanding" of the German repertoire. "We're desperate to have someone come and conduct us in the German literature and be inspired," she moans.

Bass Larry Wolfe complains about "the mass production of concerts." In an extraordinarily self-serving explanation of his work, which Wolfe will later apologize for, he says, "I'm trying to accept my job with the BSO as sometimes an artistic outlet and sometimes a bread job, and hopefully I'll outgrow it artistically and financially." Wolfe, of course, is not alone in such feelings. But the article fails to clarify how complicated such feelings are, or that players might say they felt this way to mask problems of their own. And only one person—a retiree—who has enjoyed his BSO job is given a chance to say so.

Principal violist Burton Fine says of the music director's interpretations, "Often, I have the impression that [Seiji's] too concerned with the individual trees to get the shape of the forest right." An unnamed musician says, "[Seiji] can memorize a menu, a telephone book, perhaps even *King Lear*, but he wouldn't understand the poetry of the composition." Another unidentified player, the article reports, is critical of how Seiji schedules rehearsals.

The writer of the story, a freelancer named Linda Corman, interviewed Seiji last summer at Tanglewood. His "confessions" appear to respond to the players' comments, as though a debate were being held. The winner is declared in the tone of the story, set by a subhead: "He's weak; he's indecisive; he's responsible for the Boston Symphony Orchestra's low morale and lack of musical consistency. Yes, says Seiji Ozawa, but . . . " In the end, the article hedges everything by quoting several people on the subject of what a difficult, even impossible job Seiji has.

For Charlie, the worst part of the article comes as Corman briefly recounts, as an example of Seiji's alleged poor personnel management, the episode in which Seiji tried to fire Charlie. " 'I should have said [right away], You are not good for Symphony,' " the story quotes Seiji as saying of Charlie. " 'It's a sad story.' "

When Charlie reads these words, he is furious. He knew someone was writing a story, because Linda Corman tried to interview him and he refused to speak with her. After his arbitration hearing in 1984, his lawyer and the BSO's had agreed that their clients would not discuss their differences in public. Since that time, Charlie has kept quiet about what happened, resisting the temptation to criticize Seiji and working very hard to put his life and career back together. And he has assumed that no matter what Seiji thought about Charlie, he wouldn't talk about it, certainly not with a writer for the city's largest monthly magazine.

But Charlie had also hoped that there were things about his playing Seiji liked. Now he can see that those hopes are futile. There can be no mistaking the meaning of Seiji's comments. Though Charlie cannot bring himself to use these words, he has been humiliated.

Charlie finds it ironic that of all the people mentioned in the story, he is one of the few who isn't quoted, when he has more reason than any of his colleagues to sound off. But what upsets him most is to see his name here, paraded to make a point that has nothing to do with his playing. He feels used. And he feels frustrated that he has no way of responding publicly to what Seiji said.

Charlie calls his lawyer, who fires off a letter to the BSO. But the damage to Charlie's ego and reputation has been done. Soon, the orchestra will perform Mahler Five, perhaps the most important piece for Charlie that has been programmed since his arrival in Boston. Charlie can't believe he is going to have to play it under these circumstances. How is he going to get through the week of rehearsals and the three concerts? How will he react if Seiji stops him during a rehearsal? And what will the critics say if he makes a mistake? What will his colleagues think? He feels his world will be at stake with these performances.

For the BSO, the *Boston* article is a public relations disaster, though no one in the press office will complain to the magazine. Officially, the organization's response is silence. No one rises publicly to Seiji's defense, as though it were in bad taste to acknowledge that the piece was published. But soon, on the bulletin boards backstage, the Players Committee posts reminders to players. In language that would chill a journalist's heart, the notices advise players to watch what they say to reporters.

Depending on one's perspective, Seiji's absence at this awkward moment can be viewed as a glaring example of bad timing or a blessing in disguise. His first response when he hears about the story is to ask a member of management the meaning of the word "confession." The BSO would like people to think that is Seiji's only reaction, but the article angers him very much. Like a politician in a dirty campaign, he will maintain he hasn't read it. In fact, with his absurdly busy schedule, someone else probably read it for him, but he knows what it said. "Please don't mention it," he says afterward when asked to discuss it. He has banished it from his mind, he says.

But Seiji is more than aware of how some of his players feel about him. In fact, a focal point of the article is Seiji's admission that he has made mistakes with his orchestra, for which he is to blame. Though the article did not balance this admission with a sense of what Seiji—and his players—think he has accomplished, Seiji knows he is being scrutinized. He speaks frankly about this in his interview, but clearly without the realization that the case against him would be so one-sided. He believes his relationship with most of the musicians has been improving.

But about his comment on Charlie he will only plead ignorance of the lawyers' agreement that he would not speak. Neither publicly nor privately will he take back what he said. The implication is clear and, to Charlie, frightening. Since Seiji wasn't successful in his attempts to fire Charlie, he wishes Charlie would leave.

TEN

*B*ut for Charlie there is no choice—he has to stay. And so a few weeks later he has to perform Mahler Five for the first time.

For any trumpeter, Mahler Five is a very difficult piece. From its beginning, Charlie's part is as exposed as anything written for the trumpet: He plays a solo fanfare. And throughout the rest of that first movement and in three of the other four, there are numerous places that will require a wide range of dynamics, subtle shading and exuberant fortissimo, and a keen attention to what others are playing. To Charlie, the performance looms as one of the largest of his life.

A few hours before the concert, on a rainy, chilly day with snow on the ground, Charlie drives to Boston's Logan Airport to meet his trumpet guru, Dave Monette, the charismatic young man who makes the trumpet Charlie uses in Mahler symphonies and most other late-nineteenth- and twentieth-century works. It's no coincidence that he's flown here today from Chicago. After the pasting Charlie's taken from Richard Dyer so far this season and the depressing, threatening comments Seiji made in the *Boston Magazine* article, Charlie needs Dave's calming presence.

Dave transforms Charlie's world with that presence, and they are very close emotionally. Though Dave works with many of the world's greatest trumpet players, he daydreams about moving to New England, just to be nearer Charlie. That would make Charlie very happy. A Kundalini yoga practitioner and teacher, Dave has taught Charlie how to meditate. He speaks naturally about "journeys" he's taken, and he doesn't mean actual physical trips. "Astral visits" is a term he uses to describe how he's acquired some of his knowledge, and he speaks with such great conviction that his words have an absolutely mesmerizing impact. And his "message" comes with the best trumpets his customers have ever played.

As a trumpeter, Charlie strikes Dave as "a musician who happens to play the trumpet." Dave means that as a supreme compliment, as a way of saying that Charlie does things with phrasing and tone color that go far beyond the requisite playing of the correct notes. There is no one in the world Dave would rather hear play Mahler than Charlie.

And Charlie loves Dave as he would a son. Though they have known each other for only three years, the relationship has deepened into a strong bond. Psychologically, Dave occupies the place in Charlie's personal life that Eloise once held. But he has also become an indispensable part of Charlie's trumpeting, so much so that Charlie can no longer imagine going onstage to perform Mahler Five without his Monette C trumpet. There is not a question about his trumpet and its relationship to his playing that Charlie would hesitate to ask Dave. To Charlie, Dave is like a politician's alter ego, writing his speeches behind the scenes and bolstering his self-confidence. Dave keeps Charlie on the right track, and Charlie in turn makes Dave feel like a very important person. Charlie has also helped Dave financially by investing in his company, and he has the distinction of being the first musician in a major orchestra to use a Monette trumpet in a performance.

Like Charlie, Dave grew up in the Midwest, and he played trumpet in his teens, just as Charlie did. But Dave never had much formal instruction, and after he graduated from high school he decided not to go on to college or conservatory. Instead, he played in a dance band for a year, held odd jobs for a while, at one point worked as a janitor. Eventually, he became a trumpet technician, moving first to the Northwest, then back to the Midwest. During all this time, he was constantly experimenting with trumpet design.

Neither Charlie nor Dave can remember exactly when they met, but it was sometime in 1983, a year culminating in Charlie's near dismissal. Dave lived in Bloomington, Indiana then, and he was just finishing his first trumpets. He'd heard Charlie's name from other players, and he knew Charlie held one of the most important orchestral trumpet positions in the world. One day, without the slightest doubt that he was doing the right thing, Dave called him. Charlie's younger daughter, Erica, answered the phone.

"Hello," said Dave. "I'd like to speak with Charles Schlueter, the famous trumpet player."

"I didn't know he was famous," Erica replied.

The two men spoke on the phone again before they met, and they began to develop a rapport immediately. Charlie had always tinkered with trumpets himself. He has actually built a few, and he fusses endlessly with the many he owns. Worth many thousands of dollars, they represent a larger investment than anything else in his home. But Charlie doesn't keep them as a financial hedge. To him, they are as important as paints are to a great artist. He conducts experiments with them, constantly trying to improve his sound, to match the correct instrument with the right repertoire. Mahler, for example, sounds best on a dark, rich instrument, while for Bach Charlie switches to a higher-pitched piccolo trumpet (which he nevertheless plays with a mellow, soft sound). Charlie owns so many trumpets that he has to store some in the closet of his study. That room is a veritable trumpet museum, its shelves filled with mouthpieces, bottles of valve oil, photographs of Charlie and his friends, music, and recordings. The room is also a place where he can go and feel at peace for an evening. In his mind, it is a kind of domesticated Plum Island, right in his Newtonville house.

Back in 1983, Charlie wasn't picking up the negative signals Seiji was sending him. But he knew he was being listened to and judged very carefully. So he had a very open mind when Dave called him.

To Dave, Charlie represented everything he hoped to achieve with his new company. If he could persuade the principal trumpet player of the Boston Symphony Orchestra to buy and use one of his horns, the "crazy dream" he had been nurturing to make and sell his own horns might come true.

Charlie bought two, the second and third Dave had made. Charles Gorham, a trumpet professor at Indiana University and president of the International Trumpet Guild, had purchased the first. Adolph Herseth, the longtime Chicago Symphony principal and one of the most respected orchestral musicians in the country, bought the fourth. It was an astounding beginning for Dave, who hadn't yet turned thirty. He moved his shop to Chicago, where his own fame within the trumpet world continued to grow. But his business grew more slowly. Even after adding three assistants, he could produce only three or four trumpets a week.

Dave is terribly vague about how he makes his trumpets: He doesn't want anyone to steal his secrets. It is doubtful that anyone could, however, because Dave's greatest asset is his ear. Like Seiji Ozawa, Dave has an uncanny ability to detect nuances of sound. In Seiji's case, what the music director hears is translated into instructions to his orchestra; in Dave's, into a small but influential trumpet empire. Dave's aural insights are changing the way Charlie and others play the trumpet.

With a trumpet player as good as Charlie Schlueter or Wynton Marsalis, a slight difference in the instrument's design or construction can mean a major change in the quality of sound and how it projects. Varying the thickness of the metal or the taper of the leadpipe, for example, will alter the fundamental properties of a given instrument.

Using parts that in some cases he purchases from outside, such as unfinished pistons, Dave Monette beats out the metal for his trumpet's leadpipes, tuning slides, and crooks and braces by hand. He leaves the brass unfinished, because he thinks even that has an effect on the sound. (Wynton Marsalis disagrees, and his Monette is gold-plated and engraved with flowers.) Making a C trumpet, Dave has several prototypes, design configurations from which he works, but he leaves room for specific differences that he builds in for specific players. In addition, he takes into account where the player usually performs, since there is a great deal of difference in how sound projects in Boston's Symphony Hall and in a jazz nightclub.

When Dave first heard Charlie's playing, he was immediately moved by its dark, emotive quality. No one else he'd ever heard made a sound quite like it. But Dave also noticed right away that Charlie's air capacity was extraordinarily large. In certain situations, Dave reasoned, Charlie might sound too loud simply because he was playing the wrong instrument. So he set about making a trumpet that took this into account. Thus, Dave's work had an immediate, direct bearing on Charlie's major problem with Seiji and the orchestra, the complaint that he sometimes played out unnecessarily.

Dave began building into the design for Charlie's trumpets a kind of inherent inefficiency. He made the taper of the leadpipe very wide, so that a weaker player using one of Charlie's Monettes would have trouble making a note sound properly. But to Charlie, expelling his huge lungfuls of air, the trumpet worked just fine and actually felt efficient, because he needed all that air to counter the leadpipe's taper.

Playing a Monette, Charlie felt more secure, more certain he'd hit the right note at the beginning of a difficult phrase, more confident that the intervals within that phrase would not skip. Overall, he was less anxious about certain passages and better able to take the risks that he wanted with a sense that the basic sound would still be right. And when someone complimented him, he could now "blame" the result on his trumpet. In other words, he could begin to change his playing without admitting to himself that perhaps in some ways Seiji was right. This made it easier for him to accept the idea that he had to make some accommodations in his playing if he was going to win back the respect and support of Seiji and the entire orchestra. In his mind, he wasn't changing, he was just getting better.

But now, with the publication of Seiji's biting remarks in *Boston*, Charlie can feel the pressure against him building once more.

"At the start of the Fifth," writes Mahler biographer Henry-Louis de la Grange, "as in the first movement of the Second Symphony written many years before, the symphonic hero is 'laid to rest.' But this time the imaginary spectator—or, if you will, the symphonic narrator—does not rage against destiny; he faces it rather as a tragic but inevitable reality, in his almost impersonal resignation and sorrow, which continue even into the violence of the first interlude and the expressiveness of the second."

Charlie never reads such material. He prefers not to know what others, including the composer, think the music means. Shortly after 7 P.M., in the Symphony Hall basement, Charlie runs through his part in the music de La Grange describes. Dave listens. Charlie pauses and hands the trumpet Dave made for him to its maker. Dave wants to make certain its leadpipe is clean. Completely calm, he fusses with it for a moment, using a tool he brought with him from Chicago, and gives it back to Charlie.

"The upper end of the trumpet's register is so immensely striking that it imposes as a direct consequence the severest strain on human nerves and psychology in the entire orchestra," writes Norman Del Mar, an authority on orchestral instruments. Charlie, of course, would heartily agree, but he would not restrict his explanation for the trumpeter's strain to the instrument's upper register. The damnably difficult part of playing the trumpet, once the technique has been mastered, is finding the elusive sense of feel, the connectedness between performer and instrument that is needed for a great performance. The relationship between player and instrument rests on so many factors. When Charlie is "on," all the physical things are working and interrelating correctly and he can concentrate, as he says, on "sound connecting to sound." He can also concentrate on what the rest of the orchestra is doing and how his playing meshes with it. He will have to do that constantly in Mahler Five.

Charlie's part in Mahler Five challenges him from the very first notes, a motif built around triplets. For thirteen measures he plays utterly alone, before the orchestra joins him on a giant chord. Everything he has ever learned about the trumpet and about performing must be focused on that beginning.

"So many trumpet players try to take those first measures of triplets in five beats," Charlie's old teacher Vacchiano likes to say. They are written in 2/2, two beats to a measure. To play them as though there were five beats is easier, but then it's hard to tell what the rhythm is. The measures end up sounding too fast or too slow.

Though he insists he can't remember who gave him the idea, Charlie thinks the best meter for these measures is 6/4. The half notes receive two beats, as do the triplets, but the quarter-note rest is lengthened to a half-note rest for the other two beats. This isn't precisely what Mahler wrote, but in Charlie's view he is interpreting what Mahler wanted here. By changing the meter, he believes he can play the passage with an élan that will set the entire performance in motion. Amazingly, Seiji has agreed with Charlie.

In the final Mahler Five rehearsal this morning, Seiji seemed more tired that he had a month ago. There was little discussion of the opening and much more of the massive Scherzo, the third movement, in which the principal French horn is the most prominent player. A Japanese television crew filmed the rehearsal (for which the players will each earn an extra $233.33). All this activity, and the last-minute changes in programs and recording sessions, have accentuated the normal stir that Seiji's appearance in the hall always causes. No one feels this more than Seiji's principal trumpet player, whose life seems to turn now at the music director's whim.

Dave makes another minor adjustment on Charlie's trumpet. Dave hears Mahler Five all the time at his Chicago shop. When trumpeters stop in to test a new instrument or try out an adjustment on an old one, they often play a passage from this symphony. Dave can play the opening himself, for that matter. But not the way Charlie does.

According to Dave's belief in the metaphysical human anatomy of Kundalini yoga, the body is divided into regions called *chakras*. "Charlie's got tons of fifth chakra in his playing," Dave believes. The fifth chakra is located around a person's mouth and symbolizes communication. Dave thinks that when Seiji tried to fire Charlie, "Charlie was down in the first chakra a lot, which means survival. Most trumpet players don't get past the third, which stands for power. Charlie has a lot of fourth chakra, too, which is the heart center and stands for true compassion."

What Dave means is that the sound of Charlie's playing carries with it a huge emotional load, that in that sound Charlie expresses his humanity. Many perfectly good players never do this, but their playing is often so technically correct, even dazzling, that they build entire successful careers on their technique. They are more like musical athletes than artists.

Charlie wants very badly to hit all the notes tonight, but he wants something else even more. He spends the first half of the concert, a Haydn symphony in which he doesn't play, downstairs with Dave. And then at intermission, Charlie knows it is time to bid Dave goodbye and make his way to the stage. There is nothing he can do now but perform.

By the time he has taken his seat onstage, he is already so completely enveloped in that music that the performance might already have started.

The stage fills quickly with Charlie's fellow players. But Malcolm is not among them. He is still out with his ear infection. Seiji will miss the quality of Malcolm's sound, particularly in the fourth movement of the Mahler, the famous Adagietto scored for strings only. The other strings won't play in a different style just because Malcolm isn't here. The bowings are Malcolm's; he reviewed them at home. However, the intuitive understanding between Malcolm and Seiji, Malcolm and the other players, that enables them all to make slight adjustments during a performance can't be duplicated with the substitution of another violinist, no matter how capable. That is something that develops only over time.

Malcolm's place has been taken temporarily by the new associate concertmaster, Tamara Smirnova-Šajfar. Last year she was playing in Zagreb. Last summer she beat out several BSO violinists, including Malcolm's former wife, for her new job. Many of her new colleagues hold this against her, and she's made few friends in Boston this fall. She also speaks very little English, and that obviously hasn't helped her in her attempt to overcome the social barriers backstage. She is under extra pressure tonight, for everyone is still judging her.

By the time Seiji has come onto the stage and made a brief bow, Charlie looks as though he is meditating. He has cleared the saliva from his trumpet repeatedly and has tuned his trumpet to the proper pitch. Momentarily holding his trumpet by the thumb and fifth finger of his right hand, he flexes the fingers of his left before they grasp the instrument, which weighs about two and a half pounds. He moistens his lips and blinks quickly behind his glasses. He lifts his head and turns it from side to side to release tension, bends it forward again, lifts it again. Then, except for breathing, he doesn't move. He stares straight ahead at the one man in all the world who seems to stand between him and happiness.

Seiji stares back, then looks around at Tamara, at the other strings and the woodwinds and the many other brasses arrayed around Charlie. Seiji raises his arms, and Charlie begins.

For the next hour and a quarter, Charlie remains inside the music, inside its beautiful sonic world. So does Seiji, and so does the orchestra. Though there are momentary lapses of intonation in a few spots, this is a performance that quickly startles its listeners to attention with the splendor of its sound. It is also a performance that moves. Charlie sets its tone at the outset, and the others respond, with Charlie in turn responding to them. Seiji lets Charlie and the orchestra play out, but in control, and everyone gets into the spirit of this energetic, bounding performance. Only in the Adagietto for strings does the mood perceptibly change with the extremely slow tempo and elegiac lyricism of the music. But Seiji has paced the performance so well that the Adagietto seems also a transition to the boisterous conclusion with its brass chorale. And when the orchestra reaches that, Charlie lets himself go, playing with all his verve and strength.

But there is much more to his playing than a letting go. As early as two thirds of the way through the first movement, Charlie adds an element of longing and mystery. Mahler has marked this spot "molto portamento" and "espressivo." Portamento is a term most commonly used to direct the strings to bridge the interval between notes with a kind of slide that picks up the pitches in between. Very rarely is a trumpet player asked to do this, since the effect is not proper, strictly speaking. The instruction is Mahler's way of saying what the passage should sound like rather than how it should be played, but Charlie knows what to do.

"It's really an ultra-refined glissando," he says. Using breath control, he inflects the slurred sound the way a singer would. This is very tricky, because he could easily end up playing the wrong note rather than just appearing to move by it. With the addition of his dark color, he makes the passage especially beautiful without being sentimental.

Very few trumpeters are capable of this precision and nuance. Most must choose between the two, or the choice is made for them. This is the kind of playing that originally got Charlie his job, and hearing it now is thrilling and moving to Charlie's fellow musicians and to the audience.

At the end of the piece, Seiji remains motionless for the three and a half beats of rest Mahler has marked in his score. But the audience can't stand the silence. Cheering immediately follows the finale, and there are even some whoops and hollers from the crowd, which doesn't often applaud this way in Boston. Seiji gives Charlie one of the solo bows. As though he were still in his trance, Charlie acknowledges the clapping and shouting with an almost stilted motion of his head. He appears not to realize what he has done. In fact, Charlie does not yet comprehend the full significance of his performance tonight, of what he has proven to himself if not to his colleagues. He doesn't flash a wide smile. He doesn't raise his trumpet in triumph. He is exhausted from playing and from the strain before.

Later, Charlie wonders if the bow Seiji gave him is a sign that their relationship will improve. But Charlie ought to know better. Seiji is not likely to make a public display of his personal feelings, whatever they are.

As a matter of fact, Seiji usually just goes offstage after a piece and asks Bill Moyer who should get the bows. At that moment, Seiji is too wound up from the performance to remember everyone who played well and he doesn't wish to omit anyone. Moyer at this point functions like a chief of protocol, whispering in a head of state's ear the name of an ambassador's spouse in a receiving line.

But no one in Symphony Hall has better ears or a better memory than Seiji. He, too, has heard something in Mahler Five that he will remember. He knows Charlie came through, though he still gives the first bow to principal French horn Charles Kavalovski for his solo in the Scherzo. Seiji knows the orchestra played well and that he, Seiji, was "on top" of his conducting, as Malcolm would put it. Even the *Globe* gives everyone a rave, though Richard Dyer sent a substitute. (Charlie, though, is still miffed, because the reviewer neglects to mention him by name. Actually, none of the players are named, but the review salutes the performance as "darkly sumptuous, massive, and exultant, or powerfully brassy.")

Whether Seiji says anything to Charlie will depend on how Charlie continues to perform and how Seiji feels. Seiji does take his time. To an impatient Charlie, waiting for praise from his music director, it seems like forever.

ELEVEN

*T*he next few weeks into mid-December are the most frantic of the season for the orchestra and Seiji. There will be five performances of Mahler Two, with two of the five performances in New York's fabled Carnegie Hall. And plans are now complete to record the symphony beforehand in Boston. Having just flown back from a brief visit to Berlin, where he was guest conductor of the Berlin Philharmonic, Seiji will need all his storied powers of concentration and self-discipline, plus some good luck, to get through this taxing time.

The bewildering array of rehearsals, concerts, recording sessions, player auditions, and social events is more than anyone should be expected to cope with. All the players complain about the scheduling. Some blame it on Seiji's being away too much, causing a crunch whenever he's in Boston. But his artistic administrator

Costa Pilavachi points out that Seiji's with the orchestra almost half the calendar year, which is more than almost any other conductor of a major American orchestra. So the players complain about Costa.

He has too much power over what we do, they say. We should be deciding what we play, some of them argue. Costa would demur, speaking in his elegant English with a European politeness. He dresses in Continental-cut suits, and even his clothes bother a few of the players. But what really bothers them is his access to Seiji.

Seiji depends on Costa to take care of all the programming details he clearly doesn't have time for. It was Seiji's decision to do Mahler Two, but Costa worked with Anne Parsons to fit the symphony into the calendar and to line up the soloists.

At the beginning of December, Malcolm was to have been soloist in a Vieuxtemps violin concerto. But Malcolm is still recuperating from his inner-ear infection. Though he has been in the hall recently to listen to audition tapes of some violinists, he can't perform the concerto, nor is it certain that he will be back playing in time for the Mahler recording, the most significant one for him since his appointment as concertmaster. For the Vieuxtemps, Costa has suggested that the orchestra substitute a Hindemith work that Seiji conducted in Berlin.

Seiji wanted to do a piece commissioned by Canadian composer R. Murray Schafer that he premiered in Japan last year, so Costa fit it into the schedule. Called *Ko Wo Kiku,* the piece is on the first program Seiji must face now.

Inspired by a Japanese incense ceremony, the performance calls for Seiji to come onstage and begin the ceremony. He does this with great dignity, in contrast to some of his players, one of whom says afterward, "This is not what I studied to do. I'm humiliated." Another player says the ceremony goes against his religious beliefs and he is excused. Yet another gets excused by citing a medical reason to avoid incense. Many other players wish they had such valid reasons to be absent.

Ko Wo Kiku also features basketballs in the "instrumentation."

Percussionist Arthur Press laughs afterward about the basketball he had to bounce onstage during the piece. "Now I want my shirt hanging from the Symphony Hall rafters," he jokes, referring to the Boston Celtics' tradition of honoring their champions in the Boston Garden.

Following a Friday afternoon performance of the piece, Costa and Karen Leopardi, the secretary he shares with Seiji, accompany the music director to a Symphony Hall reception to mark the opening of an exhibition of photographs taken on the orchestra's Japanese tour the previous winter. While Costa tries to anticipate whom Seiji may encounter at the reception, Karen keeps track of the time so Seiji won't be late for the next event on his schedule. Costa thrives on the heightened sense of occasion Seiji creates, while Karen secretly wishes for some peace and quiet.

The triumvirate of Costa, Karen, and promotion coordinator Kim Smedvig, a glamorous Smith graduate married to former BSO trumpeter Rolf Smedvig, hover around the music director whenever he's in his dressing room or attending a nonmusical function in the hall. At such public times—even for an interview, if his picture is being taken—Seiji wears a herringbone sports jacket and his "casino tie" (purchased for a visit to Monte Carlo, where men are required to wear ties to be admitted to the casinos). Costa, who never has to remember to put on his tie, is the most important member of the trio because of the work he does to arrange programs and soloists. But all three function together as a protective unit for Seiji, controlling others' access to him and responding to whatever request may suddenly pop into his head. Once, greeting two old friends after a concert, Seiji wanted his photograph taken with them, but a photographer was not present. Costa immediately conferred with Kim, and they both searched madly to find a camera before Seiji's friends left.

So used to such service and deference is Seiji that he seems unaware of the personal cost to him and the institution of his being cut off from most spontaneous human contact in the hall. Granted, he has to worry about little else than his work. But he misses out on the interaction with others, especially with orchestra members, that could add richness to his life. And even some of the office employees think of him as a stranger in their midst. Few can readily cite an instance when he surprised them with a kindness. Almost no one believes he knows the names of more than a half dozen of the nonmusicians in the hall. (For that matter, many of the musicians sometimes wonder if Seiji knows who they are.)

Coming from a culture where the group is valued more than the individual, Seiji actually thinks of himself as Americanized when he's in Boston. It does not seem to occur to him that his star status is not only a contradiction to his background but a deeply galling affront to his musicians. Nor has anyone who works for him had the courage to say so. He ought to be a sympathetic listener. In private, he is warm and gracious, remembering to compliment a guest, empathizing with what others tell him about themselves. He does not think of himself as better than others, but he has fewer and fewer opportunities in Boston to convey this attitude to people.

When he makes his appearance at the photography reception, it is just that: an appearance. Someone who didn't know him might conclude he is shy. He stays for an appropriate time and then his cortege escorts him away.

Several musicians also attend the reception, many with their spouses. Veteran violist Jerry Lipson, a summer golfing companion of Malcolm's despite the difference in their ages and athletic abilities, worries about his friend and colleague's continued absence. So privately does Malcolm live when he's not at the hall that most of the players in the orchestra are not aware of the reason for his having missed more than a month of the season.

"I think it's his heart," confides Lipson.

Charlie Schlueter brings his wife to the reception. It still isn't easy for her to come to the hall, but she and Charlie celebrate by drinking large quantities of saké. There was no bow for Charlie from the music director today, perhaps because Charlie missed his last note in the Hindemith piece. But Charlie is feeling expansive after the stunning string of Mahler Five performances.

The *Ko Wo Kiku* premiere elicits a deserved tribute from the *Globe's* Richard Dyer. But Seiji continues to receive a mixed response from his Boston critics. In two recent *Boston Phoenix* articles, that weekly's critic, Lloyd Schwartz, praised October's *War Requiem* and *Drala*, but said he'd heard little else he liked in the season so far. Heaping scorn on Seiji, Schwartz was particularly disdainful of some Ravel performances. "The *Valses nobles et sentimentales* and *La Valse* . . . struck me not only as Ozawa's worst Ravel performances but also as the worst performances of these pieces I've ever heard."

Schwartz's tone was so completely negative that it seemed a parody of the worst invective a critic can write, especially since Seiji's San Francisco performance of the same *La Valse* a month earlier had earned a *San Francisco Chronicle* toast of "champagne and sushi to Ozawa. It was sensuous and sensational as it could be."

The disparity between Seiji's reviews locally and elsewhere has long followed such a pattern. The pattern reverses itself when guest conductors come to Boston; they invariably win praise. Familiarity in music seems to breed contempt. But in Seiji's case the situation in Boston is complicated by the deep cultural and personal differences that separate him from the people who write about him for a living. Seiji's contact with the Boston media amounts to little more than occasional, prearranged photo opportunities. Once in a while he agrees to an interview or holds a press conference, but he never has dinner with a writer, never engages in spontaneous give-and-take when someone runs into him in the hall. (No one runs into him outside; he spends most of his time at home.) So the critics seldom give him the benefit of the doubt, as they almost always do a guest conductor.

But Seiji makes genuine mistakes, too, and these take a toll on his players' morale and on the perception his critics have of him.

Because he is so busy, he sometimes chooses the most expedient way out of a thorny situation. Then, when it is necessary to deal with the consequences, he tries to avoid them.

Bowing to pressure from the Dutch recording company Philips, Seiji and the orchestra's management have agreed to use different soloists for the Mahler Two recording. Even though the orchestra is partially subsidizing the recording (the total bill will be about $120,000 in direct labor costs alone), the orchestra's management has gone along with replacing Edith Wiens and Maureen Forrester for the recording. Philips feels that because Maureen has recently recorded the piece with another orchestra (St. Louis) and because Edith is not sufficiently well known, the BSO recording will sell more copies if it has other soloists. Though there is an understanding within the recording industry that a soloist doesn't record the same piece for a different label within five years, exceptions are often made.

But as Costa Pilavachi explains a little too smoothly, "It's important to have good soloists to enhance the salability and distinguish from the competition. Maureen and Edith knew from their agents this was in the works. As far as I was told, they were completely understanding."

Indeed they were. "Someday it will be me," hopes Edith, while Maureen already has too many recording credits to her name to miss adding the prestige of this one. But privately her pride is hurt.

The singers chosen for the recording are two of the most famous and sought-after opera stars in the world. Mezzo-soprano Marilyn Horne, on hold while there was still a strike possibility, has been formally engaged to replace Maureen, although she hasn't signed the actual contract. And Seiji personally called soprano Kiri Te Kanawa, who has never before sung this piece. They performed together a year ago at Tanglewood and Seiji loves her voice.

Seiji has also made the extraordinary offer of flying to New York for a piano rehearsal with the new singers, despite his having a concert the night before and a BSO rehearsal the next morning. He didn't have to do this. He could have fought Philips on the replacement of the soloists and avoided the necessity of this extra rehearsal, as well as any tension between the two sets of soloists on the day when they will both perform the same piece with the same orchestra, a few hours apart.

And, because Te Kanawa will be singing at the Metropolitan Opera the night before the Mahler recording session, the BSO will have to get her to Boston for the recording. Costa has had to put off the start of that session to one o'clock in the afternoon—even though the orchestra has its Mahler concert that same night. This has greatly annoyed the players and put additional pressure on Seiji. Costa has also had to secure a release from the Metropolitan to let Te Kanawa record, and he's had to get advance permission of the musicians' union to be able to rerecord her part on a separate track, should she arrive exhausted from her opera engagements and therefore in poor voice at the recording session.

This is the first major commitment to the orchestra by a recording company in several years. The investment signifies a growing respect for the BSO and its music director that could lead to further acclaim—and more recordings. And it is an opportunity for Seiji to add to his international stature as a conductor whose work matters to others.

Early the next week, Peppino drives Seiji to New York to rehearse Mahler Two with Marilyn Horne and Kiri Te Kanawa. Seiji is extraordinarily happy this morning. The orchestra played very well at last night's Pension Fund concert, and Malcolm returned for part of the performance. Though he hasn't recovered completely, he plans to be at tomorrow's Mahler Two orchestral rehearsal. Better than anyone else, Seiji understands the difference Malcolm makes in the string section, and how his sound inspires the whole orchestra and reflects on Seiji. Tamara has distinguished herself as a substitute, but the orchestra needs Malcolm's musical leadership. And Seiji wants him performing the many small solos in the Mahler.

Only the two singers, along with Kiri's husband, Costa, and Tanglewood Festival Chorus pianist Martin Amlin, attend the piano rehearsal in a small auditorium at CAMI, Columbia Artists Management, Inc. Seiji wanted to minimize what could go wrong, so he asked Costa to engage Martin, a pianist he trusts. Seiji has refused to let anyone else come because Kiri is quite nervous, since the piece is new to her. In fact, when Seiji called her to ask her to be the soprano soloist, she had to go out and buy a score to familiarize herself with the music before she replied.

But Seiji works both of the singers hard, even Marilyn, who has sung Mahler Two many times and recorded it with Claudio Abbado and the Chicago Symphony.

The day after his trip to New York, Seiji uncharacteristically takes a moment of rehearsal time to congratulate the players for their work in the Pension Fund concert.

"I enjoyed very much the two Brahms concertos," Seiji says beaming. Daniel Barenboim was the piano soloist at the concert, squeezed into the one open slot on the orchestra's calendar. "You played like symphony." As they do when they applaud a soloist, several string players tap their bows on their stands. Is their praise for Seiji, for Daniel Barenboim, or for themselves? "When you want to listen to a soloist, you listen so well," continues Seiji, attaching deep significance to his choice of verb. "Listen," as he uses it here, means the sympathetic ability to play *with* a soloist in a true collaboration. "I really enjoyed it."

With these words, Seiji ends what amounts to a speech for him and the Mahler rehearsal begins. Without a single further remark, Seiji glances to his left, as if to reassure himself that Malcolm, in his familiar blue cardigan (but sans moustache), has indeed finally returned, asks for movement five, and with the motion of his baton gets a sudden thunder of sound. The confidence he feels is unmistakable, but Seiji has no intention of letting the orchestra rest on its recent successes. With a determination that is frightening in its consuming focus, he's going to make his players forget he ever got a bad review.

Only a few minutes into the rehearsal, he stops the orchestra to say, "Excuse me, we have a funny echo. Something's different."

The place in the piece that bothers Seiji comes at the first of the three passages in movement five where part of the orchestra plays offstage. Seiji wonders aloud whether the door off the stage has been opened improperly.

"Why do I hear something different?" he asks. "Is something changed?"

He reminds the offstage instrumentalists to play in the same position as they did in October. Again they play, again Seiji stops them. Still puzzled, he turns to Bill Moyer, standing in the first balcony. "At the end of the rehearsal," Seiji says, "we'll try with no one else here." Seiji means he will dismiss most of the orchestra before the break and rehearse "Der grosse Apell" to get the proper opening of the door.

At the break, Seiji chats with Jules Eskin and with Malcolm, who began practicing again only four days ago. Malcolm is doing everything he can to stay healthy, even remembering to wear rubbers over his shoes this morning. He forgot to take the rubbers off until he was onstage, ready to play, so he left them by his chair near the podium, where he and Seiji now continue their conversation about the rehearsal.

Seiji wants to test the acoustics. "For some reason, it's not the same as October," says Seiji again.

Listening above, in the first balcony, Seiji's other assistant, Carl St. Clair, suddenly realizes what's wrong. Seiji's last memory of the piece is from a concert and now, in rehearsal, the hall is empty (though a large curtain is suspended from the ceiling near the front of the auditorium, to compensate acoustically for the missing people). He leaves to tell Seiji, who can't spend any more time on this problem. He needs a short break himself, to get ready for the chorus and soloists, who will join the orchestra shortly to continue the rehearsal.

The chorus comes onstage to rehearse at 11:45, followed by the soloists.

With everyone on stage, Seiji begins rehearsing the Mahler Two finale without a fuss. At one point he conducts while carrying on a simultaneous conversation with John Oliver.

The dependable choral director wants these new performances and the recording to go well, because he knows that the chorus will be scrutinized by the New York concert critics and that its singing will be compared to other choruses when the record comes out in a year. Much is therefore at stake for him.

But an undercurrent of unfocused discontent, absent when he leads a rehearsal or speaks with Seiji, animates John's private feelings. What he'd really like to do is raise herbs, he sometimes says, only half joking. Five years ago, he seriously considered quitting music. "Music is something that people with money buy," he says disdainfully. He yearns someday to be rid of the grind, but he can't let go.

"In a performance, you obliterate time," continues John, explaining why he persists. "You become anonymous. Every single note is infinite. You expand time. You're untrapped."

Like everyone else at this final rehearsal, he can feel the emotion taking hold of him as the musicians reach the end of Mahler Two. Despite their familiarity with the work, the performers seem overwhelmed with the sound they have just made, and they remain momentarily silent afterward.

Seiji breaks the spell. "Is that maximum organ?" he kids organist

Jim Christie, who sits at the movable console, positioned for this piece far to Seiji's left. Everyone laughs. The huge Aeolian-Skinner pipe organ is one of the few such grand instruments permanently installed in an American symphonic hall. Its powerful sound adds an extra luster to the finale of these Mahler performances. Christie, in much demand around the city and elsewhere, must be present for the entire rehearsal, even though he doesn't play until the conclusion.

"You know this so well," Seiji tells the chorus. "Can you stay for fifteen more minutes? Then you don't have to be here for the Friday rehearsal." The chorus, many of whose members have had to skip work to be here this morning, responds with applause. It sings for a moment a cappella, then with full orchestra.

"Thank you," Seiji says to the chorus. Then, looking at Maureen Forrester, he asks, "Do you want to do 'Urlicht'?"

"Whatever," she replies.

Now, while some in the chorus get up to leave, others stay still, frozen by the beauty of the song's magic notes. And Maureen sings "Urlicht" with such certainty of phrase and meaning and such quiet passion that upon her finish the entire orchestra breaks into thunderous applause. Elsewhere in the hall, in cramped offices where the orchestra's administration works, the sound of Maureen's voice comes through on a closed-circuit speaker system. Most of the employees normally pay little attention to it, but now many of them stop to listen to Maureen.

Though she would never say such a thing, Maureen sings as if she is intent on proving to Seiji and the orchestra's management that she should have been engaged for the recording. She smiles with satisfaction at the applause when she's done.

But Maureen Forrester likes Seiji. She admires the way he keeps his own counsel under great pressure. "And he almost meditates before we start performing. He has great inner control." She is also certain that the music affects Seiji emotionally. You can see this, she says, by looking at his eyes as he conducts.

*   *   *

As he does after each rehearsal, librarian Marty Burlingame checks with Malcolm to see if there are any bowing changes.

Later that afternoon, Seiji and Malcolm and the audition committee reassemble on an otherwise empty stage for the finals of violin auditions to choose three new members of the orchestra. Through bits and pieces of Mozart and Brahms and Beethoven the six finalists play, pared over the autumn from an initial applicant pool of over three hundred.

After years of practice and dedication, the finalists must stand alone, one by one, trying in a few minutes to convince their select audience to make a decision that may affect the rest of their lives.

For Seiji, this audition is one more duty in the midst of too many others. But he is notoriously careful about picking people for his group, and today is no exception. Only one of the finalists is chosen, an unassuming but very talented young woman from Los Angeles, Bonnie Bewick. Seiji speaks to the two runners-up, a gesture he doesn't have to make, thanking them for coming and suggesting to them what they should work on before applying again.

After the Friday night performance of Mahler Two, Ed Barker confesses, "This piece is hard. I get tired." Orchestra manager Anne Parsons believes the performance was better than those in October, but she worries that the orchestra may not be ready to record yet. Her belief is characteristic of the sniping that people who supposedly work for Seiji direct at the orchestra when he's out of earshot.

Immediately after the concert, the stage is rearranged by the house crew and the recording engineers, with different seating and a maze of microphones and wires, so that the BSO's Mahler Two can be digitally encoded into 1's and 0's for compact disc posterity, what Carl St. Clair calls "Mahler on demand."

TWELVE

$\mathcal{H}$oping the extra rest will clear up the bronchitis that bothered him after the concert, Seiji planned to sleep late on Saturday morning. He doesn't hear Peppino park the Lincoln in his driveway. But the sound of the burglar alarm Peppino's knock sets off a moment later wakes him instantly. The alarm sends a signal to the Newton police, who immediately dispatch a squad car to Seiji's house. In several years of devoted duty to Seiji, Peppino has never before come for his beloved maestro at the wrong time. Deeply embarrassed, he apologizes repeatedly to Seiji, whose voice still betrays symptoms of a sore throat.

Peppino could not have chosen a worse moment to make a mistake than at the start of this terribly demanding day for Seiji. But Peppino, too, is tired this morning. And he has good reason for forgetting the morning's arrangements. Last night, he drove to New

York City to pick up Kiri Te Kanawa after her performance of *Die Fledermaus*, and they set off for Boston around midnight. Peppino dropped her off after 3 A.M. at the Four Seasons Hotel, where Kiri requested a room in which the previous guest hadn't smoked and stipulated no maid service, so she, too, could sleep as late as possible this morning before faithful Peppino drove her to the hall.

Seiji quickly forgets he's tired when he gets to the hall. He's all business and wastes no time getting started. Though there will be repeated takes and retakes of the music they will all record today, there will be no second chance with the chorus and soloists after this session. The playing must be good, and Seiji will have to sustain a high level of motivation and execution throughout.

They begin at the end, with the hushed choral "Aufersteh'n" in the last great section of the final movement. Kiri stands as soon as the chorus sings its first note. While he conducts, Seiji picks up a telephone receiver that has been mounted by the podium. Producer Wilhelm Hellweg, with whom he was worked before, is calling him from the basement control room.

A talented, deeply committed musician—he plays both the piano and the French horn—Hellweg is the technical mastermind behind these recording sessions. Without him, the recording session would quickly degenerate into chaos. He has to keep Seiji and the orchestra on the schedule he has mapped out. He has to serve as an intermediary between the performers and the other engineers and technicians who operate the recording equipment. And he must remain unflappable, never letting his own emotions influence those of the performers. In short, he must be a musical magician.

He's a taskmaster but with a love of what he does. Seiji respects that as much as his considerable technical skills. Hellweg constantly cajoles, but he has a good sense of humor and pace. And he's very smart. He understands the psychology of performers, because he has been one himself. And his work in the control room is a kind of spoken performance. He speaks in a mellifluous voice with an insistent, assured tone that at moments of crisis veers into a bark. He wants this recording to be successful as badly as Seiji does.

Without a break, and without putting down the phone, Seiji leads the chorus, orchestra, and new soloists through the test run, its principal purpose the proper setting of the microphone levels—a whole run-through just for that. As Marilyn Horne—Jackie, as all the musicians call her—stands to sing, Seiji kneels to speak with Kiri, who sucks on a throat lozenge. Both soloists have been positioned near him, rather than with the chorus, to make communication easier.

Rapidly, to catch up with the music, Seiji turns several pages in his score. Though he conducts as usual from memory, even in this recording session, he uses the score today for reference between takes. He needs it to check occasional notes and markings, to help him with the large number of things he keeps in mind simultaneously.

Simply conducting won't suffice now. He must maintain a perfect rapport with the soloists. And as he concentrates on the music, he must be ready to respond to the telephone interruptions from Wilhelm Hellweg. Furthermore, he must make the bizarre fact of these constant calls seem as natural a part of the recording session as the movements of his body, in order to preserve an illusory sense that this is a performance. While alert to the basement activity he cannot see, he must conduct as if this were a concert.

But this recording session is very different from a concert. After the climactic concluding chords, Seiji immediately sits down on the podium to speak again with Kiri. Jackie leans over to hear what Seiji is relaying about the sound, which Wilhelm has reported to him on the phone. They decide to listen together in the control room, so Seiji dismisses the orchestra.

Downstairs in the control room, Seiji sits on the middle chair before a table, flanked on one side by Jackie and Wilhelm and on the other by Kiri. Behind them stand John Oliver and several members of the orchestra, including Charlie Schlueter. The first note seems to be missing from the tape, but Seiji thinks that's funny. Of more concern to him is a missing Malcolm, who is slow getting to the control room. He sends Costa Pilavachi to find Malcolm, and Tamara as well.

As the playback commences, Seiji sways in his chair, as if he were conducting. He makes comments about what he hears. To John Oliver after a choral passage: "I like that." To Kiri: "You came in too fast."

Out of Seiji's earshot, one of the extra trumpet players hired for these performances mutters to Charlie, "What a way to start." He wonders how his lip will hold up.

Jackie wants to say something. "I don't want to tell you what to do," she says with false modesty. She suggests that she and Kiri sit with the chorus. Seiji and Wilhelm agree.

"The chorus sounds wonderful," she adds. "Which chorus is this?"

Seiji and Wilhelm have already decided that the next take will be a passage requiring neither soloist. "I'll stay down here," says Jackie in the hallway, "if there's no smoke." Seiji bounds up the staircase.

As soon as the take is over, Seiji picks up the phone and listens attentively to Wilhelm.

"Chorus, I think we've got that section," he reports. Most of the singers chuckle.

Seiji reminds the violas about one of their entrances. Charlie asks a question about his penultimate notes. The soloists return to the stage, where they sit this time with the chorus. The next take proceeds smoothly until Wilhelm once more interrupts with a request to begin again. Seiji signals for that beginning, but one of the wind players drops his mouthpiece. Another stop, another start eat up time that will be precious later.

For fifty minutes, until 2:40 P.M., the musicians work to get as much of the fifth movement on tape as they can. With her passages done first, Jackie leaves the stage to applause. After another vocal take, Seiji gives Kiri an okay sign with his fingers. People she's asked have told Kiri that her entrance is the most difficult passage in her part, so she tells herself it's easy. But it isn't. She's in terrific voice this afternoon, despite her Met performance of last night. Her singing lacks some of Edith's warmth, but the top notes are strong and firm.

Just before Seiji asks her to sing again, Charles Kavalovski says he can hear the organ's air conditioner. Wilhelm suggests leaving the organ out of one take. The technical work will all be done in Holland, where Wilhelm lives. There the engineers will be able to marry the two separate takes, one with the organ and one without, and people listening to the finished recording will never know.

Finally satisfied, Seiji calls for another twenty-minute intermission. Downstairs, Jackie wonders what Wilhelm thinks of the recording so far.

"Do you like it?" she asks him.

"I like it very much," he answers truthfully. But there's still too much to do for him to relax. He's under orders from Philips to avoid overtime.

John Oliver, wondering if his chorus can leave, asks whether Sarah Harrington should line the singers up and have them "file to the parking lot." Seiji, not getting John's joke, says he can't decide until he's heard the tape. Impatiently, he waits for the correct playback. "Would you buy a quicker machine for next time," he says, annoyed.

"Yes," says Wilhelm.

"Chinese maybe," continues Seiji, trying to be funny.

Jackie joins in. "Where is the machine made?"

"Switzerland," says Wilhelm. Now it is his turn to be annoyed. He doesn't like questions that imply the engineers don't know what they're doing.

"O Glaube," deadpans Jackie.

Jackie's digitally taped voice suddenly comes through the speakers, riveting everyone's attention in the small, crowded room.

In his chair, just as he would on the podium, Seiji thrusts forward as she sings. He appears to be listening for something indefinable. Not content with surface sound, he's listening for expression, for emotion.

"Very strong statement that time," Seiji says to Jackie afterward. The compliment is also intended to remind Jackie that this is Seiji's recording, not hers. He's in charge.

Malcolm and Wilhelm discuss a poor passage in the next take. "My fault," insists Seiji apologetically. "I hope we have a better one." Wilhelm responds with a quick "Oh yes."

As the chorus on the tape intones the word "leben," the assistant personnel manager, a retired horn player named Harry Shapiro, mimics Seiji's motions for Tamara Smirnova-Šajfar's amusement. Seiji can't see them. Nearing "Sterben," Seiji fixes his eyes on the low ceiling. His head shakes. Now Jackie makes believe she is conducting, her hands spread, head back, as the chorus sings its last note. The sound of the chorus and full orchestra seems too much for the loudspeakers. Seiji smiles. "Beautiful," says Kiri, joining the recently convened mutual-admiration society.

Harry Shapiro reminds everyone that the orchestral break has almost elapsed. "One minute," he says. It's time for the performers to get back onstage.

Seiji still hasn't decided if he wants to rerecord any of the choral passages, so he sends word that the chorus must stay, but not onstage. No sooner has someone left to deliver this message than he and Wilhelm listen again to the first "Aufersteh'n." The playback continues. Kiri asks to hear a take on a different tape. One of Wilhelm's assistants points to the clock on the wall. The tension now is almost unbearable. They're running out of time.

"It's recording time now," the assistant says. "It takes four minutes to change tapes," he adds.

Seiji reiterates that the chorus must stay. "Too important," he says. Before leaving the room, he asks Wilhelm if he can make the trumpets' first entrance following the chorus a little softer. Seiji doesn't want a scene with Charlie today, and he has apparently decided that asking Wilhelm to do this is easier than asking Charlie to play the passage softer.

"Of course," replies Wilhelm. He shares Seiji's concern about the trumpet's volume level. But he's been very impressed with their playing today. The trumpet sound is going to stand up very well in the finished recording.

Though Kiri has to get back to New York, Seiji asks her to stay until he's certain he doesn't need her again. "Do you mind waiting?" he inquires.

"No," she sighs. "I've come all this way."

Onstage, Jackie sits by herself, surrounded by the chorus's empty chairs. She sings a few measures of "Urlicht," choosing the spot near the opening after the trumpet chorale. Seiji signals the start of taping to the orchestra. They play the end of the Scherzo and then Jackie sings, one hand holding her music, the other in a pocket of her jacket. Silence follows her singing. Seiji picks up his phone.

"Ten-minute break," he announces.

Downstairs again, the main participants listen to "Urlicht." The trumpet chorale sounds too loud. "It wasn't that loud onstage," insists Charlie. He means the microphone placement makes the trumpets seem loud. He doesn't like Wilhelm's slight rearrangement of the players' chairs, but he keeps silent on this point. He's beginning to feel tense now, and he can't let that hurt his playing. But Wilhelm can't take time to reassure Charlie.

Ralph Gomberg's oboe playing sounds flat. "I thought we were only going to do the fifth movement today," Gomberg complains. "I brought the wrong reed." Oboists constantly change reeds, and Gomberg would have brought another for his delicate part in the fourth movement.

At one point as he listens to "Urlicht," Seiji says, "That's good." Near the end of the song, Jackie shakes her head, as if to say she knows she can do it better. The time is now nearly 3:30, which leaves about an hour and a half to the recording session, including breaks.

"What is it then that delights you when you hear music?" Mahler once asked. "What makes you light-hearted and free? Is the world less puzzling if you build it out of matter? Is there any explanation to be got from your seeing it as an interplay of mechanical forces? What is force, energy? *Who* does the playing? You believe in the 'conservation of energy,' in the indestructibility of matter. Is that not immortality too?

"Put the problem in any form you wish, you will always reach the point where your wisdom turns to dreams."

Pushing to put Mahler's Second Symphony on record with his own name next to it, Seiji is too intelligent to dream the result will be any kind of immortality. By one count, this will be the twenty-ninth complete recording of the piece since 1924, when the Berlin State Opera Orchestra under Oskar Fried first recorded it. And one of those other recordings is also Seiji's (with the New Japan Philharmonic).

Here in the hall, the people around Seiji take for granted the human dimension of his ambition. "I must hear the chorus and soloists before I go today," Seiji says. "They don't come back on Monday. I don't want to lose any recording time, but this is important."

Dutifully, the engineers find the right tape. Perhaps Seiji is still remembering that first time he heard the chorus in Mahler Two, in Vienna with Bernstein conducting. That was Lenny's Mahler. This is Seiji's. In this almost helter-skelter atmosphere of a late-twentieth-century digital recording session, he's comparing many versions. No one in this crowded room can help him do this. In the midst of all these talented, opinionated people, he's on his own in making certain that it's his version of Mahler Two they record. For this to happen, he must feel right about himself, because that self is his instrument. If he isn't confident, no one else will be. His certainty today defines the session's success, more than the playing and singing.

The rest of the afternoon is a mad dash. John Oliver and assistant conductors Pascal Verrot and Carl St. Clair remain in the control room with the engineers and Harry Shapiro and watch Seiji and the orchestra on the closed-circuit television monitor. Jackie is out of view, but they hear her voice clearly on the speakers as the next take begins. During a brief break, Jackie asks a question about tempo near the end of the song. Seiji listens politely, but without any intention of making a change.

Jackie has trouble with the octave interval near the end. "Sorry, I can't make it," she says. They try again.

"That was beautiful," one of the engineers says, but just to be sure, they repeat it. She misses a D.

"Sorry, I've got phlegm in my throat." Another stop, another start.

"Once more," coaxes Seiji.

St. Clair thinks the source of the problem is Jackie's insistence on not taking a breath shortly after the D, during the long phrase. Impressed, he says, "She's trying to sing it as it's written," without the breath.

"I think we've got this," Wilhelm finally announces. But there's no time to celebrate. Immediately, he moves to the next problem.

"One thing we have to repair is the beginning of the trumpets," he says dispassionately.

The trumpets try it. Charlie hates this stopping and starting. He thinks the whole experience is musically false. He misses the edge a live concert gives, its replacement the maddening pressure to play correct notes.

"Late," reports Wilhelm of their entrance. "But," he adds, as if afraid he sounded too harsh, "the balance was perfect."

They try again, but Wilhelm remains unsatisfied. "I'd like one more in the can," he tells Seiji on the phone. "That sounded manufactured."

Start. Stop. Start. Stop. Start. Stop.

"This is hard," trumpeter Peter Chapman says in the control room, as he pulls for Charlie and his colleagues to make it through the passage, which he doesn't play.

"Thank you very much," Wilhelm interjects, speaking again to Seiji on the phone. "I think we've got this one."

Now Jackie wants to record the last six measures again. And so they do, eliciting from Wilhelm an "Okay, excellent." His tone is that of a surgeon, commenting on an operating procedure. But afterward, during the subsequent break, Wilhelm repeats this compliment in person. "That was beautiful," he tells Jackie sincerely. But he also means, "We have to move on." The time is 3:55.

"Can we listen?" Jackie asks.

"Will you kill me if I say no?"

The playbacks commence with the choral passages recorded earlier, but Jackie remains in the room to hear "Urlicht." She won't take Wilhelm's answer as final.

"Can you make the flutes softer?" Seiji asks Wilhelm as they listen to the double pianissimo entrance of flutes and oboe just before the conclusion of the chorus's first section. Some orchestras leave out the flutes at this spot in recordings, to be certain the chorus is sufficiently hushed.

Pleased with the pitch, Seiji feels confident now that what the chorus sang will work. "Send the chorus away," he announces matter-of-factly, meaning the chorus members can break now until tonight's concert.

John Oliver decides his singers need a reward. He tells them they don't have to report back at the hall until 7:45 for the 8 o'clock concert.

Meanwhile, Seiji turns to bid goodbye to the soloists. "Thank you very much," he says to Kiri, and they embrace, a rare public gesture for Seiji. "I appreciate," adds Seiji.

Graciously, Kiri shakes the hand of every single person in the control room. She has done what she was asked to do, and she sees no reason to remain any longer. Leaving, she has about her an air of musical royalty, mingled with a down-to-earth relief that her assignment is complete. She smiles broadly and then she disappears.

But Jackie doesn't want to go. Still concerned about the last take of "Urlicht," she holds her ground firmly. She'll not let any record producer be the judge of her voice.

"You don't know my voice," she informs Wilhelm imperiously. "I do." He doesn't reply. But she still doesn't leave.

"How much recording time left?" Seiji asks.

"Thirty-seven minutes," replies Harry Shapiro. Then, almost to himself, he adds, "Thirty by the time Seiji gets up there."

The orchestra plays the first offstage section, early in the fifth movement. Wilhelm interrupts with a reminder to open the stage door. "That was excellent," he says after the take. "In fact, the first bit was perfect. But then it went a little bit on the loud side.

"And one little thing," he continues. "The offstage horns were a little on the flat side." With the placement of the offstage band in the corridor, so far from the stage, this surprises no one. Instruments tend to sound flat when they are heard from a distance.

"One more shot," Wilhelm orders.

After two more attempts, Wilhelm directs everyone to the next offstage section, later in the movement. The orchestra tries it several times. Then, with eight minutes of recording time remaining, they take a break so Jackie can hear "Urlicht." It is almost five o'clock, and she has to catch a six o'clock plane to New York, but she will not leave until she's happy with the sound of her singing. She's won her little battle with Wilhelm.

"That's good,"she says of one spot. Then, "That's awful." The next receives a mixed notice. "That's not bad."

"What I've got to know is, how do we patch this?" she asks.

While Wilhelm assures her that he'll be able to splice the best spots from each take, he answers a question from Seiji about the last five minutes of recording time. To Seiji he says, "Offstage," which he follows immediately, to Jackie, with, "It will be a bit tricky. I'll promise to try if you'll promise not to kill me."

"Thank you," says Jackie. "Onward and upward with Mahler. I do this tomorrow and the next day." She has a Sunday recital, and, with Zubin Mehta leading the New York Philharmonic, she will sing the final movement of the same symphony on Monday night at a Carnegie Hall gala and some Mahler songs on Tuesday night with another orchestra and another conductor. Seiji isn't the only performer who lives in a state of perpetual motion.

"Stop talking!" implores Harry, ever alert to the clock. "Play!"

The session ends with thirty seconds to spare, but Wilhelm's take-by-take recording schedule is seven minutes behind. Wilhelm will have to figure out a way to make up this time on Monday, when two more recording sessions will be devoted primarily to the first three movements of the long symphony.

Wilhelm wants Seiji to hear the last takes, but the music director declines.

"I'd love to listen," he says. But the long Saturday afternoon has caught up with him, and he still must conduct the piece again tonight. His throat is still scratchy and he could lose his voice if he keeps talking. "I need to rest." This afternoon has been only a small part of a busy ten days, and a few hours later Seiji and the orchestra and chorus must put on their concert clothes for another performance.

The concert that night is much better than it should be after such a grueling afternoon. Instead of going through the motions, Seiji gets a second wind and the players sense it. Freed from the constraints of the recording session, they sound like they're enjoying their work.

Bounding up the stairs to see the music director, Costa can't contain his enthusiasm over what he's heard tonight. "I wish we'd kept the same cast for the recording," he says. His comment is less a criticism of Jackie and Kiri than praise for the spontaneity of a live performance.

Costa has invited Pulitzer Prize–winning composer Bernard Rands, who teaches at Boston University, to see Seiji tonight. Rands and his wife wait now at the bottom of the stairs that lead to Seiji's dressing room. They wait a long time. But Seiji doesn't budge. The dressing-room door remains closed. He doesn't mean to be rude, but he can't face another duty right now. Annoyed, Rands discusses the awkward situation with his wife. Seeing Seiji may lead to a BSO performance of one of Rands's pieces, maybe even a commission for a new one.

Costa should have invited Rands to come another time. Without speaking with Costa, Rands realizes this himself, and he leaves before Seiji's door opens. Tonight is really no time for anyone to discuss future performances with Seiji. After pushing himself all day long, the exhausted music director ought to get to bed. He has a double recording session on Monday and three more concerts next week, two of them in New York.

But, putting aside the prospect of all that work and forgetting his sore throat, Seiji impulsively decides to go to a party to which one of the BSO's photographers has invited him. And tomorrow, when he ought to rest, he and Bill Bernell have tickets on the fifty-yard line to see the New England Patriots host the San Francisco 49ers in a football game. For thirty-six hours, he's going to try to put Mahler Two out of his mind. He won't be able to do that completely, of course, but just the attempt will be a relief. He bundles up in his Eskimo coat and heads out into the city, just as he always did after a concert when he was a young man and the world hadn't discovered Seiji Ozawa yet.

THIRTEEN

*M*onday is the biggest day of the season so far for Seiji. Two more recording sessions will completely fill the schedule. Tomorrow is crammed with appointments preceding a Mahler Two concert at night. Then the orchestra leaves for New York on Wednesday, to give concerts at Carnegie Hall that night and the following one. Seiji goes home to Japan after that for Christmas and then to Europe. He won't return to Boston until late February.

But after a day off, Seiji feels renewed and full of energy to tackle the huge job ahead. Despite all the stops and starts on Saturday, he knows a lot has gone right. The chorus sang superbly. The new soloists did more than a creditable job, and the orchestra has played really well. Though this is not a time for reflection, Seiji believes the musicians are coming into their own as a group molded by him. He's especially proud of the strings, but he's also pleased with the work of all his principals, even his principal trumpet player. With rotating vacation weeks and other leaves, as well as the varied instrumentation of different works, the orchestra's principals do not often play together as a unit with the entire orchestra. Seiji's group has been growing stronger as an ensemble in response to the challenge of Mahler.

But it will be very hard for Seiji to keep everyone's motivation high today. The players are tired after their labors last week. And, unlike Seiji, they see no end in sight. For him, this week will be a culmination to be followed by a much-needed break. Most of them, however, face a week of Christmas Pops afterward and then the continuation of the regular season with guest conductors. The musicians mustn't let thoughts of what's to come distract them. Their natural human reaction to last week is to let off a little now. It will be up to Seiji to maintain their intensity by the example he sets.

Shortly before ten o'clock on Monday morning, before the official beginning of the day's first recording session, Seiji sits in the control room, sipping tea and reviewing Saturday's session with Wilhelm and Malcolm Lowe. Malcolm mentions a "spot of an intonation problem" with a fifth-movement pizzicato, a passage of notes plucked by the strings.

"I didn't hear it," says Seiji.

"One or two takes weren't good," Malcolm insists.

Wilhelm intercedes. Fixing the problem will involve some "tricky cutting," he explains, "but no need to worry." In fact, there are typically half a dozen mistakes per minute of recording time. So Wilhelm doesn't worry about one in particular, unless it stands out. He's more concerned that after all the work on Saturday afternoon more than half of the piece still remains to be recorded.

Bill Moyer has been waiting to ask about using three extra minutes the orchestra agreed to add to the recording sessions. After a dispute about the official starting time on Saturday, the Players Committee voted this concession. Because microphones set up in the hallway for the offstage instruments may pick up traffic noises from outside the building late in the day, noon is the quietest time for offstage recording. Seiji and Wilhelm decide to spend the bonus minutes then, rerecording "Der grosse Apell." Bill hurries from the room to report this decision to the orchestra, already assembled onstage, and Seiji follows. Wilhelm listens impatiently to Bill's announcement on the closed-circuit television in the control room, where curmudgeonly Harry Shapiro notes, "That took thirty seconds to say."

"Ready for recording," says Wilhelm. "Take twenty-eight. Rolling."

For the first time in its recording of the symphony, the orchestra begins at the beginning of the piece. After a quick stop to retune, Seiji cautions the cellos and basses not to relax the tempo just before the French horns come in. Several more starts and stops bring the orchestra through the exposition section of the first movement. A mysterious noise onstage prompts one of the engineers in the control room to quip, "Another musician coming in," while the orchestra continues playing through the movement's first development. No such labels mark the score, but the rough overall form lends itself to block-by-block recording takes, which Wilhelm painstakingly planned before these sessions began. His plans look like a movie director's shooting charts.

"The levels on that last part were perfect," reports one of the engineers.

"Of course, of course," responds an assistant of Wilhelm's. He has brought two with him. One of the assistants, a gregarious, bearded man named Onno Scholtze, is chiefly responsible for adjusting the balances among the fifteen microphones. The number is far smaller than it would have been just a few years ago, before the advent of digital electronics. With fewer microphones, the sound of the finished recording will be closer to that on the stage. (Some companies now mike in only one or two spots in the hall, to give a sense of the sound from a "live" listener's reference point.)

Conscientious, dependable John Newton, Wilhelm's recording engineer, operates out of his own Boston company, one of the first involved in digital recording. If he makes a mistake or his equipment breaks down, a portion of the recording could be ruined. But Newton, who has made over twenty recordings with Seiji and knows the kind of recorded sound the music director wants, is serene. He worries only that an airplane carrying one of the tapes to Holland later might crash. He has a total belief in himself and the machinery he brings with him: two Sony tape recorders and two Studer mixing consoles. An assistant actually operates the tape recorders, while Wilhelm and Onno preside over the consoles, constantly checking track levels and making minor adjustments in the myriad dials and switches.

The engineers take their work as seriously as the performers, but try to keep their contribution in perspective. "There's a lot you can fix in editing," Newton says. "But you can't make well-played notes if they don't exist."

Bill Moyer has returned to the control room to remind Wilhelm of the clock. Wilhelm picks up his phone and says, "Okay, Seiji, why don't we take a twenty-minute break." Wilhelm and Seiji use the break, mandated by the musicians' contract, to listen to what the orchestra's done.

Into the control room comes Seiji, followed by assistant principal bass Larry Wolfe, Ralph Gomberg, Jules Eskin, and several other players. Gomberg kids Seiji about the rehearsal glasses the conductor wears during these sessions (although never in performance), while principal cello Jules Eskin leans over Seiji's shoulder to hear the first full take. "That's together," Eskin says to Seiji. A few measures later, just prior to Gomberg's entrance with another oboe and the English horn, Seiji asks Wilhelm, "Would you make this part more diminuendo?" Playing thirty-second-note tremolos for two bars, the violas and second violins here must keep a steady stroke as they get progressively softer. "This is very hard," Seiji says.

Even harder to play, the lovely ascending C-scale entrance of the first violins at the first development challenges the ensemble ability of the strings. The two violinists at each stand split their parts, one violinist playing the scale an octave higher than the other. They must all keep the spacing between the drawn-out notes in unison while using a light bow. Malcolm, who has joined Seiji and Wilhelm at the front of the control room, worries that the duration of the notes isn't even. They listen silently as the playback continues through more of the first part of the piece, culminating in the fiendish opposition of legato eighth notes in the violas and second violins and pairs of slurred sixteenth and eighth notes in the cellos and basses, each slur ending in a staccato with a sixteenth-note rest. "Very difficult, but we did okay," concludes Seiji. He means to sound encouraging.

Reviewing with Wilhelm what he has just heard, Seiji seems oblivious to the departure from the room of the musicians who have been listening with him. But he's thinking about them as he responds to a question from Wilhelm about an upbeat in one place and a timpani entrance in another. He must pace their progress, pushing them for their best playing without tiring them. And he must conserve his own energy. With each of his comments instantly noted on Wilhelm's charts of the piece, Seiji must focus on every problem the piece presents without wasting the emotional reserves he will need a moment later when he returns to the podium. This entire day is becoming a performance for him, with the breaks in the actual recording as much of a job as conducting.

Wilhelm listens carefully as the orchestra plays, hears a tiny misintonation, nods to himself as if to say, "Okay, we can fix that later, or we have it on another take." A buzzer on the control room's clock inadvertently goes off, and Wilhelm jumps slightly in his chair. Writing madly in his score, Wilhelm tells Seiji on the phone that a spot in the basses' playing at the beginning now sounds "calculated." Upstairs, Seiji apologizes to the players for the continuing, maddening repetition.

Neither he nor Wilhelm, who continues talking on his telephone hookup with the music director, ever mentions Mahler. But everything they do is motivated in some way by the notes in the score, which both men have before them. Mahler himself was a notoriously picky conductor when he rehearsed, and he probably would have approved of this intense effort to get everything right. But when Mahler conducted he could impose his will on his players without recourse. They had no union to protect their rights. Seiji and Wilhelm don't fear an actual backlash, but they are both aware of the limits to which they can take these men and women before their orders will be met with deaf ears.

"To figure five," directs Wilhelm on the phone to Seiji. Then he changes his mind. "We had a little bit of a horn kick, so to 'pesante.'" By "kick," Wilhelm means an intonation mistake.

One of Mahler's frequently used markings, "pesante"—literally, in English, "heavy"—occurs here midway between figures five and six. Seiji relays Wilhelm's message to the orchestra, but he makes it seem to the players that the decision is his. The musicians do as they are told.

"Okay, excellent, we got this one," Wilhelm soon says. After two long takes, the orchestra reaches the end of the first movement.

At the twenty-minute break, Seiji changes his shirt as usual, taking another from a closet off the control room, each one with the hand-sewn butterfly trademark of the designer Hanae Mori, a personal friend of Seiji's. At one of Seiji's favorite Boston shops, shirts like this sell for several hundred dollars apiece.

Charlie and several other players join Seiji and Wilhelm in the control room. It's now noon, but Seiji has no intention of sticking to his schedule. "The orchestra is on now," he says with excitement and a hint of pride. He is beginning to sense that this recording may turn out to be very good, and he needs to keep his and the orchestra's concentration on the first movement.

Turning to Pascal Verrot, who was to conduct the offstage players during "Der grosse Apell" now, he adds a cheerful "Sorry." Pascal will have to wait. Wilhelm, meanwhile, is thirsty. With great gravity, he asks those around him in his imperfect English: "Is there someone to organize a cola for me?"

The playbacks in the control room commence at figure 16, where Mahler has changed the familiar motif of slurred, paired sixteenth notes and eighths into groups of thirty-second notes and eighths. For four bars after figure 16, half of the basses and cellos play alone like this in unison, continuing as other instruments join in. Very delicate, the effect requires adept coordination by the players under the precise beat of their conductor.

"It seems more together than it has been," says Ed Barker. Seiji credits the demands of the recording session for this accomplishment, and everyone in the room laughs at the idea that the distracting stops and starts could actually be improving their ensemble. Then, seven measures after figure 16, Seiji's tone changes. "The pitch is bad there," he says. "Why?" No one answers, and the tape continues. A quarter note the trumpets play sounds "artificial," Seiji tells a silent Charlie Schlueter. Deeply insulted, Charlie keeps his mouth shut. He can't afford to talk back.

Addressing Barker again, Seiji makes a rare, personally revealing comment about the music.

"With this piece," Seiji says, "we have a problem. With all of Mahler. How much together? How much feeling?"

Few people are in the room to hear him. Most of the players are elsewhere for the break, drinking coffee, reading, smoking in the lounge, where the shade has been pulled down while someone naps. But they would all understand what Seiji has said, and some of them would seize on his words. They wish he would share with them his discoveries about the music, instead of constantly harping on their mistakes. They wish he would reveal more of himself.

Yet some of them sense that there is about their music director a growing purpose, a grasp of something new and deeper in his conducting of Mahler Two. He may not talk about it, but it's there in the motions of his body. And, though they don't want to admit this, the result is revealing itself in the extremely high quality of their playing.

"How do you like my tempo primo?" Seiji asks Wilhelm.

The descending chromatic scale with which the first movement ends is marked "Tempo I," meaning the tempo is the same as at the beginning of the piece, "allegro maestoso." But the direction has caused much confusion, because Mahler changed his mind, both about the opening tempo and that of the closing scale. Like many conductors, Seiji chooses to compromise here, taking the scale at a tempo somewhat between that of the opening and the "schnell" ("fast") that Mahler at one time indicated.

Wilhelm seems baffled by Seiji's question, as though he were being asked to praise the maestro for something that is none of his business. Perhaps to make up for the silence with which he greeted Seiji's question, Wilhelm turns to Harry Shapiro after Seiji leaves the room and says enigmatically, "When Seiji makes up his mind, he's extraordinary." But he should have said something to Seiji. Wilhelm is the only person here who can tell Seiji he's doing a good job. The players never do and never will. And Seiji needs positive reinforcement just as much as they do. He must get it from what he hears in their playing.

"Seiji loves the sound," Harry Shapiro says to himself. So does Harry, who played French horn in the orchestra for forty years until he took on his present duties as assistant personnel manager in 1976. He has caught Seiji's enthusiasm. "Seiji says the orchestra is playing hot."

But before the orchestra can go on to the second movement, several patches from movement one remain. Wilhelm deftly gets Seiji to do what he wants. "Well, unfortunately, we need one more of this," he says after a rerecording of a difficult bar for the trumpets and trombones before figure 20. "Oh, that was excellent," he reports after another spot goes well. "Oh, that was good. One problem before twenty-seven. Horns and trumpets. Can we start at 'nicht schleppen'? In fact, up to twenty-seven, up to the end. That's a nice finish-off."

Wilhelm and Seiji talk on the phone about mutes. At figure 5 of the second movement, the string players begin with the small comblike clamps that fit over the strings at the bridge and lessen their vibrations. "Don't put on mutes until I signal," Seiji reminds the violins. They try the section again.

The second violins flub a pizzicato at figure 12. "Oh God," mutters Bill Moyer's assistant, Bruce Creditor, in the back of the room, worried about the time.

"Thank you, very well done," says Wilhelm a few minutes later, the problem corrected and the second movement over.

With another twenty-minute break, only fourteen minutes remain in the morning recording session. Wilhelm and Harry double-check their computations of this figure, just as Seiji asks about the same thing. He calls his office as he once again changes his shirt. That makes three or four this morning. The tape continues through figure 5 as Malcolm arrives.

"Did you hear the beginning?" asks Seiji, looking up.

"I just got here," Malcolm replies.

"It was very good."

As Seiji speaks, the tape has reached a soaring, lyric line the cellos play against the muted pizzicati of the violins and violas. "Cello sounds good," continues Seiji. "That's nice. Very nice."

The tape keeps going, and as the movement nears its end, Seiji allows himself and the players a unique compliment. "Okay, that sounds like Boston Symphony." Then he quickly adds, "Too fast, I know. But the Saturday night performance went too slow. That was on my mind. This is good now." Excitement among the players and engineers in the control room is growing. There is no grumbling now about the schedule. Suddenly, everyone wants to keep going.

During each playback, the closed-circuit television continues to display a silent view of the stage, where some of the players stay to practice. Now, with the playback of the second movement over, the members of the orchestra who have been listening to themselves in the control room leave, while Seiji and Wilhelm decide what parts of the movement need rerecording.

"What time do we start?" asks Seiji.

"One minute."

"Uh-oh."

Anne Parsons has joined the group in the control room. Her presence is intended to remind Wilhelm that both Philips and the orchestra want to avoid overtime.

A frantic series of short recording takes begins, with Wilhelm alternately marking his score, talking to himself, and watching the clock. At three minutes before 1 P.M., the orchestra stops when the pizzicato at figure 12 again doesn't go correctly. Another start, another shake of Wilhelm's head, and something drops onstage.

Stop.

Starting once more, this time five measures before the dreaded pizzicato, the take goes smoothly until one of the strings strikes a wrong note nine bars after figure 13. The clock shows 12:59. But the music continues.

"There goes our bonus," sighs Wilhelm to Harry Shapiro, beating the rhythm with his pencil. They're going to keep recording past one o'clock and use up the extra three minutes. "I hope we can make it," Wilhelm adds. Harry stands. Wilhelm grimaces.

"Tell me when," Wilhelm says anxiously, meaning when time runs out.

"I'll tell you," Harry assures him.

"Thank you, Harry." With only a little more than fifteen bars to go—just over a page in the score—Harry has to stop the session. The time is up. Nervous, relieved laughter erupts in the control room, releasing the tension that the engineers have been under. This may not be a healthy way to make music—or to live—but it's exciting.

Seated on the couch in the room's rear, Pascal Verrot waits for Seiji and Wilhelm to reschedule the offstage instruments' rerecording. With all of the Scherzo to do and a few spots in the fifth movement to fix, the afternoon session will challenge everyone's endurance. Clearly, "Der grosse Apell" can't wait until the end. Rush-hour traffic will make too much noise then. Even at three o'clock, when the final session begins, the streets outside the hall may clog, creating havoc for the hallway mikes.

"We'll stop the traffic," jokes Seiji, as he grins mischievously. "We'll get three girls," he says, and with his hands mimicking the motions of a traffic cop he demonstrates their assignment. End of discussion.

With Seiji gone, trumpeter Peter Chapman lingers to hear himself in Saturday's final take of "Der grosse Apell." And Malcolm asks Wilhelm about his first-movement solo, played antiphonally with the flute. It is one of his the most difficult spots in the entire piece.

Finding the note on which he starts, a G two and a half octaves above middle C, presents Malcolm with several alternatives in the left-hand position switch the passage requires. He elects to change his fingering rather than his hand location and therefore uses third position, which enables him to find the high G as though it were a fingered octave above the G he plays earlier.

There are countless tiny moments like this in the piece, for many of which Malcolm makes quick, instinctive decisions. But this one required longer thought, in addition to the years of playing and practicing before he could execute fingered octaves. And beyond the sheer technique Malcolm must master here, he keeps within himself a deep sense of what he calls "the musical context, the line, musically." He must think about how Seiji takes this place in the piece, how it fits in with the rest of the movement. And he must think about how each individual passage of the piece is moving, even in this recorded performance with its stops and starts. And always he must think about his intonation—getting that G in the passage correct—within the playing of the entire ensemble.

"I think it's okay," says Wilhelm, but Malcolm wants the reassurance of his own ears. While he and Peter Chapman wait for the playbacks, Malcolm asks about the Monette trumpet, with its distinctive unpolished brass, that Peter holds in his left hand. "I'm just trying it out," Peter explains. Peter can't decide if he wants to make the fifteen-hundred-dollar investment in an instrument that will match Charlie's. He's not yet convinced it will help his sound, and that's a lot of money to spend (though far, far less than the thirty-thousand dollars that one of Malcolm's bows costs).

Malcolm's question reveals how unobservant of Charlie he has been. The Monette trumpets look like no others, and Charlie has been playing them for three years now, certainly time enough for Malcolm to have inquired before. But Malcolm hasn't been paying attention to Charlie's brand of trumpet. Like Seiji, he's been listening to Charlie play. He thinks Charlie has "done some good things" in his playing—not exactly a vote of confidence, but praise nevertheless. He missed hearing Charlie in Mahler Five, but he remembers the Prokofiev, and he can certainly hear Charlie today. But he doesn't say anything to Charlie. The trumpet remains a foreign language to him, even though he's the concertmaster.

Their idle chat is interrupted by music, and Peter and Malcolm listen to the trumpets playing. Then Peter goes and Malcolm remains to hear two takes, numbered 31 and 34. After the playback of 34, Malcolm immediately decides the first one sounded better. He smiles and leaves, at long last, for a late lunch.

Flanked by his palace guard, Seiji attends a buffet lunch hosted by the house crew in the Cohen Annex. Wilhelm comes also, as does a cheerful Bill Bernell, who'll be with Seiji through the rest of the week. Wearing a bright red sweater, Bernell greets former colleagues with warm greetings and animated conversation, while the music director remains withdrawn. The menu features wild game, including venison, cooked by the hall's stage manager, Cleveland Morrison

By 2:30, with the meal over but the occasion continuing for the house crew, the musicians who didn't attend the lunch have started to drift back to the hall. Charlie plays alone in the basement in his usual spot near the practice rooms. In a marble-tiled bathroom, someone hums a pizzicato from the first movement. Shortly before three, Bill Moyer announces over the backstage public address system that offstage players in "Der grosse Apell" should tune their instruments onstage, with the rest of the orchestra. A few minutes later, Moyer is onstage himself, waiting for the musicians' attention before signaling the beginning of the final recording session for Mahler Two.

Seiji looks tired when he returns to the podium. "No need to hurry some things," says Wilhelm philosophically. But his calm quickly becomes worry when Seiji reports from the stage that one of the extra French horn players hasn't checked in.

"Oh dear," Wilhelm says. It is his polite way of swearing.

Already, for intonation purposes, he and Seiji have removed one of the four offstage horn players from "Der grosse Apell." What should they do? Seiji suggests a further postponement, but Wilhelm vetoes the idea. "Traffic noise problems later," he reminds Seiji. "Let's try it with two," he says, meaning just half the horn complement.

Later, in Holland, the engineers will tinker with their dials, making the digits that encode the sound seem like four horns. Seiji explains the problem and its solution to the orchestra.

"That discussion took four minutes," Harry Shapiro observes dryly. But Wilhelm ignores Harry. He won't be pressured by someone else.

For several takes, the players fuss with getting their instruments properly tuned. At first, the piccolo is flat, the timpani sharp. Wilhelm directs that the stage door be shut completely. He likes the resulting sound quality but feels it seems too far away. As the participants piece together "The Big A," the rest of the orchestra members sit idly. With recording time literally money, they earn their fee here doing nothing.

Humor breaks the tension in the basement control room, where the rigorous, repetitive emphasis on getting things right has drained everyone's energy. Finally, after four takes, Wilhelm tells someone, "The offstage is finished. You can start making noises in the hallway."

At last they turn to the Scherzo, which they play straight through. Thirty-seven minutes have elapsed since the episode of the missing horn player. Another twenty minutes will pass during the first afternoon break, which Seiji again spends with Wilhelm in the control room.

"Our horn player is here," Bill Moyer reports. But no one pays attention. They don't need him anymore.

Freelance trumpeter Randy Croley waits to hear himself in the offstage takes. He's proud of himself for being here, and he's beginning to feel he's part of the orchestra. But the playback of the Scherzo consumes the entire break, and there's no time for Randy's offstage playback. "I guess I'll have to buy the recording," he jokes, hiding his disappointment.

The next several takes focus on small spots in the Scherzo. The orchestra and Seiji work backward and forward, making corrections in a sequence that Wilhelm directs. After about twenty minutes of painstaking patching, they have worked themselves back to the beginning of the movement, just as they might were they shooting scenes of a movie. Then, with a few tentative stops and starts, they reach the middle of the movement and continue without stopping.

"That was basically well done," says Wilhelm on the phone to Seiji. "Two exceptions."

Earlier, Wilhelm lectured Charlie on the crescendos and diminuendos at figure 40, the Scherzo's little waltz, as though Wilhelm were a trumpet player. Yet this is the moment in the piece that makes Maureen Forrester weep when Charlie plays it. In the control room during a break, Wilhelm admonished, "Don't make the crescendos too fast." Charlie hated this order. The crescendos in this passage are what give it character, and the way he takes them is personal, dependent on his feelings for the passage and his sense of what Mahler wanted. He thought it was none of Wilhelm's business to comment, and he hasn't changed his mind.

But it is Seiji who says, "You could play out a little more at forty." Seiji thinks the whole passage could be louder, while Wilhelm is telling Charlie to slow the rate at which he makes his crescendos. Charlie is getting confusing signals, and this only makes him madder. He has to work very hard to resist the temptation to tell Seiji that he knows how to play this waltz. But he tries to do what he's told.

"Trumpet sharp," Wilhelm says to Seiji over the phone.

"Volume good. Don't go too high pitchwise," Seiji translates the message a little more tactfully.

It's not surprising that Charlie should sound sharp. That often happens when a trumpet player feels on the spot and forces the notes. Charlie takes a deep breath and they try again.

Wilhelm's still displeased.

"Sounds a bit careful. Manufactured. Everyone watching for everyone," he says to Seiji via the phone.

Seiji paraphrases this to the orchestra in shortened form: "Too careful." Charlie might have answered, "I could have told you so," but he keeps quiet. Sitting near him, Randy wonders why Seiji is picking on Charlie. It seems to him to serve no musical purpose. Clearly, the two men are still at odds with one another.

But Seiji means nothing personal. And he likes the next attempt at the waltz. So does Wilhelm. Seiji flashes an okay sign to the orchestra and immediately instructs the players to return to the beginning of the movement, to the first ten bars.

Unbeknownst to Seiji, there is a small crisis in the control room. With about seven minutes left before the next break, one of the engineers confesses, "I haven't got enough tape for that much time." Wilhelm is very angry.

Soon, forced to break early, Seiji pauses for yet another shirt before listening to the latest playbacks with Wilhelm and a few of the players. Timpanist Everett Firth worries that he played a wrong note during one passage.

"Did you do this each time?" Wilhelm asks him.

"No. The last time."

"It will be okay."

As if to celebrate this good news, Firth passes out sugar-coated peanuts to everyone.

"I splattered a B flat," confesses Charlie Schlueter.

"It won't matter," Wilhelm assures him. There's another take of the same passage with the note played correctly.

With only eighteen minutes of recording time left, the participants debate what should still be rerecorded. Boldly, Charlie mentions a spot in "Urlicht" that he sensed went faster than it should have. Surprising him, Seiji agrees and tells Charlie to find the other trumpet players. "Short time," he adds. "No kidding." Charlie disappears on his errand.

"We could use the extra three minutes again," Seiji continues. He wishes they hadn't spent it in today's first session, when they let the clock run past one. "We still have concentration."

"Come on, Seiji!" implores Harry Shapiro at exactly 5:27, the end of the break. "Let's go."

Fixing the fourth movement's trumpet part goes easily. So does a minor correction at the beginning of movement five. But the remaining time seems too short to Wilhelm. He has one last place—a trumpet entrance in the fifth movement, after the trombone chorale—that he wants to fix. And Seiji wants to start with the trombones.

"That's okay," says Wilhelm, but fretting inwardly.

Two false starts follow. "Someone has water in their tuba," says Wilhelm, meaning one of the trombones has some saliva in its slide. Two minutes and fifteen seconds are left.

"Come on!" Wilhelm says.

Something drops on the stage floor. Ninety seconds to go. Wilhelm crosses his fingers.

Charlie forgets the earlier tension over the Scherzo's waltz. He and the trumpets enter nicely, and Wilhelm lets the music continue. The recording session ends.

Seiji comes downstairs one last time to thank Wilhelm. "Tough, tough," he mutters about the afternoon. At this triumphant moment of the week, he is too tired to savor his accomplishment. Besides, there is no one here he can share it with.

Seiji leaves quietly, without Karen or Costa for once, and walks back to his dressing room. He will not see Wilhelm again until the spring, when he will hear a tape that combines the eighty-three takes of the three recording sessions into one finished, sequential version of the symphony. He must approve that tape before Philips can begin manufacturing copies for sale to the public.

But Seiji knows that the lasting result of what the orchestra accomplished in these three recording sessions, and all the rehearsals and concerts that preceded it, will not be the fancy package available in record stores a year from now. The real significance of this extremely concentrated effort for Seiji is that the orchestra played for him today the way he wanted it to. He insisted on the players' total concentration and best effort and he got it, got the sound he asked for.

He has no idea how this will carry over into tomorrow, when the orchestra will perform the piece again, or in January and February, when the orchestra will be performing under one of its many guest conductors, or in the spring, when the season will conclude with the single most difficult piece of music Seiji will have conducted since he came to Boston, Alban Berg's opera *Wozzeck*.

As he heads upstairs before Peppino drives him home, there are no outstretched hands of greeting from the players or others backstage. He makes a lonely figure as he passes the bulletin boards and coffee urn and vending machines. No one slaps him on the back. No one shouts, "Bravo!" Most of the players have already left; a few have returned to the house party in the Cohen Annex. During the entire last recording session the party continued, and a few members of the house crew are still there, oblivious to Seiji and to Mahler.

The engineers immediately begin dismantling their equipment, unplugging wires and packing microphones. Though Wilhelm is still keyed up, when someone mentions the party to him he gladly shifts his focus. "Let's have a big beer!" he says. "Let's get drunk."

FOURTEEN

*S*eiji calls his secretary, Karen, when he gets up on Tuesday morning and orders her to cancel all his appointments. He talked with Bill Bernell after the recording session until around 1 A.M. last night and now he doesn't feel like doing anything. He has another Mahler concert tonight, and Wednesday morning he will fly with the orchestra to New York for the two Carnegie Hall concerts, that night and Thursday night. He's still bothered by the sore throat he's been fighting since last week, his house is a mess, and he hasn't packed yet for New York.

But mostly he's very tired. It would be a waste of his energy to spend it on meetings. He needs to gather himself now for these last Mahler performances or much of what he has accomplished with the orchestra will be wasted. But he must also focus on one performance at a time the rest of this week. No one in the audience will care what else he's been doing or how that has made him feel. Each concert is a new event, and the minute Seiji forgets that he may as well retire.

To his orchestra and his audience, he must prove himself worthy of his artistic rank each time he conducts. He couldn't rest on his laurels even if he wanted to. He hopes with the final Mahler Two concerts to showcase his orchestra—and, by extension, himself. First, however, he's got to get some more sleep.

But because Seiji won't be back in Boston for two months, Costa and Karen have lined up a long series of appointments for him today. A tenor who wants to perform with the orchestra is flying down from Montreal for an audition. An out-of-town journalist who's been asking for an interview since last summer is coming for it. George Kidder, the incoming president of the symphony's board, is scheduled to speak with Seiji. Kenneth Haas, who will take over as managing director of the orchestra in March, has flown here from Cleveland to meet with Seiji. And Bill Bernell is expecting to spend a couple of hours with the music director, continuing their conversation about future concerts.

Karen gets on the phone and manages to catch the Canadian tenor before he leaves for Boston. The rest of the people are already in the hall or will be shortly, so they will find out about the change in plans in person.

Seiji has decisively indicated his priorities. The board president and managing director will have to wait. The journalist can make another date for his interview; the tenor can try again to audition. Eventually, Seiji will attend to these matters, but not now. The only thing that matters to him today is his conducting. Seiji knows that if he leads a good concert tonight, Kenneth Haas and George Kidder will be there in his dressing room afterward to congratulate him. If he fails, they will still pay their respects, but repeated failure will lead to a situation that no number of kept appointments can rectify.

But the possibility of that kind of failure isn't on Seiji's mind. The success he seeks isn't a matter of competence. No one, not even his worst critics in the press or in the orchestra, accuses him of being incompetent. But the questions that many of them raise when they assess Seiji go to the heart of the single most important issue in live music, which is the emotional impact of a performance. Where does the emotion come from, and how in a symphony orchestra does the conductor summon it? Is it in the piece or the playing?

"When you go to a concert, you want to feel something is happening," says Malcolm. Echoing him, principal trombone Ron Barron describes what he thinks should be a listener's experience. "When you leave, you want to feel something was *done*, that it wasn't just another playing of the piece." But Barron believes that when Seiji conducts the result is too often just that: "He plays the piece rather than performs it." Barron thinks Seiji emphasizes technique over style, which he defines "not as metaphysics, but as phrasing, intent, balances, proportion." Nevertheless, Barron allows that when the playing under Seiji is very good, the concert can be successful. Of course, he gives the credit for the playing to the players.

In fact, very few of Ron's colleagues give Seiji the credit, although they are quick to jump on the music director when they play badly. When lapses in concentration, caused principally by the distractions of their leafleting, marred their Opening Night playing, they blamed Seiji for not being "visionary" enough in his interpretation. Now, playing the piece well, they cite their excellence as musicians to explain their success. Seiji can't win.

But the deeper debate here turns on Seiji's view of the music and his perception of what makes a performance work emotionally. Seiji's Mahler is an extreme example of what he has been emphasizing since the season began: keen attention to the score and superb ensemble sound. He does permit certain veteran players "to take liberties," as Marylou Speaker Churchill would put it, holding on to a certain note in phrase, slightly changing the tempo in another. But Seiji still resists many of the liberties his principal trumpet player suggests, and he takes very few himself.

This refusal puts him in good company, though out of fashion with many other contemporary tastes. A whole school of conducting, reared on the impassioned example of Leonard Bernstein, takes Mahler as raw material for an exegesis of the conductor's life. But very few conductors can get away with this often. In the wrong hands, the effect wears thin because it is self-aggrandizing; even in Bernstein's epic grasp, the apocalyptic experience is frequently too draining to repeat. Seiji's Mahler, on the other hand, is music a person can hear again and live with. But Ron Barron is right: It requires terrific playing.

Thirty years since he first heard a Western orchestra, Seiji is still in love with its sound, but his ear has become more refined. He wants in his orchestra both greater clarity and greater richness of sound—"color, harmony, blend," as he says—and the only way to do this is to choose excellent players and then drill them in rehearsal. But Seiji's goal is not a band of obedient soldiers. He welcomes the response of his players, as long as it serves the same shared goal, his ideal beauty of sound. But they must often understand what he wants without his telling them, and they must have his confidence to make suggestions he hasn't thought of. No one intuits Seiji's wishes better than Malcolm.

To Seiji, Mahler is preeminently a creator of beautiful sound. And Seiji's approach to Mahler Two reflects that vision, both in his rehearsals and in his concerts. He respects Mahler's achievement too much to make more of it than is already in the music, as if to do so were a presumption. As a consequence, his interpretation is probably much closer to the way Mahler wanted the piece conducted. As much as possible, he removes himself—not to take away his emotion, but to reveal Mahler's. After one of Seiji's good performances, a listener is apt to have noticed the composer, not the conductor. But one is not possible without the other. Seiji's self-effacement masks a total commitment to the music. But it also leads to trouble when his players don't understand him or, worse, disagree. Then they quickly become a disparate group of individuals without common purpose, each advancing a separate agenda or none at all. When this happens, as it did in the rather lackluster Haydn symphony that was paired with Mahler Five, the orchestra's sound becomes boring.

It is no wonder that Seiji and Charlie Schlueter have had such a tense relationship, given their very different musical personalities and philosophies. Though he, too, means to serve the music, Charlie approaches a piece in very passionate, individual terms. To him, a Mahler symphony is more than beautiful sound. It is life and death. When Charlie plays Mahler, all of his own triumphs and terrors are poured into his playing, so that a really fine performance can become a haunting, harrowing transcription of everything he knows about people, love, time. When he's playing well, Charlie's Mahler will both thrill a listener and break the listener's heart.

Seiji's sensibility is no less responsive, but his emotive qualities are more refined and disciplined, more schooled. And he looks for meaning and beauty in the score. It is ironic that when he appointed Charlie, Seiji thought he had finally found the trumpet sound that would help him do that.

"I wanted a dark brass sound, *dunkel*, which is not only a color but also a sensitivity," Seiji told Richard Dyer at the start of Charlie's first Boston season in 1981. "It may take two years to get what we want, but we will be the first major orchestra to try to do it seriously." Instead, after two years, Seiji wanted to fire Charlie. At the beginning of this season, he still wished he had been able to. Now, however, Charlie has played so well most of this fall that getting rid of him would be even harder than when Seiji tried earlier. And, though no one has apparently said this to Seiji, it would also be unjustified. But Seiji's a jury of one in these matters, and the jury's still out.

Charlie, too, is trying to recover from the exhaustion of the two recording sessions yesterday, but for him the best thing is to keep busy. He spends Tuesday afternoon teaching in one of the practice rooms at Symphony Hall. The teaching relaxes him for tonight's performance.

It's been almost four weeks now since Charlie's triumph in Mahler Five, and he's still carrying around in his wallet one of the good reviews he received for those performances. None of the local critics have come to these repeat performances of Mahler Two. Charlie feels good enough about his playing to wish they had.

Like all the other players, Charlie has no idea what the recording they just made will sound like when Philips is finished with it. Nor, of course, has Seiji said anything to him about how he played. Charlie resents his music director's continued silence. And he's still bitter about the *Boston Magazine* piece. Seiji has said nothing to him about that, either. So Charlie continues to worry that if he makes a mistake Seiji will jump on him again. He's getting tired of living in a perpetual state of fear caused, he thinks, by Seiji's inability to communicate.

Charlie's pupil Eric Latini, a shy and unassertive student at the New England Conservatory of Music, waits at the stage door. On their way back to the practice room, Eric confesses to Charlie that he didn't have much time to practice this week.

"How little?" Charlie inquires.

"Maybe one hour," answers Eric.

"That's okay," Charlie says, adding with unnecessary kindness, "It's good to take a break. I didn't play Sunday." Charlie doesn't tell Eric that when he was a student he always came to his lessons prepared. He does not believe in lecturing people about their work habits or motivation. He thinks one of his daughters may have lost interest in piano because he pushed too hard. And he hates being pushed himself. Whereas Malcolm's face always lights up when a friend tells him about a son or daughter taking music lessons, Charlie remains equivocal. He always goes out of his way to hear his students perform, but he would tell anyone to think twice about a career in music after what he's been through.

Eric begins his lesson with an exercise built around slurred intervals and unslurred arpeggios. Taking his usual huge breath, Charlie hums each phrase Eric plays. He also conducts with his pencil and beats time with his feet. He tries to help Eric relax. "You have more time for the D than you think," he says when his pupil misses that note.

Charlie calls such problems "trumpetitis," and he always includes himself as a fellow sufferer. Another common symptom of trumpetitis is "end-of-the-phrase syndrome," in which the player misses the very last note of a phrase. This happens when the rest of the phrase goes perfectly and the player says to himself, *Phew, I didn't screw anything up that time*, and then proceeds to make a mistake.

Now Eric has trouble with an A-flat arpeggio. He plays it again. "The recovery is more important than the mistake," Charlie tells all his students.

Eric continues to an ascending and descending chromatic figure, followed by an arpeggio in B. He plays this very nicely. "There," says Charlie. "The hardest one of all came out the easiest."

Charlie stares at Eric's rib cage through his gold wire-rimmed glasses, saying nothing for a moment. Then he squeezes Eric's chest with his hands. Eric seems amused.

Tracing an imaginary line on his student's body as he speaks, Charlie says, "Tightness in the rib cage: tightness in the fingers."

Inside the front cover of Eric's etude book, Charlie writes the number of the next etude Eric must learn. He takes a sip of his coffee. In little more than two hours, he will perform Mahler's Second Symphony for the third time in five days, not counting rehearsals and recording sessions. Teaching Eric's lesson has kept him from thinking about Seiji for an hour, but suddenly now he's conscious again of the time and the coming concert. "Well," he says, "I think I'm going to let you go."

Leaving his trumpet in his locker, Charlie walks to Amalfi's for dinner, where he runs into Joe Conte, a freelance violinist who plays frequently with the BSO. He takes a seat next to Conte at the bar. Charlie orders a gin and some linguine. In an era when many in the orchestra favor health food and Perrier, his tastes seem bizarre to some, but not to the regulars at Amalfi's.

Neither man discusses Mahler. "You think about a performance when you're ironing your shirt," Conte explains, but not now, an hour before you take your seat onstage. How will tonight's performance go? Like almost all the players, Joe won't predict.

Charlie pays for his dinner and returns to the hall. He changes his clothes, gets a cup of coffee, and walks to a place in the basement near where Eric had his lesson. Beginning with a few arpeggios, Charlie feels a tightness that concerns him. He tries some more notes. He remembers what he told Eric about the rib cage. He takes a deep breath and then another. For a short time, he doesn't play at all, just breathes. Then, finally, he brings the trumpet to his lips. From a distance, the note that comes out sounds as warm and natural as a human voice.

The time is 7:30, half an hour before the scheduled start of the concert. Most of the players spend the minutes before the concert socializing while they warm up. A few practice early onstage, but most remain backstage talking.

Many of the players are thinking this evening about the absurdity of their schedule. As violinist Jenny Shames puts it, "We always seem to go out of town when we're tired." Like most of her colleagues, she can't believe that their first trip of the season to New York is taking place right after the recording sessions.

Freelance trumpeter Randy Croley has no complaints about the schedule. For him, the New York concerts mean added income, and the continuation of his role as an extra in the orchestra. He passes the preconcert minutes in conversation with organist Jim Christie. A veteran at waiting out these nerve-racking moments, Christie admits his hands were shaking during the recording session on Saturday. The two men talk about Charlie. Christie says the quality of Charlie's playing in "Urlicht" on Saturday struck him deeply. "It was almost like a flügelhorn. So rich." A flügelhorn characteristically sounds darker and richer than a trumpet.

"Seiji really seemed into the recording yesterday," observes Croley. "That spills over." But it still bothers him that Seiji stopped Charlie as often as he did during the recording sessions. He does not think Seiji knew what his comments in the magazine article would mean to Charlie, does not think Seiji would consciously have intended to be that cruel. And for everyone's sake, he hopes the war between the two men will end.

Randy is relieved that Charlie has recovered enough to play as well as he has the past month. So perhaps Charlie will stop being so hard on himself. But Randy wishes that more of Charlie's colleagues would recognize Charlie's musicality, the way he picks up on phrases played by others, the way he phrases his own notes with small but significant shadings of color and emphasis, much as a great violinist does. Very few brass players even understand this, Randy thinks. They're too concerned with themselves, he believes, whereas Charlie thinks about the music "and bares his soul."

The Tuesday night concert is a deeply felt one, and prolonged applause after the performance brings Seiji repeatedly back to the podium for bows. As always, he invites John Oliver to join him onstage, but tonight John is very unhappy. Some of his singers were sick tonight, and he thinks his chorus tried too hard to compensate for the absentees. Offstage, he apologizes to Seiji, but the music director thinks John is overreacting.

Charlie gets the first solo bow, and there are many others for his colleagues, but none for Malcolm, whose feelings are hurt. Did Seiji forget about him?

George Kidder takes it upon himself to meet the soloists afterward. "I'm the new board president," he says with a patrician air to Maureen Forrester. "Thank you for what you do." Maureen smiles regally. She still loves such attention.

Clutching a pen, Nina Keidann, the young singer who joined the chorus in September, also calls on Maureen. Nina has been waiting for this moment all fall. Thrusting her pen at the famous contralto, who personifies to Nina everything glamorous and beautiful she has dreamed about in music, Nina nervously asks for her autograph.

The next morning, Harry Shapiro's voice comes over the p.a. as the musicians prepare to leave for New York. "Four-minute call for the bus," he says. His words only momentarily interrupt conversation among the musicians gathered backstage in Symphony Hall for their bus trip to the airport and flight to New York.

Randy Croley is beginning to think about auditioning for the opening in the trumpet section. After the glorious experience of recording Mahler Two, he thinks he might like the job very much. Despite all the problems Charlie has had, the romance of what he does for a living has taken hold of Randy's imagination. Life with the orchestra, and with Charlie, has gotten under his skin.

Gregarious Andre Côme joins the group, carrying one trumpet with him while another has been shipped on ahead. Andre looks for "the smoking bus," but there isn't one. Smokers get their own bus only for trips of more than an hour and a half. But nothing seems to make Andre angry, and he's soon entertaining friends with jokes. He's quite pleased with the way he played a short solo at the end of the first movement last night, one of very few for second trumpet. But he has no delusions about competing with Charlie. He served on the audition committee that recruited Charlie almost six years ago. And he knows of Charlie's respect for him, which is why they play so well in tandem.

The plane is late leaving. "The auxiliary power just quit on us," the pilot announces, but everyone's too tired to get worried about the plane's takeoff. A bumpy descent brings the plane into La Guardia Airport shortly after two, where gray, slightly foggy weather greets it. Buses wait outside the terminal to transport the players to their Manhattan hotel, a trip that takes more time than the Boston-to-New York flight.

Passing Carnegie Hall, the players can see a line of people waiting at the box office to buy the few remaining tickets for tonight's concert.

At their hotel, media and production manager Nancy Phillips waits for the orchestra to arrive. Phillips, who acts as the advance person on these trips, traveled to New York yesterday. She and Harry Shapiro greet each of the players, giving them their room keys and answering questions about the arrangements for their visit. The players might be campers on a field trip.

Suddenly, the hotel's fire alarm goes off and the elevators stop working. At the main desk, an elderly woman who survived the Coconut Grove fire demands that her accommodations be moved from a room on the eleventh floor. The players, many of them amused, wait in the beige lobby with its low ceiling while firemen investigate. Shortly before 4 P.M., the alarm is found to be false. A minute later, another goes off, triggering another delay. Now some of the musicians are annoyed. They have a concert to play tonight and this is no way to get ready.

Oblivious to the problem, husband and wife, Ron Wilkison and Patti McCarty, both violists, finish a late lunch next door at the Carnegie Deli. After driving to New York from the Berkshires on their own with Bratsche, their beloved dog, they have already separated themselves from their colleagues. They do this often. But Ron, usually laid back, is animated when talking about being here today. "I particularly love playing at Carnegie Hall," he says, a thick paperback spy novel next to him on the table. "And I love the pastrami at this deli!" He and Patti place a takeout order for the friend who's sitting for Bratsche, who's already had a run in Central Park.

Charlie Schlueter disappears to visit an art museum with Martha, who came down to the city earlier to see their daughter

Erica at school. Looking at the paintings will take his mind off the concert, though he's not visibly nervous about it. Charlie has been playing in Carnegie since he was a Juilliard student, when Bill Vacchiano put his best pupil on the substitute list for the New York Philharmonic.

By six o'clock, John Oliver arrives at Carnegie Hall, where the excessive heat onstage makes it seem that all the renovation money went toward a new furnace. "It will be a hot performance." He smiles at his own weak joke.

Physical evidence of the $50 million renovation of the building is everywhere the public can't see: cans of paint, unfinished wallboard, and dust fill the backstage. And despite the renovation, the backstage is still very cramped, and the musicians have to hunt for private spots to warm up.

John is quite annoyed that the Carnegie renovation budget did not include new chorus risers. But the view of the hall from the stage is spectacular: red seats, gold trim against white walls, and the dizzying tiers of four balconies.

Martin Amlin tries out the piano, positioned onstage for the chorus's warmup. He's thrilled to be back in New York again, only a week after being here with Seiji and the soloists for the recording. His job seems to be getting more glamorous every week.

Organist Jim Christie has also arrived. Sitting at the organ console, he fusses with a dial that tunes the instrument and confers with the technician, who knows neither the orchestra nor Mahler; he's here simply to be certain Christie has no complaints, other than the disgrace of having an electronic organ in this hall instead of a real pipe organ.

By 6:40 P.M., the singers have taken their places. When they have all done so, John Oliver sees anew how poorly designed the risers are. "This is just an outrage!" he exclaims. "I'd build new risers for you, but we don't have time." He moves a few people who can't see him. Then, at last, they begin.

"Aufersteh'n, ja aufersteh'n."

He asks the second tenors and basses to sing this alone. "Last night," he tells them, "your singing made me want to flee the hall. The first time I've ever felt that way." Somewhat unfairly, he's using the incident to shock them into singing as well as he knows they can tonight.

In just a few minutes, the chorus must vacate the stage so the orchestra can use it. But John remains very calm. Now that he's gotten the risers and last night out of his system, he seems unhurried, even tranquil. And he knows that the performance will not start on time. Otherwise, the concert would end before 9:30—too early for the patrons who compute entertainment time by the dollar.

John asks Martin to conduct while he sits in the auditorium to test the sound. The chorus sings only a few bars before John tells it to stand up. "It's a fabulous sound without the curtain," he says, referring to the removal of a curtain as part of the renovation. "Very beautiful. Can you hear it?" Actually, what most of the singers can hear is two trumpet players warming up in one of the backstage rooms behind them.

"It's a fabulous sound, it really is," John repeats. He is now genuinely excited over what he hears—and about conducting his chorus on this stage.

"Second tenors," he says, "make more of an effort to sing with the beat. You're so busy trying to make that noise you get ahead."

Again, John momentarily leaves the podium, but this time Martin continues playing the piano. The chorus is nearing the conclusion. "That's dull," he tells them on the word "Sterben." "That will never get through the orchestra," he says.

They start again and he stops them again. "The first note was good, the second . . ." He shakes his head. "Find a way to get through, right to the vowel." He leaps back onto the stage, almost catching a foot on the edge. Now, repeating something he has told them ever since the first rehearsal in September, he stresses the hush at the start. "Everything at the beginning has to be much less substantial," he says. "Don't let it come up."

The chorus sings "Aufersteh'n." Peter Chapman enters through a side door. Carrying his trumpet, he walks across the stage and exits. The chorus keeps singing. The brief scene has the surreal quality of a Fellini movie. But it underlines how very focused everyone is on his or her own individual part in the evening's performance. Peter doesn't even seem to notice the chorus is there.

"Do you realize that, except for one take on the recording, you haven't gotten this kind of atmosphere?" says John. "You need to do it tonight," he continues. They try one last time. "Yes, that's it," he says, arriving at the climax of his preconcert performance. Once the concert begins, he will have nothing to do but listen. And, as he knows only too well, Seiji will get most of the credit for the chorus's singing.

A few minutes later, Marty Burlingame walks onto the stage and starts distributing the players' parts. They've been corrected against brand-new ones, which the BSO had to rent for copyright reasons because of the recording. Marty resents the extra time this took to arrange—and the added expense ($925 for the first performance and $460 for each of the other four this month, plus additional fees for the recording sessions and broadcast rights).

Soon, the musicians who play offstage in the finale begin to take their places, some in concert dress, others still in street clothes. Malcolm pokes his head out.

Seiji appears, looking sporty in charcoal wool pants and a blue sweater. Anne Parsons trails him, while Costa stands on the podium, mimicking a conductor. But Seiji's not in a joking mood. For the next few minutes, he leads a rehearsal of the offstage playing, to check the acoustics.

At the second offstage section, Seiji asks assistant conductor Carl St. Clair how many bars before figure 22 of the fifth movement he should start conducting.

"Two," says Carl.

Without a score before him, Seiji begins at precisely that point. But he hears something offstage he doesn't like.

"Somebody's practicing," he says, annoyed. They try again.

Carl: "We need the door open a little here. There, that's much better. An inch more."

Seiji: "No."

Charles Daval: "It's louder than it was in Boston."

Harry Shapiro: "It will be different when the audience comes. It will be all right."

Now it's time for "The Big A." "We didn't call flute, piccolo?" asks Seiji, wondering where those players are. Harry goes to get them. Seiji can still hear a French horn practicing. "This is crazy," he says. But that's as close as he comes to losing his temper.

While Harry locates Doriot Anthony Dwyer and piccolo player Lois Schaefer, Seiji remains silent and motionless, almost as if he is meditating. When they arrive, he leads them through "Der grosse Apell," then asks everyone to join him by the podium.

"Okay, may I talk with everybody? Everything was quite loud, nothing to change. Go with quality, beautiful quality. Balance was very good. Pitch was not bad. Good luck. Thank you very much."

Seiji lingers a moment longer, looking at the stage from the wings. Then he leaves for his dressing room. Some of the players think it would have been good to have rehearsed the whole orchestra, instead of just the offstage players, were there time and money. But Seiji's not worried. In fact, he's excited about the performance—and relieved that in little more than twenty-four hours, this long siege of Mahler Two will end.

*   *   *

Marty resumes putting out the parts. Malcolm walks out to try the sound on the new stage. At 7:30, the doors from the lobby into the auditorium are opened and patrons begin to find their seats. One after another, they pause to look up and around. Beyond the back doors, in the lobby itself, people push past the ticket takers. The BSO's Mahler Two at Carnegie is a sellout.

Though the players find the new acoustics hard to adjust to onstage, they all work hard to make this performance connect. They sound like an orchestra that wants to be playing Mahler. The performance has life and energy and the audience picks this up. There is little coughing or other crowd noise, and when Seiji begins the finale many people literally move their heads, jolted by the enormous sound of the full brass.

Loud cheering and repeated bravos greet the conclusion. Again, Charlie Schlueter receives the first solo bow.

After the concert, a long line of people waits to see Seiji. "Where is the maestro?" asks an admirer at the door to the packed dressing room.

"Right next to you," someone points out.

Soon, Peppino will drive the maestro to a private dinner party in the BSO limousine, which he brought down earlier today.

The newspaper reviews the next morning praise the performance. *The New York Times* commends the concert "more for its ensemble brilliance and precision than for conveying the kaleidoscopic mood shifts and angst-on-sleeve feeling that one listens for in Mahler's symphonies." The *New York Post* calls the concert "inspired

... as if [Ozawa] had contemplated the mysteries of the universe from the Big Bang to the birth of the tiniest quasar." While this purple prose amuses some of the players, they are all pleased.

The BSO's Mahler is a hit, and seats for Thursday's performance disappear quickly. Nina Keidann purchases one of the last for her mother, who has flown here from Kentucky. Nina has to choose between a seat with cramped leg space and one with an obstructed view. She chooses cramped.

Charlie slept poorly Wednesday night after a few postconcert drinks at Mulligan's, an old pub across the street from the hotel. Now, on Thursday, he's fighting a cold, and the rain he encounters on his walks next door to the Carnegie Deli doesn't make him feel any better. An early lunch—matzoh ball soup and a Heineken—lifts his spirits a little. But he's quite agitated today, as though he has finally acknowledged something he realized a while ago but didn't want to face.

Seven or eight years ago Charlie took several weeks off from playing the trumpet because of "tightness." When he came back, he was just as tense. He wondered if he would ever come out of it. He wondered if he should look for "another line of endeavor." "The mind is weird," he says when he recalls this episode in his career.

"My teacher in St. Louis, Ed Brower, had a great attitude toward the trumpet," Charlie recalls. " 'Look at Stan Musial,' he used to say. 'One of the great hitters of all time, he has a lifetime average just over three hundred. He goes to the plate and he figures, "Shit, I got one coming " ' "

Charlie feels he's had one coming for quite some time now. Seiji hasn't said anything to him yet, and he knows that after tonight the two men won't see each other for two months. Since there will be no chance for a talk after the concert, when another large group of people is certain to crowd the music director's dressing room, Seiji is clearly going to leave for Japan without a word to his principal trumpet player about that magazine article of almost two months ago or about Charlie's subsequent superb playing.

Back in his hotel room after lunch, Charlie meets with Bill Moyer and the young, outgoing bass trombone Doug Yeo to discuss the trumpet audition that will be held later in the winter to replace Charles Daval, the audition Randy is considering trying. The bed in Charlie's room is covered with music and preliminary paperwork for the audition.

The phone in Charlie's room rings. It's his old teacher Bill Vacchiano, calling from the downstairs lobby. Each time the orchestra travels to New York for concerts at Carnegie Hall, Charlie calls Vacchiano ahead of time and arranges to get together with him. Vacchiano takes the subway in from his home in Queens—he's lived there all his adult life—or the bus from Juilliard if he's been teaching.

"If I had to play for him now," Charlie says, "it would put me in a catatonic state. A forty-five-minute lesson with him was worse than playing under any conductor." But Charlie looks up to Vacchiano as he does to almost no one. He particularly respects his teacher's musical and human values. This sweet, considerate person, without whom Charlie would probably not have had his present career, is a reminder to Charlie of the heights he scaled as a young man.

Charlie feels he owes him a debt of gratitude that he will never be able to repay, but these visits are one way he can show Vacchiano that he remembers. To share with Vacchiano a moment of his life is for Charlie an unqualified pleasure, a reward in itself for having persevered.

Today Charlie wants to take a photograph of Vacchiano with the Monette trumpet that Charlie and many of Vacchiano's other former students recently presented to him. But the real purpose of the meeting for Charlie is just to spend some time with the one musician he knows to whom he no longer has to prove anything. Without hearing any explanation from Charlie, the seventy-four-year-old former principal trumpet of the New York Philharmonic will know how his student, now almost fifty, feels. In very different circumstances, he's felt the same way himself. While he never had to fight for his job in an arbitration—there were no arbitration provisions in his day, nor was he ever fired—he sat in the principal trumpet's seat under some of the sternest conductors of his day, including Toscanini. He knows the pressure Charlie lives with daily, and he respects as only another performer can what Charlie has accomplished. He also thinks the world of Charlie.

Vacchiano takes the elevator up to Charlie's room, where the audition meeting continues. He is wearing a plaid shirt and a tie under his jacket. His face is deeply lined. Charlie sees in that expressive face the life of a man who has survived many ordeals, including the death of his only son.

Charlie introduces Vacchiano to Doug Yeo as the informal meeting breaks up.

"It's an honor to meet you," says Doug. "I grew up on Long Island and used to listen to you play on the radio." The four men talk shop for a few minutes, and then Yeo and Moyer leave.

Vacchiano places his Monette, which he's brought in an old Yamaha case, on the bed and takes the instrument out. Gold-plated, it bears an inscription commemorating its presentation.

Miles Davis also studied with Vacchiano briefly at Juilliard in 1945, an experience that Davis does not recall fondly. But Vacchiano's chief memory of Davis is affectionate. "One day Miles came for a lesson and he's smoking this *long* cigarette. And I said, 'Miles can I try that?' And Miles looked at me and said, 'You don't want to try *this*.' That was no tobacco cigarette." Vacchiano chuckles whenever he tells this story.

Vacchiano asks if he can try Charlie's trumpet. Charlie hands him his Monette C, and after just a few notes Vacchiano says he likes the feel of it better than his. Vacchiano tries his own Monette again.

"Here," Charlie says to him, removing the caps from the bottom of his trumpet's valves. "Try these." The valve caps from Charlie's instrument are weighted differently, and on Vacchiano's trumpet they subtly change the tone color. Even changing the degree to which these caps are tightened can produce a change in the sound of a responsive instrument played by a skilled musician. Vacchiano likes Charlie's sound. He says simply but with great conviction, it "sticks in your mind afterwards."

Because his wife is ill and the subway ride back to Queens takes an hour, Vacchiano can't attend the concert tonight. Nor will he invite Charlie to come out to Queens with him. In all the years they have known one another, Charlie has never been to Vacchiano's house.

But Vacchiano poses for the photograph. He holds the trumpet in both hands, as if it were a baby and he were afraid of dropping it. Charlie holds the camera in the same way. He doesn't want anything to go wrong with this picture. He'll send a print of the photograph to Dave Monette, who's certain to be pleased by the implied endorsement, but mostly he wants to preserve this moment on film for himself. Though his teacher is in remarkably good health, Charlie never knows when he will be seeing Vacchiano for the last time.

The two men leave the hotel for a snack. They walk slowly, in no hurry to get anywhere, as they continue the dialogue they began thirty years ago. They talk about other players, pieces, halls, conductors. They swap jokes. In no time at all, Charlie has completely forgotten Seiji. Proudly, he tells Vacchiano about the Mahler Five performances a month ago. "I'll send you a tape," he promises.

An hour before the final concert in Carnegie Hall, the soaring soprano voice of Edith Wiens can be heard in one of the labyrinthine hallways above the stage door. From farther away, upstairs in what's been dubbed the Captain's Walk, the Tanglewood Festival Chorus sings an ascending series of syllables, "de-ee-ah" and so on.

Karen Leopardi, whose time in New York has been spent trying to keep up with such requests from Seiji as producing instant tickets from the box office for unexpected foreign guests, looks forward to "a month-and-a-half reprieve" afterward. Feeling a little full of himself during his last visit to New York while he's still acting general manager, Dan Gustin, wearing a big bow tie with his tuxedo, keeps an eye out for some of "the important people." They include wealthy financier and publisher Gilbert Kaplan, a Tanglewood patron and a man with an intimate connection to Mahler Two.

Kaplan, who owns the original manuscript of the score (there is one in a copyist's hand, minus "Urlicht," at Yale), has had a facsimile of it published at his own expense, page for page, in a limited edition of one thousand copies that sell for $150 each. Kaplan has also become a good enough conductor of Mahler Two to have led the London Symphony Orchestra in a critically acclaimed performance of it. He travels around the world to hear every performance he can. Three days ago he attended the Carnegie Hall gala that concluded with its fifth movement, and of course he is coming tonight.

In the facsimile, which includes letters by Mahler about the symphony's composition and essays by Kaplan and by Mahler scholar Edward R. Reilly, even the color of the ink Mahler used has been copied, with its dramatic change from black to purple just before the climactic "Aufersteh'n."

Mahler's manuscript, completed in 1894, reposes in a climate-controlled room in the Pierpont Morgan Library on East Thirty-sixth Street, where Kaplan has put it on loan so that scholars can peruse it. Strict rules govern its use: When turning its loosely bound pages, the reader must take care not to touch the actual staves and notes and must not have a pencil in hand. "The worst thing for the manuscript is use," says one of the librarians there. But few people look at it, since it's easier to examine the facsimile, a copy of which Seiji owns.

*   *   *

By 7:30, a full half hour before curtain time, many musicians have already taken seats onstage. Malcolm Lowe practices his short solo in the first movement, then stops to say hello to an old friend who has walked down the center aisle. Malcolm's still getting used to the new Carnegie acoustics. Certain things sound too much like glass, he feels, because the hall's acoustics are too bright. But he doesn't complain. In fact, he acts as though it adds to the challenge facing him and the orchestra. Still, he hopes no one tries to "improve" the acoustics of Symphony Hall.

Martin Amlin, the chorus pianist, finished with his piano playing for the evening, pokes his head through the doors to the box seats, looking for an empty place. He finally finds one, just before Seiji makes his appearance to warm applause, several minutes after eight.

Seiji seems in special control of himself tonight. He's still making small adjustments in the way he conducts the piece. The kind of coil into which he went before releasing himself at the start has been modified into a more standard downbeat. But the real change is internal. Moved by the beauty of the sound he hears, Seiji seems to let himself go, at once guiding the playing but also following it, as his players bring to life all the details they have worked on so hard.

The performance begins well and gets better. The orchestra under Seiji has rarely sounded so good. In their excitement at what they hear, several people in the usually sophisticated Carnegie audience commit the supposed vulgarism of clapping upon the first movement's end. The orchestra shares Seiji's mood. Tonight, in this historic hall, the players seem to sense his conviction about the integrity of the music's beauty. They make the BSO sound once again like the aristocrat of orchestras.

*   *   *

The musicians change quickly after the concert, so they won't miss the bus that takes them to La Guardia. Trumpeter Andre Côme shares a bottle of Scotch in the back of one of the buses. Randy Croley feels suddenly empty, no longer a part of the group. His work with the orchestra over for now, he's heading home for the holidays on a flight to Tennessee.

Delta Flight 1436 leaves New York late in a driving rain that rumor says is snow in New England. It's 12:30 A.M. before the plane is airborne, and almost immediately the timid wish they'd stayed on the ground. Even seasoned flyers remain in their seats, with seatbelts buckled because of the turbulence. Andre and Peter Chapman sit together. Noticing a new trumpet case Charlie bought in the city, Peter calls to him across the aisle: "Must be for that cheap trumpet you use."

Charlie doesn't answer Peter. He's not sure whether he's feeling the effects of Andre's Scotch or of the past ten days. During the concert tonight he was so tired that, sitting still with his head almost buried in his lap when he wasn't playing, Charlie lapsed into a kind of trance. A stranger might have thought he was ill. But his playing of the Scherzo's waltz again made Maureen Forrester weep, and he nailed the high C in the finale. Now, Charlie can sense the anticipation of a release from a period of great stress, even the possibility of something new to come. He still wishes Seiji had said something to him, but he has become almost inured to the music director's silence. Or so he likes to think.

Charlie feels himself beginning to doze. He stretches in the space around him. Though the plane is nearly full, with almost the entire orchestra and chorus flying back together, the seats to either side of him in the plane's rear smoking section are empty. Going through more turbulence, the plane bounces as though it were landing, and one or two people gasp. A moment later, in the midst of this spirited, frightened crowd, Charlie is asleep.

229

FIFTEEN

W hat day is it?" John Oliver, exhausted after a week and a half of Mahler rehearsals, recording sessions, and concerts, looks up at his chorus members. It is early Friday afternoon at Symphony Hall, barely twelve hours since everyone returned from the New York concerts. But there is no time for either the chorus or the orchestra players to relax and enjoy the success they had there.

While Seiji has gone home to Japan, where he will conduct his annual Christmas Day performance of the Beethoven Ninth, most of the orchestra must immediately begin Christmas Pops, a week-long series of holiday music and other light fare that is immensely popular with audiences, although not with most of the players. These concerts, many led by Boston Pops conductor and movie composer John Williams, are very profitable for the institution.

The Tanglewood Festival Chorus sings, too, and it has a

rehearsal for the first concert with the orchestra. "From Kiri and Marilyn to this," says John, shaking his head over the jarring contrast as the chorus warms up with a few carols.

Since the orchestra's principals are contractually excused from Christmas Pops, Malcolm, still recovering from his ear problem, takes off to visit Colleen's family in Vermont and his in Canada. But for Charlie the holiday period will be brief, since he's agreed to give a solo recital in January at Boston's Gardner Museum. Still, a short break ought to restore at least some of his energy, and he's genuinely looking forward to several of the guest conductors who will take Seiji's place during most of the winter and early spring. For eight weeks, Charlie won't have to dwell on what the music director's thinking. That seems like a nice Christmas present.

January brings the first of the many guests, Klaus Tennstedt, from Germany. A former concertmaster, Tennstedt has conducted the BSO before, and most of the players like his taut, driven approach to such composers as Beethoven, whose Seventh Symphony concludes one of Tennstedt's Boston programs.

For Charlie, playing under Tennstedt is galvanizing. He knows Tennstedt likes him, and Charlie's playing reflects that awareness. Even the Boston critics take notice. Substituting for Dyer again, Richard Buell in the *Globe* extols "Charles Schlueter's shining trumpet sound" in a review of a Dvořák symphony. Charlie's new year has started very well.

So has Seiji's. He is typically an excellent guest conductor, well received by other orchestras and other critics. With the New Japan Philharmonic he often tries out pieces he wants to do in Boston, while in Europe he has had particular success over the years with the Berlin Philharmonic and with opera. This winter he receives accolades in Paris for a new production of Strauss's *Elektra*. The experience is another boost to his confidence and reputation, an additional new lease on his musical life that will propel him through the remainder of the Boston season.

And Seiji's Boston players receive a similar shot in the arm whenever he's away. Charlie's other personal favorites include Bernard Haitink and Leonard Bernstein. "Sometimes it just seems he's on an ego trip," Charlie says of Bernstein, "but if he is, it's because he's so passionate. He has no inhibitions." For Charlie, as well as for most of the other players, performing under Bernstein is an intense, exasperating experience they wouldn't want to repeat every week. But once a year it can be gloriously exhilarating to play for a conductor who says, "You have to *kill* to make music. You have to give everything you have."

Charlie vividly remembers the last time the BSO played under Bernstein. Whereas Seiji says very little to the orchestra about the meaning of the music they are playing, Bernstein often seemed to say too much during the rehearsals for that performance of Tchaikovsky's Sixth Symphony. But it all mattered. Were Seiji to attempt a similar approach over the course of the season, his players would probably rebel. But the source of Bernstein's success in the Tchaikovsky lay in his ability to inspire the players, to make them believe what they were doing was special. Seiji invariably assumes the players must know this or should.

At that first Tchaikovsky rehearsal, Bernstein sauntered toward the podium, his brown boots striking the floor. Deeply tanned, his hair silver, he was wearing gold-rimmed glasses and, next to the watch on his left hand, a gold bracelet. Passing the podium, he stopped in front of Malcolm and the two men embraced. Then Bernstein moved to the center of the orchestra and threw his arms around Doriot Anthony Dwyer. Handshakes with a few other principals accompanied personal shouts of greeting to those out of reach, before Bernstein finally ascended the short step to the podium. Already, Bernstein had established an atmosphere totally different from Seiji's.

Reverently, Bernstein talked about the Tchaikovsky, which he told the musicians he had not conducted for sixteen years, since he'd left the post of music director of the New York Philharmonic. The BSO, Bernstein supposed, had probably played the piece "two hundred times." For this performance, he had bought brand-new parts for the players. Seiji would never do such a thing. It is expensive and, from his perspective, unnecessary.

Sweat showed on Bernstein's face a few minutes into the two-and-a-half-hour rehearsal. He addressed the bass section. Before the first note, he said longingly, there must be a "churchly silence." Then, at the start, the basses should seem like a "Russian church choir." Bernstein spoke in a hush, and there was silence as he raised his baton. He had made the musicians feel they were engaged in the creation of art.

But not all the players were impressed by Bernstein's remarks. Some were annoyed with his verbosity.

"Gorgeous!" Bernstein exclaimed. It was his favorite word, and he used it to great effect, drawing out the first syllable like an old-time Hollywood agent describing a blonde. He discoursed on dominants and subdominants. "One more time, one more time," he pleaded with a clarinet during a break in the first movement. "You're so important. You're the only one with the D sharp." Seiji never cajoles the players in such a tone, which is one reason they can play for him concert after concert. No adult would happily put up with Bernstein's constant preacherly requests regularly.

Tchaikovsky wrote the second movement of the symphony in quintuple meter—five beats to a measure, a quarter note receiving one beat. Bernstein spent several minutes getting the players to see that within the 5/4 measures, three beats are followed by two for some instruments while two beats are followed by three for others. "These things take time," he said later, "but boy, are they worth it." Bernstein saw this section of the symphony as "ambiguity, and ambiguity is the secret of music." Seiji rarely makes such statements, as though he is too modest to indulge in grand generalizations. And he would probably disagree with this one, believing as he seems to that music is one of the few unambiguous things in life.

Moving constantly around the podium, Bernstein frequently got off to speak directly with one of the musicians. His face registered rapid changes in emotion: A smile followed a frown; a rasping voice alternated with singing. "This is the story of a starry night," he sang during the rehearsal as the violins played the rondo theme. When it didn't sound right to him, he stopped the orchestra and said, "This is Tchaikovsky's most beautiful ballet music. Beautiful girls dancing." Raising his arms above his head, he mimicked a pirouette as the playing resumed. It was a gesture that no other conductor in the world would make.

Later, Bernstein became agitated when he twice detected inadvertent crescendos by the violins during their upbowings and similarly incorrect diminuendos on downbowings. As if to flaunt his own nonchalance about Bernstein's biting criticism of this mistake, one violinist reached behind himself and undid the shoelaces of a colleague. Further risking the conductor's wrath, the violinist then told the man next to him a joke. Bernstein did not notice, but when another violinist seemed not to be listening to him, he stared at the man and said sharply, "I'm talking to *you*." Seiji would have to be considerably more provoked to make such an outburst.

As the rehearsal reached its scheduled conclusion, Bernstein asked the players if they were willing to remain on overtime for the fourth and final movement. This question caused confusion, with some of the musicians mumbling assent and others getting up. Bernstein put the matter to a vote, while a violist disappeared to summon one of Moyer's assistants in case he was needed to mediate. "Raise your hand if you can stay," Bernstein said.

About a third of the orchestra members raised their hands. More indicated they could not—or would not, unless ordered to. Bernstein conferred with a few of the players closest to the podium.

He asked for another vote. Again, the result was negative. Many musicians were already standing as Bernstein, admitting defeat but furious, looked at them and said, "Okay, go to hell."

In all his years with the orchestra, Seiji has never sworn at it like that, though that would probably do him and his players a world of good. In any event, the BSO didn't hold what Bernstein said against him, even if some members believed he'd gone too far. They rehearsed the rest of the piece the next day, and the performance was sizzling, a Tchaikovsky Six like no one else's. The tempos were generally much slower than Seiji's, but it was the little things the players remembered afterward. "Lenny made me see that the piece is about appoggiaturas," Charlie said, referring to the many notes that too often sound only ornamental. Bernstein had made them into a metaphor for the yearning the piece expresses.

Charlie likes Bernstein and certain other guest conductors because they make him feel affectionately noticed. How gratifying it would be if just once after a particular passage Seiji were to look at Charlie—or Malcolm, or Marylou— and say, "Gorgeous."

Dressed uncomfortably in a three-piece woolen suit for his January recital, Charlie checks his templates in a small room off the auditorium of the Isabella Stewart Gardner Museum. It is a few minutes before three on a bitterly cold Sunday afternoon. Through a door of the room, Charlie can see one of the Rembrandts the museum owns, in a gallery that looks out on a lovely interior courtyard. Peeking through another door, he can see a large crowd filling all the chairs of the auditorium for his three o'clock recital. His wife, Martha, is here, and one of their daughters. Many of their friends have come, including most of Charlie's students and several of his orchestral colleagues. The members of the trumpet section take seats in the back, perhaps hoping Charlie won't notice them right away. They know how nervous he feels. No reason to make it worse.

The ubiquitous Martin Amlin, Charlie's chosen accompanist for the recital, is relaxed and convivial. Used to all manner of stage fright (from a student's audition for the chorus to a famous soprano's rehearsal for a Mahler recording), Martin nevertheless seems baffled by Charlie's anxiety. He knows what it's like to feel jittery, and he, too, can be high–strung in conversation. But he loves to perform, loves being center stage. Doesn't Charlie?

Almost shyly, Charlie walks through the door of the auditorium at a few minutes past three, followed by Martin. He acknowledges the applause with a small nod of his head, licks his lips, licks his mouthpiece, peers over his glasses at Martin, and begins. He's chosen four works, all by twentieth-century composers, one of whom is a friend. None of Charlie's selections, which include a piece he plays on the flügelhorn, are showpieces with fancy fingering or sustained high-register notes. The virtuosity they require is more subtle, calling for delicate phrasing, difficult slurs, long breaths. Most of all, the music he plays demands the kind of sound that Charlie has been refining since he was a young man.

After each piece, Charlie and Martin leave the front of the room. But Charlie takes no long breaks; he seems in a hurry to be done. He plans no encores, though after the last work the audience would gladly welcome many. The best piece on the program, Charlie's finale, is the Sonata for Trumpet by Paul Hindemith.

As the afternoon light fades outside, the room fills with a sound so dark it might be hastening the night. But there is a warmth in the sound, a rich texture that seems synonymous with the colors and shadings of the Rembrandts in the next room. Everyone is deeply moved. Charlie himself is affected by the piece, which he privately believes he plays better than anyone else in the world. No one would disagree this afternoon, but no amount of applause afterward will change Charlie's mind about playing some more

He does stay afterward to greet people though, and it is nearly half an hour before everyone has had a moment with him or Martin, who gracefully accepts compliments for his accompanying. Charlie seems embarrassed by the effusive compliments his fans shower on him. And he organizes no party to visit Amalfi's bar nearby.

When the last person has said goodbye, he and Martha and their daughter head home quietly.

Stage fright is far from uncommon. It has been recognized as a medical problem by the International Conference of Symphony and Opera Musicians (ICSOM). Nearly a quarter of the musicians in a recent ICSOM survey said they suffered from it at least occasionally. Interestingly, the highest incidence was among brass players—partly because their instruments are so prominent that even a small, relatively easy part can make a player anxious. And, of course, many pieces are filled with very difficult parts for the brass.

Moreover, in many works, regardless of difficulty, the brass go long periods without playing anything. In Mahler Two, for example, there is little brass playing in the second movement. In the typical Mozart or Haydn symphony, a brass player may have only a few notes in the entire piece—if he plays at all. "The most nerve–racking time is when you sit too long without playing," says principal trombone Ron Barron. "I'm not nervous when I'm on the spot [with a solo]. I'm less nervous. I'm involved then. In control."

Most of Ron's brass colleagues would concur. As a group, therefore, brass players tend to be higher strung than other instrumentalists. Charlie has lots of company.

The musicians in the ICSOM survey explained that they coped in various ways. Some sought counseling; other engaged in aerobic exercises or yoga. Many admitted having on occasion used a beta blocker, a prescription drug usually administered to cardiac patients. Precisely why the drug helps musicians with stage fright is not clinically clear—it is not a sedative—nor are the long-term side effects certain.

But the short-term benefits are not a mystery. One BSO player ascribes his successful audition for a higher position in the orchestra to his use of the beta blocker Inderal. The first time he competed in such an audition, he was so nervous he missed many notes. He took Inderal before his next attempt for such a promotion and was a completely different player, calm and very sure of himself and his abilities. He won promotion easily.

Though no longer as popular as they were in previous generations, alcohol and tobacco remain prevalent among performing musicians, particularly—in Boston's case—trumpet players. Their liabilities are, of course, well documented and, to a lesser extent, so are their benefits, which include their easy availability. Charlie, Andre, and Peter all smoke cigarettes, and they all drink to a varying extent. In their world of preconcert tension and postperformance letdown, the two drugs are dependable short-term company. Long term, they can also be deadly.

During his entire career, Charlie has smoked cigarettes at work and had a drink before dinner, another when he got home after a concert. Except for the colds he gets often, smoking has never seemed to bother him. He still has the largest lung capacity of any trumpet player he's ever known. The cigarettes are simply a part of his personality, like the beads he wears or the beret he bought in Japan. At home, of course, he smokes only his pipe, which he sometimes substitutes for the Winstons during the day.

But now, with a relatively light load of pieces to perform over the next month, before the schedule picks up again for him with several performances of Mahler Five on the road, Charlie has made a bold, difficult decision he has contemplated for a long time.

He does not pretend that he would be a completely different person without cigarettes. Nor does he believe that the world is going to be a better place if he does something for his health. But his dependency on cigarettes, the knowledge that he needs such a crutch to function, bothers him. And he feels the same way about alcohol. While he enjoyed the little daze Andre's Scotch put him in on the flight back from New York in December, he's usually been just a social drinker. After the magazine piece came out last fall, he didn't go on a bender. But he enjoyed his daily drinks then. It was reassuring to know they would be there.

But that bothers him, too. And when he's been with Dave Monette, who has started teaching Charlie some yoga exercises, he's been perfectly happy without drinking afterward. In fact, he's sometimes experienced a kind of serenity that is liberating. He hasn't wanted a drink then. He's wanted to play the trumpet.

So Charlie takes the step. With the same iron resolve that has driven his response to conductors, his certainty about how to play the trumpet, his willingness to take risks, he smokes his last Winston and has his last bourbon. Simultaneously, Charlie quits cigarettes and alcohol. He still smokes his pipe, but he never bums a cigarette from anyone. And he starts drinking Perrier or nonalcoholic beer. He doesn't cheat once.

The physical change in him is quite immediate. In only a few weeks he looks better. His complexion is brighter and he appears more rested. He doesn't clear his throat as often. And, though he continues to enjoy cooking—his Italian and Indonesian dishes make dinner at the Schlueters' a coveted invitation—he keeps on a regimen with his exercise. He starts to lose the extra weight he carried in his middle. Eventually, he'll need to get some new clothes.

Unlike many people who give up cigarettes or alcohol, Charlie doesn't seem fidgety or irritable. After only a few days of this new life, he is confident enough about his success to tell others what he's doing. The only reward he gives himself is to spend the money he's saving on some expensive imported tobacco for his pipes. Otherwise, his routine and habits remain the same. He still goes to Amalfi's for dinner before a concert, though he resents the $2.50 charged for Perrier and is annoyed the restaurant won't carry nonalcoholic beer for a customer who spends between $100 and $150 a week there. He still sits at the bar there with his friends. He still drinks black coffee while he checks his templates in the Symphony Hall basement.

And he still feels an edge in himself when he walks onstage. He always will. But he puts the edge into his playing more than he ever did. To those listening to him closely, his sound is even warmer and richer. He's still the same Charlie, but something's different. Something's been going on inside him, and the absence of cigarettes and alcohol is only the outward manifestation.

Charlie is really looking forward to playing Mahler Five again now. Lately, he's even taken to joking about Richard Dyer's reviews, which now usually ignore him. He's thinking of calling Richard up, he mentions one day at the hall. "Maybe I'll ask him out to lunch," Charlie says with a broad smile. Of course he never will.

Much has happened in Charlie's life since he won his arbitration. Charlie believes he has met his music director more than halfway, and he would like to think he has something to do with the way the orchestra's esprit de corps has grown.

Charlie wants more than ever to remain in Boston. He feels he belongs here, and he feels his playing this winter has proven again that he deserves to be. He also feels good about himself, good about the decision to quit cigarettes and alcohol. He feels he has taken charge of another part of his life, said goodbye to something that was part of him for a quarter of a century. He wants to look ahead now. Recently he's even calculated how much he'll earn if he keeps playing in the orchestra until he's sixty-five years old (about as much as one of his favorite Boston Celtics stars gets paid in a year)

Just before Seiji returns, the orchestra performs Shostakovich's Thirteenth Symphony, *Babi Yar*, with Kurt Masur conducting. Music director of the Gewandhaus Orchestra of Leipzig, Masur appears regularly with the BSO, and Charlie respects his mastery of the German repertoire. He also enjoys playing for him because he feels that Masur, like Tennstedt, recognizes him as a fine player. Last year, Masur gave Charlie a special bow.

The Shostakovich alternates moods. Parts of the piece are bleak and depressing, others are satirical. Charlie responds to this range of emotion with playing that is by turns touching and boisterous. He never hides his feelings after a concert, and his happiness this late-winter afternoon is a certain indication that he knows he played well again.

He wishes Seiji had heard him today.

SIXTEEN

The week beginning at the end of February is Mstislav Rostropovich week. For Seiji and the orchestra, it is also the start of an early spring. In the joyous atmosphere created by the presence of the great Russian cellist, the hall is a happy place.

Seiji almost misses the start of the week because his mother-in-law is very ill, and he won't leave Japan if her health does not improve. This news sends his aides scurrying to find a substitute conductor for the series of concerts with Rostropovich, who is considered too eminent an artist for the orchestra simply to use one of its assistant conductors.

But the search proves unnecessary. Seiji decides at the last minute he can conduct the concerts, which mean much to him personally. He and Slava, as Seiji calls the cellist, work very well together. Their recording of Dvořák's Cello Concerto has recently been released, and Rostropovich reportedly thinks it's the best recording of that piece he's ever done. The Dvořák is among six works that will be rotated in several concerts, which commemorate Rostropovich's sixtieth birthday.

Seiji's return to Boston ushers in another crazy round of rehearsals, concerts, and orchestral functions. But the tone for the rest of the year is set by the bright spirits of Rostropovich. His contagious warmth as a person and musician affects Seiji, the players, and a huge crew of television reporters who congregate daily for interviews with him.

Seiji blocks out the stress of his mother-in-law's illness and concentrates as he always does on the present. That ability continues to astonish his players.

"The very happy birthday thing," as Seiji characterizes the Rostropovich concerts in his inimitable English, calls for too much music for the orchestra to rehearse properly. The Boccherini concerto on the first program was last performed by the orchestra in 1915, and Seiji had never even heard this piece by the obscure eighteenth-century Italian composer whose speciality was chamber music. "We weren't ready," complains a violist the next day, but no one else seems to mind. Rostropovich wins a rave in the *Globe* from Richard Dyer, who goes on to praise the orchestra as though it were not the same group he panned in the fall. "Under Seiji Ozawa, alert and supportive," Dyer writes, "the BSO sounded fabulous."

After a Friday afternoon performance, Rostropovich and Seiji embrace backstage, not for any camera's benefit but as an expression of their mutual affection. "It's unbelievable what he does," Seiji says of the cellist. Later, Rostropovich meets Seiji and the orchestra's principals to review the Vivaldi concerto they will play on Saturday. Then Rostropovich leaves for another television interview, during which an old friend pokes his head into the dressing room and says in Russian, "Your father's here!" Everyone is in such good humor that the poor joke strikes those who hear it as enormously funny.

Music director of the National Symphony Orchestra in Washington, D.C., Rostropovich cannot seem to resist the urge to conduct, even when he plays the cello. But he does that conducting with his expressive face, raising his eyebrows, furrowing his forehead, and moving his head, all the while staying in a kind of trance brought on by the beauty of the music. He listens intently to the orchestra and whenever he can watches Seiji, who frequently turns his head to the left to peer over his shoulder at the cellist. At these moments they look like two musical friends exchanging knowing glances. The orchestra members seem to realize that the feeling between the two men is genuine, and they catch it in their own playing. The audiences for the Rostropovich concerts, all sellouts, sense it, too. There is virtually none of the sneezing and coughing from the audience that usually accompany any concert.

Seiji also spends part of the week listening to the finalists for the open trumpet position. He decides quickly and firmly on Tim Morrison, who played in the orchestra a few years earlier before joining the Empire Brass for two seasons. (Feeling he's not yet ready for such a jump in his career, and not interested in the Boston Pops principal work that goes with the job, Randy Croley doesn't try out.)

An appearance by Seiji at the orchestra's annual fund-raising benefit, "Salute to Symphony," precedes a locally televised concert he conducts for that same purpose. He also leads two rehearsals for the Mahler Five–Haydn One Hundred concerts the orchestra will perform on the road. He wishes after a so-so New Haven performance that there'd been three rehearsals, but he doesn't let it upset him. His standards for the orchestra have simply gotten higher, and he's sure the musicians' playing will pick up again in Philadelphia or Washington, as it does.

He gives Charlie the first bow in Washington, the last stop on this mini-tour. "Seiji must still be feeling guilty about the magazine article," Charlie says afterward, but he's joking. Seiji still hasn't said anything to him, but Charlie's feeling too good about himself to complain. He hasn't had a cigarette or drink in over a month now.

The upbeat mood lingers through the spring. One warm March Friday afternoon, assistant conductor Carl St. Clair lingers in the library, checking parts for several youth concerts he will·conduct in a few weeks. Spontaneously, he says to the others in the room, "Nice day, nice music."

Many of the musicians give concerts of their own. A chamber music recital draws a small but enthusiastic crowd to a church in suburban Watertown, Massachusetts, where violist Patti McCarty and two other women—a singer and a pianist—perform seven works by American women composers. Patti seems completely unaffected by nervousness and plays with zest and conviction. To be a soloist is what she dreams of.

Her husband, Ron Wilkison, doesn't come. "He was afraid there wouldn't be any other men here!" Patti says afterward. He's just bought a new computer, and he spends the evening of Patti's recital at home, perfecting his understanding of an investment program that he humorously hopes will make them wealthy.

In early April a special nonsubscription concert presents the world premiere of a work commissioned for the Tanglewood Festival Chorus, Donald Martino's *The White Island*. The piece is not a hit with the players, some of whom joke backstage about tickets being given away. John Oliver conducts; he's just returned from a cross-country trip to audition singers for this summer's Tanglewood classes. There's a big party in the Cohen Annex afterward. There, wearing pastel sunglasses and matching socks, Richard Dyer steers the *Globe's* society reporter, Carol Flake, around the crowd and tells her facetiously he'll "look for people who will say nasty things" for Flake's column.

Malcolm apologizes to Dan Gustin for missing an administrative meeting he'd been asked to attend as concertmaster. But he isn't sorry about the reason that kept him away. "I had to practice," he says, certain that that excuse covers just about anything.

The week's vacation Malcolm took to go cross-country skiing in Vermont, after all the time he was out sick in the fall, prompted one of the Friday afternoon grande dames to turn to the woman sitting next to her and remark, "He's never here." Some of the players complain among themselves, too. But few will criticize the concertmaster's playing. This winter, in the difficult solos in Strauss's *Ein Heldenleben*, Malcolm's sound was soaring and lyric, his playing in the upper register delicate and precise.

Charlie continues to thrive on his sobriety. He's been trying different kinds of nonalcoholic beer, and he's thinking of boycotting Amalfi's if the bar doesn't start stocking one of them.

By an informal count, he's had only one rough review all winter, a description of the trumpets as "blatant" in a Strauss work. He continues to credit his Monette trumpet for his playing. But his excited response to the Tanglewood schedule reveals how much he has changed. During the second July weekend, the orchestra will perform Strauss's *Alpine Symphony* and, the following night, Sibelius Two and Scriabin's *Poem of Ecstasy*. All call for heroic work by the trumpets, especially the Scriabin, during which Charlie will have to play many demanding, extended solos. Then, on a Sunday afternoon in early August, there will be another performance of Mahler Five, followed later in the month by Mahler One (which the orchestra will perform several times next season in Boston). The summer will end with yet another work in which Charlie and the brass are prominent, Verdi's *Requiem*.

Charlie wonders what his lip is going to feel like after the night he plays the Sibelius and the Scriabin, but he's almost boasting when he says this. Better than do Costa and Seiji, who approved this program, he knows how good he'll have to be that night. And in that sense, the program is a sign of their confidence in him, not in the particular brand of trumpet he happens to play. Charlie doesn't seem to have realized that yet, but he can't wait for the summer. He begins to tell his friends about it, hoping they will be there.

By April, Seiji's spirits are buoyant. He has had a reunion engagement in Toronto, where he was music director in the early 1970s. And *Time* magazine has published a favorable article about him, focusing on a documentary on him that was shown nationally in late March on PBS. Produced by a subsidiary of CAMI, Seiji's management agency, the film conveys a confident, intelligent, humorous man who loves his work. In substance and style, the film is the complete opposite of the *Boston Magazine* profile last fall. To the administrators who work with Seiji, the release of the film conveys a message more important than its content: Seiji's a star.

But Seiji is more excited about his orchestra than about himself. His confidence stems in part from a tape of the Mahler Two recording he's just heard. It was sent from Holland for his approval, and listening to it has confirmed Seiji's belief that this is the best recording he's made with the orchestra. He's thrilled with his group's playing, but he doesn't tell them so now. They have too much to do, and he wants to choose the right moment, perhaps this summer. As Charlie knows very well, Seiji never hurries these things. He always waits, to be certain of his convictions.

The most important work of the spring for Seiji and the orchestra is a semistaged presentation of Alban Berg's tragic masterpiece of betrayal and murder, *Wozzeck*. Six rehearsals have been scheduled for three performances of the opera, the single work Seiji will conduct during the week between Passover and Easter. A large cast of singers, headed by soprano Hildegard Behrens, and the Tanglewood Festival Chorus join the orchestra for the most complex piece Seiji has ever conducted in Boston. Oboist Alfred Genovese, who used to play in the Metropolitan Opera's orchestra, spreads word that the Met had many more rehearsals for *Wozzeck*. For a while, some of the players take this as a sign there will be trouble. But the opposite is clearly the case.

For the orchestra to learn this piece so quickly is astonishing. Fully half the players have never performed the complete, three-act opera before, since the only previous full BSO performances took place in 1969, before Seiji became music director. Dedicated to Mahler's widow, Alma, the score calls for a Mahler-sized orchestra, and each of the parts is extremely complicated. Yet Seiji commits the entire work to memory. In the basement den of his Newton home, its wall-length bookshelves filled with all his scores, Seiji reviews the piece early each morning before Peppino drives him to the hall for the day's rehearsal. In his specially bound, personal copy of the score, the German text has been translated into Japanese. But that is the only help he receives, astounding Charlie and the other players, who all must put in extra practice hours on their own individual parts.

Seiji works the musicians very hard, taking charge at each rehearsal as if he'd been conducting the opera for years. His famous concentration is so total that he seems completely undistracted by the presence of an unusually large number of visitors. One night the entire board of trustees attends the dress rehearsal, "for development purposes," Anne Parsons explains to the players in a memorandum. (In other words, the trustees' attendance is a reward for the monetary gifts they are expected to make.)

During a rare quiet moment in the midst of the *Wozzeck* rehearsals, Seiji takes Charlie aside for a brief talk. Charlie's heart is pounding. He knows he's playing *Wozzeck* well. Even his colleagues in the trumpet section, who rarely talk about one another's playing, have said so. "The high, soft sections are so difficult, and Charlie does them very well," says Peter Chapman, impressed. What could Seiji want from him now?

Their talk is brief; Seiji as usual has lots else on his mind this week. But Seiji says the words that Charlie has stopped hoping he would hear, that he really thought Seiji would never use. Without actually taking back what he said to the *Boston Magazine* reporter, Seiji apologizes for speaking to her about Charlie.

Later, Charlie wishes Seiji had said more. But nevertheless, with unexpected suddenness, Charlie has been liberated from a tension that had become a constant in his life. He knows he will always think twice before he speaks with Seiji, and he will always wonder how he and the music director ever became at odds in the first place. But something very significant has changed in their relationship. The war is over.

As if to assure himself of this, during another rehearsal Charlie walks over to the podium after Seiji calls for a break and asks Seiji about a passage.

Except for Malcolm and a few others, most of the musicians have left the stage, and the auditorium seats are dark and empty. Stepping down from the podium, Seiji looks over Charlie's left arm, which is pointing toward the questioned spot. He nods his head in recognition of the question's appropriateness. And then Seiji answers Charlie, all the while still looking at the music, and as he does his right arm reaches around his embattled trumpet player and pats Charlie on the back.

The day before the final *Wozzeck* performance, a very happy Charlie celebrates his forty-eighth birthday.

Wozzeck is presented with one "set"—a platform in the center of the orchestra on which the singers perform. Wearing simple costumes, the cast act out their parts with gestures, highlighted by effective lighting. The story and the music rush toward the tragic conclusion in a dizzying succession of short scenes, culminating in a supremely moving sequence of full-orchestra chords. Symphony Hall is hushed when the piece ends, very quietly, and for several seconds there is a kind of gasp in the audience, finally followed by sustained cheering, as if that release was in response to a collective catharsis. Seiji knows these performances are a supreme achievement, and he says later that conducting them was like participating in chamber music: He wasn't really needed. "*Wozzeck*, the last performance, I just enjoyed it."

After the *Wozzeck* performances, hailed even by Richard Dyer as "overwhelmingly powerful, theatrical, emotional and compassionate," the end of the season's Liszt and Bruckner are almost an anticlimax (though piano soloist Krystian Zimerman's playing in several performances and recording sessions is kinetic).

But Dyer mixes abuse with praise for the music director and orchestra in his season summary. And he adds with what must have been unintended irony, "A rocky year for the BSO trumpets." Richard Dyer hasn't spoken with Charlie since the day they met on the train in Japan and, many feel, hasn't listened to him in a long time either. By the time these words have been published in the *Globe*, Charlie and the other principals are in Japan, where the BSO Chamber Players will tour for two weeks. Seiji's there, too. Soon he will conduct the first-ever radio broadcast of digitally encoded sound. Eventually, Seiji will return to the States via Paris and Berlin for the opening weekend of the Tanglewood summer season in July.

Charlie spends much of June in Wyoming, teaching at the Grand Teton Orchestral Seminar. There, on a Saturday in the middle of the month, he receives a call that shatters him emotionally once again. It's about Andre Côme, the second trumpet and Charlie's friend, who checked into a hospital the day before for long-planned surgery. Fifty-three years old, Andre has been literally at Charlie's side during all of Charlie's six seasons with the orchestra. Now, Charlie learns, looking out the window at the Rockies, Andre is dead.

SEVENTEEN

*C*harlie immediately flies home to play in the memorial service for his friend. Afterward, painfully, there is nothing to do but return to Wyoming. The first Tanglewood rehearsal is still two weeks away, and keeping busy has always been Charlie's best antidote to distress.

Because Andre would have been out recuperating from his surgery had it been successful, the orchestra had already engaged Randy Croley to take his place until he would have returned. Randy, who spent most of the winter at home in Tennessee, will join the orchestra again temporarily, this time as fourth trumpet, while Charles Daval will remain at third and Peter Chapman will play second. For Randy, this is a tremendous opportunity to show Charlie and the rest of the orchestra that he can play with them over a period of time, not just for one concert or a special piece. Randy is a little in awe of his responsibility, but his first, overwhelming emotion is sadness at Andre's death.

Charlie no longer participates in conversations about his friend. He'll listen to others swapping stories about Andre, but he won't add any himself. He tries to accept the death and move on, hard as that is. Only a few years apart in age, the two men were kindred spirits in some ways. Like Charlie, Andre had a wonderful sense of humor and great affection for other people. And also like Charlie, he was neither pretentious nor arrogant. But Charlie can't bring himself to talk about him now.

Charlie does give his blessing to Peter Chapman's suggestion that there be some kind of concert in Andre's memory during the summer, but he lets Peter organize it. The best thing he can do during the long summer season is play his heart out, and he does. For Charlie, this summer becomes one continuous fantastic performance, as though his whole life has been a preparation for it.

From far away, beyond the crowded section of the huge lawn near Tanglewood's outdoor auditorium—the Music Shed—the stage on summer concert nights seems a giant, bright jewel in a magic kingdom. The air smells of cut grass and picnic food. When the voices of concertgoers quiet before the music begins, wineglasses tinkle, a baby cries, and then the applause for the conductor wells up from within the Shed and wafts over the lawn and the lake beyond.

Tonight is Saturday, July 11, and the conductor is a Russian, Gennady Rozhdestvensky. This is the second night of the second Tanglewood weekend of the summer. It is hot and sticky, but not uncomfortably so. The Shed, which seats five thousand, is quite full, and several thousand more people are spread out on blankets and seated on folding chairs on the beautifully kept, weedless lawn. Scattered throughout the large, buzzing crowd are a few dozen friends of Charlie Schlueter's. They've come from as far away as

Chicago and as near as Stockbridge, the next town, to hear Charlie play.

It's intermission now, almost ten o'clock. The concert began with the wonderfully melodic Second Symphony of Sibelius and a Moussorgsky song cycle. Rozhdestvensky last conducted the BSO in 1979. A balding man, with what hair he has left long and trailing behind his ears and down his neck, Rozhdestvensky wears glasses when he conducts. He doesn't use a podium, but stands right on the stage floor, with the musicians on risers before him. Sometimes, his paunch swelling with his breathing, he hardly moves the rest of his body, as though he didn't really think the players needed much guidance from him. In fact, during the rehearsal for a different concert, he skipped over several parts of another symphony, astounding the players by announcing that they must already know it. In response, they have performed tonight with self-indulgent assurance and fervor. Charlie and two other trumpets raised the roof of the Shed with the Sibelius symphony's final, sweeping chords. Typically, this piece closes concerts on which it is programmed because most other works sound anticlimactic after it.

But after intermission comes the Scriabin. Finished in 1907 by a composer best known for his virtuosic piano pieces, the *Poem of Ecstasy* is a mishmash of overused themes and overdone orchestral effects that would probably never be performed today were it not for the first trumpet's part. There is nothing else in the trumpet literature like it: long sustained high notes, difficult slurs, complicated rhythmic and dynamic effects, all brought together in the main, repeated theme of the piece, which Scriabin called "Self-assertion." At its most climactic, that theme overrides the huge sound of the entire orchestra, which plays at the same time. This is less a piece of music than a trumpeter's orgy.

Charlie waits out the final intermission minutes backstage with the aplomb of a man who would rather be playing the Scriabin than doing anything else in the world right now. With Dave Monette, who's flown from Chicago for this concert, he checks his trumpet's valves to be certain they have the proper amount of Tom Crown valve oil. He makes no cracks now about mistakes, no references to blowing the performance he is about to give. He laughs about having to play this piece after the Sibelius. Dave chats with the other trumpeters—the score calls for five—who have all either bought or ordered Monette trumpets. By the fall, the entire BSO trumpet section will be playing Dave's instruments.

With the p.a. announcement for the players to be onstage, Dave leaves to find his seat in the Shed. Just three years since Charlie first played a Monette trumpet here, Dave's dream of running his own company has grown beyond his wildest imagining. But more important to Dave tonight than his good fortune is the change in Charlie since then, even since the late fall when Charlie played Mahler Five.

With Martha, and with many thousands of strangers, Dave waits now in the darkened Shed for the Scriabin to begin. Charlie's entrance doesn't come right at the start. The orchestra plays first, but the music is clearly pointing toward the trumpet. And then, suddenly, there is the Schlueter sound. Perfect intonation tonight. Clear, golden tones, with generous vibrato as the theme begins to soar. Long before Charlie hits a high E flat, everyone listening realizes this performance is in a class of its own. Many in the audience have never before heard trumpet playing this sure and appropriately full of itself, and even players in the orchestra, notoriously judgmental of one another, sense that their colleague is coming into his own—that he is playing again as he did in his audition.

Charlie doesn't miss one note in the Scriabin, and when the piece concludes the Shed erupts in the kind of shouting usually heard at a sporting event. Ever so slowly, Rozhdestvensky walks offstage and then returns. The shouting continues, and Rozhdestvensky stops and points toward the trumpet section, toward Charlie. It is the only solo bow he gives. Charlie stands and lifts his head, and the other trumpeters and then many of the other players join in the applause.

Later, Charlie's friends gather by a kind of portico to one side of the Shed, on a small expanse of lawn near the Tanglewood Tent, an outdoor bar for the orchestra's patrons. They wait there while Charlie changes his clothes backstage. Wearing a loose-fitting sport shirt that hangs outside the belt of his pants, smoking his pipe, and carrying his trumpet in a leather case over one shoulder, Charlie walks through the door to the porch. Spontaneously, the cheering begins all over again, his friends and wife clapping and crying, "Bravo! Bravo!" in the fragrant summer air of this night of nights in Charlie's career.

Charlie is overcome. He stands still for a moment to gather himself. Finally, he begins to greet people. Many give him huge hugs. To Martha and Dave and those who know Charlie best, the happy emotion of this moment is almost more than they can bear.

"Let's go skinny-dipping," says Martha. Dave and a few others have decided to cool off at one of the beaches on the Stockbridge Bowl. Martha wants to go and she wants Charlie to come along.

Charlie smiles, but he's so exhausted he can almost begin to feel his legs giving out from under him. And he's had enough of other people tonight. He only wants to be with her. Without his saying so, she understands.

The swimmers go and, gradually, so do the others. The Shed is now completely empty. Perhaps somewhere in the vicinity a guard still walks the quiet grounds, but to Charlie and Martha it looks like they're the last to leave. They can't see anyone as they walk along one side of the Shed, toward the canopy leading to the parking lot reserved for box seat holders and some of the players. The warm night is filled with insect sounds and the occasional distant drone of a car. Charlie is staying at a bed-and-breakfast run by Ron Barron as a summer sideline to his trombone playing. Martha's here only for the weekend, she will go back to Boston to paint. They head out together now, Charlie's loves, his trumpet and his wife, to either side of him, one on each arm.

Three weeks later, outside the Shed, the sun shines on the Berkshire hills, and the air on this first Sunday in August is hot and muggy. Congressional hearings on the Iran-Contra affair have made headlines all summer. FOUR HUNDRED DIE AS IRANIAN MARCHERS BATTLE SAUDI POLICE IN MECCA, reports *The New York Times*, which many Tanglewood listeners have brought with them to the afternoon's final BSO performance of Mahler Five this year. Some in the audience have been stationed on their blankets since the gates opened at 12:30, two hours before the opening notes of the concert.

Malcolm is absent today. His health is fine, but he has been on the golf course since early morning. He is golfing because he was a soloist a week ago and has an extra day off in return. The summer still has a few weeks to go, and Malcolm will be a soloist again with the orchestra soon. But right now Malcolm is happy about his game. He's even planning to play in a tournament the last weekend of the season, when the orchestra and chorus will perform the Verdi *Requiem*. He's going to ask the pro at the Stockbridge Golf Club to give him the latest Saturday afternoon starting time, so he can play in the morning's Verdi rehearsal. Then, on that Sunday, he'll ask for the first morning tee time, so if he's lucky, he'll just get in his Sunday round before Colleen picks him up and takes the short cut from Stockbridge to Tanglewood for the afternoon concert.

One or two of his colleagues are jealous because he isn't here today for Mahler Five, but Malcolm has contributed to this performance already. The bowings are still his, and following his lead, the strings will play their parts the way Malcolm does, which for this composer is with a dark, rich sound that beautifully complements that of Charlie and the brass.

Once again, the orchestra is on, this time with a piece of music worthy of the players' finest abilities. The players realize it, too, but few will ever credit Seiji for the quality of the work they put into preparing for this performance. Actually, the musicians seem to play best when they're a little angry at their conductor.

A tremendous roar erupts when the symphony ends. Seiji calls for solo bows from the orchestra's different sections by miming the shapes of the instruments they play. When Seiji doesn't do that for the clarinets, Buddy Wright stands anyway and takes his own bow. The audience in the Shed stands, and many crowd into the expensive front seats, simply to be nearer the stage as they cheer.

Soon, the Shed has emptied and Seiji appears to make a brief toast to the Tanglewood ushers, who have gathered in the back of the Shed for a party in their own honor. Peppino has parked the Lincoln Continental to one side of the Shed and stands waiting to drive Seiji home. Wearing a T-shirt now, Seiji drinks part of a beer and then quickly departs.

In the Tanglewood Tent, Charlie is feted by Roger Voisin, the elegant principal trumpet for many years (Charlie's position has been endowed in Voisin's name). Charlie declines Voisin's gracious offer of champagne. So Voisin buys him a Perrier and toasts his playing in the Mahler.

Later, relaxing in his house on Stockbridge Mountain, with its spectacular view to the west, Seiji reminisces about the Mahler Five concert. Seiji's family was here for part of the summer. His son played basketball in a court with fiberglass backboard at the end of the driveway. Now his son and wife have returned to Japan. Seiji's alone in the house, except for his cook and his daughter, whom he is teaching to drive the family's Tanglewood car, a Mercedes.

"The orchestra knew this piece," Seiji says with great understatement. "But it could have gone either way." Not until ten minutes into the Mahler, after Charlie's stirring fanfare and much of the first movement, did Seiji admit to himself what everyone else listening could also hear. Until then, he was still wary of how Charlie would play.

Conducting the Mahler, Seiji paid special attention to his principal trumpet player. There is still tension between the two men, and Seiji comments that he still has to "control" Charlie when there is a fortissimo. But Seiji has decided Charlie is "a good musician," and he follows his comment with a laugh. "We control each other!" he says. Seiji means that he knows Charlie watches him, too.

After the last Tanglewood concert of the year, Seiji's mother, a small, dignified presence in her son's musical life, keeps him company in his dressing room, where he sips champagne with several people retiring from the orchestra. A few of the other players poke their heads in to say goodbye until the fall. In the hallways, the players gossip about the orchestra's new cause, Seiji's handling of the replacement for retiring principal oboist Ralph Gomberg. BSO member Alfred Genovese won the audition committee's endorsement, but Seiji has instead made him "acting principal," a temporary replacement.

Seiji leaves his dressing room now and walks outside to the Tanglewood Tent. There, some of the players and singers mingle with patrons over drinks. Seiji has been asked to thank the benefactors, but he turns his remarks into a brief impromptu speech about Andre Côme and another orchestra member, violist Bernard Kadinoff, who died very suddenly during the summer.

A few days before, Seiji and many of the orchestra's players performed in a memorial concert for Andre. The stage in Tanglewood's Theatre–Concert Hall, a smaller auditorium across the lawn from the Music Shed, was crowded that night with musicians from different eras in the orchestra's life. Charlie and his three immediate predecessors as principal trumpet played together for the first time, as did Malcolm and his predecessor Joseph Silverstein. The program was varied, ending with the stirring overture to Handel's *Music for the Royal Fireworks*. All the musicians donated their services, with proceeds from ticket sales going toward a Tanglewood scholarship in Andre's name. The playing in every piece was not perfect, but the musicians were united that night as performers. They had all at one time in their lives been members of the orchestra with Andre, and that night, as a tribute to his memory, they played in concert.

Now, Seiji links Bernie's name and Andre's with the Verdi *Requiem* he has just conducted. Choking on emotion, Seiji can finally only repeat himself, "Thank you, thank you," and he leaves.

After the closing of Tanglewood, the lovely grounds are soon deserted. In the administrative offices, secretaries quickly pack their files for shipment back to Boston, where preparations will immediately begin for the next season, a month away. The Tanglewood gift shop still displays posters of Seiji Ozawa, and Tanglewood sweatshirts in gray, green, and purple, but the store is closed until the following summer.

Now, past that shop and through the gate, left unlocked for the occasional tourist, water sprinklers send their spray into the late-summer air, on cool nights already smelling of early autumn. Beyond the lawn's vast horizon, the leaves in a few of the trees have started to show some seasonal color. The Shed stands empty, the eaves of the old auditorium creaking in the wind. The orchestra's year is over.

"Every year is critical," Malcolm says. "Even most weeks, most concerts." This past year has seen the reemergence of the orchestra in its Mahler cycle as a major recording ensemble, and the reaffirmation in its *Wozzeck* concerts of its great ability with very difficult repertoire. But even more important, the year has been one of personal growth for Seiji and his group, growth in their spirit and their ability to work together.

"The orchestra is always in transition," Malcolm concludes. "But there are threads that remain, building a tradition, building a personality. That's what music is all about. It is such a true yet abstract image of life. It can't be anything but that, a reflection and expression of life."

Seiji stays in the Berkshires a few more days to celebrate his fifty-second birthday before going home to Japan for several weeks.

Malcolm and Colleen are getting married, and then they're returning to Stockbridge, where Malcolm is going to compete in the golf club's championship. He thinks he has a good chance of winning.

Charlie is driving west to visit relatives in Du Quoin and to see Dave Monette in Chicago. He's going to call on one of his old trumpet teachers who is now in a nursing home. And Charlie is thinking about buying a word processor. He's planning to use it to write a book about how to play the trumpet.

SOURCES AND ACKNOWLEDGMENTS

*M*ost of this book is based on my own reporting over a period that began in 1984 with a magazine piece about Malcolm Lowe's appointment as concertmaster and continued the following year with a monthly magazine column about classical music in the Boston area. During the 1986–87 BSO season, I attended most of the orchestra's concerts and many of its rehearsals, traveled with the orchestra on some of its tours, and spoke with most of the musicians and BSO staff in a process that went on after the season ended. Eventually, I made over one hundred trips, principally to Boston and Tanglewood, to interview and observe the people who appear in this book. The BSO did not officially authorize my work, but it would have been impossible to complete my research without the cooperation and help of a great many people connected with the orchestra.

I am especially grateful to Seiji Ozawa for the time he gave me and for his permission, jointly with that of the Players Committee, to sit in on rehearsals and recording sessions usually closed to visitors. Likewise, my thanks to John Oliver for welcoming me to his rehearsals and to the chorus auditions, and for agreeing to several interviews.

Malcolm Lowe answered countless questions about his music making and shared with me his life at home, in the hall, and on the golf course. Many others in the orchestra accepted my presence backstage and spoke with me about what they do. Most of their names already appear in my narrative of the 1986–87 season; to all of them, a collective thanks—and a personal one to Amnon Levy and, for their hospitality, Ron Wilkison and Patti McCarty.

Charlie Schlueter entrusted me with the story of his life and career and even let me play several of his trumpets. More than any other person, he enabled me to explore the world of the orchestra offstage. He was patient and kind; he introduced me to his family, his friends, and his students; and he was open. He never refused to answer a question or asked to speak off the record. He asked nothing in return, nor did he question my judgment when it was clear from what I said that we disagreed about some point or person or performance. My thanks to Charlie are many and deep.

My thanks also go to the many BSO staff members who figure in the text. Others helped me behind the scenes. In the press office, Caroline Smedvig and Vera Gold made my way easier at the start and happy always; Lesley Ploof, Joyce Spinney, and Bernadette Horgan responded graciously to all my requests and offered me their phones and desks. Special thanks to Bill McRae at the stage door and Marty Burlingame and James Harper in the library. And thank you, Bruce Creditor, Kath Fitzgerald, Patricia Halligan, Nancy Knutsen, John Marksbury, Cleveland Morrison, Nancy Phillips, and James Whitaker.

In addition to the other people—musicians and nonmusicians

alike—mentioned in the book, I am grateful to the Carbondale (Illinois) Chamber of Commerce, Larry Davis, Terry Kahn, David Maguire, Stephen Parkany, Maurice Peress, Harold Prenatt, William Rotkiewicz, Henry Rubin, Chris Sorrentino, Robin Stone, Joel Upton, and Bruce Wilcox.

Secondary material about the BSO is rich and plentiful. I am indebted to the BSO's Steven Ledbetter and Marc Mandel for their fine notes in the orchestra's program books. The orchestra's own *The Orchestra Book* (third edition, 1983–84) was a good place to check biographical facts. *Symphony Hall, Boston*, by H. Earle Johnson (Boston: Little, Brown and Company, 1950) was a useful historical resource. The files and current issues of *The Boston Globe* were invaluable, including an early article on Charlie Schlueter by M. R. Montgomery.

For general musical references, I consulted the following:

Apel, Willi, and Ralph T. Daniel, editors. *The Harvard Brief Dictionary of Music.* New York: Washington Square Press, 1960.

Del Mar, Norman. *The Anatomy of the Orchestra*, revised edition Berkeley and Los Angeles: University of California Press, 1983.

Grout, Donald Jay. *A History of Western Music*, third edition. New York: W. W. Norton and Company, 1980.

Kennedy, Michael, editor. *The Concise Oxford Dictionary of Music*, third edition. Oxford: Oxford University Press, 1980.

Moravcsik, Michael J. *Musical Sound: An Introduction to the Physics of Music.* New York: Paragon, 1987.

Peyser, Joan, editor. *The Orchestra: Origins and Transformations.* New York: Charles Scribner's Sons, 1986.

For more specific musical background and references, I also consulted:

American Symphony Orchestra League. *Principles of Orchestra Management*. Washington, D.C.: 1985.

Bate, Philip. "Valve." *The New Grove Dictionary of Music and Musicians*. New York: Macmillan, 1980.

Chambers, Jack. *Milestones 1*. New York: Beech Tree, 1983.

Dundas, Richard J. *Brass Musical Instruments*. Cincinnati: Queen City Brass Publications, 1986.

Epstein, Helen. *Music Talks*. New York: McGraw-Hill, 1987.

Fishbein, Martin, Susan E. Middlestadt, et al. "Medical Problems Among ICSOM Musicians: Overview of a National Survey." *Medical Problems of Performing Artists*, Volume 3, Number 1 (March 1988).

Flesch, Carl. *Violin Fingering*. London: Barrie and Rockliff, 1966.

Forrester, Maureen, with Marci McDonald. *Out of Character*. Toronto: McClelland and Stewart, 1986.

Galamian, Ivan. *Principles of Violin Playing and Teaching*. Englewood Cliffs, N.J.: Prentice-Hall, 1962.

Hart, Philip. *Conductors: A New Generation*. New York: Charles Scribner's Sons, 1979.

Horne, Marilyn, with Jane Scovell. *My Life*. New York: Atheneum, 1984.

Horowitz, Joseph. *Understanding Toscanini*. New York: Knopf, 1987.

Philipson, Susan. "A brassy touch makes a Monet of a Monette." *Chicago Tribune*, October 4, 1987.

Porter, Andrew. *Musical Events*. New York: Summit, 1987.

Rubin, David M. "Ronald Wilford: Maker & Breaker." *Musical America*, September 1988.

Steinberg, Michael. "Ozawa, Seiji." *The New Grove Dictionary of Music and Musicians*. New York: Macmillan, 1980.

Tarr, Edward H. "Trumpet." *The New Grove Dictionary of Music and Musicians*. New York: Macmillan, 1980.

Because so much of the music performed by the BSO in 1986–87 was by Mahler, I consulted virtually everything in print in English by and about him. Especially helpful were:

Banks, Paul, and Donald Mitchell. "Mahler, Gustav." *The New Grove Dictionary of Music and Musicians*. New York: Macmillan, 1980.

Blaupof, Hertha, editor. *Gustav Mahler–Richard Strauss: Correspondence, 1888–1911*. Chicago: University of Chicago Press, 1984.

Blaukopf, Kurt, with Zoltan Roma. *Mahler: A Documentary Study*. New York: Oxford University Press, 1976.

Cooke, Deryck. *Gustav Mahler: An Introduction*. Cambridge: Cambridge University Press, 1980.

de La Grange, Henry-Louis. *Mahler*, Volume I. Garden City, N.Y.: Doubleday, 1973.

de La Grange, Henry-Louis. "Mahler: Symphony no. 5." Deutsche Grammophon, 1985.

Kaplan, Gilbert E. "How Mahler performed his Second Symphony." *The Musical Times*, May 1986.

Kennedy, Michael. *Mahler*. London: J. M. Dent and Sons, 1974.

Mahler, Alma. *Gustav Mahler: Memories and Letters*. Donald Mitchell, editor. Seattle: University of Washington Press, 1975.

Martner, Knud, editor. *Gustav Mahler: Selected Letters*. Translated by Eithene Wilkins, Ernst Kaiser, and Bill Hopkins. New York: Farrar, Straus and Giroux, 1979.

Mitchell, Donald. *Gustav Mahler: The Wunderhorn Years*. Berkeley: University of California Press, 1980.

Mitchell, Donald. *Gustav Mahler: Songs and Symphonies of Life and Death*. Berkeley: University of California Press, 1985.

Parkany, Stephen. "Gustav Mahler: Symphony no. 2." San Francisco Symphony, 1986.

Schoenberg, Arnold. "Gustav Mahler" in *Style and Idea*. London: Faber and Faber, 1975.

Walter, Bruno. *Gustav Mahler*. Translated by James Galsten. New York: Greystone, 1970.

Quotations from Mahler's writings are taken from the above, but for translations of the Mahler Two text I usually relied on the BSO. The Berg quotation is from *Alban Berg: Letters to his Wife*, edited and translated by Bernard Gunn. (London: Faber and Faber, 1971). The Poulenc quotation is from his *Diary of My Songs*, translated by Winifred Radford (London: Victor Gollancz, 1985). Eloise Ristad's *A Soprano on Her Head* is published by Real People Press (Moab, Utah: 1982).

I also consulted *The Complete Illustrated Book of Yoga*, by Swami Vishnudevananda (New York: Pocket Books, Simon & Schuster, 1972) and *The Schwann Record and Tape Guide*.

I am indebted to Mike Kurrier at the Hampshire College Library and to Gail Sommers at the University of Massachusetts at Amherst Library. Thanks, also, to the Jones Library in Amherst, the Smith College Library, the Amherst College Library, and Howard Gersten of the Jeffrey Amherst Bookshop.

The revised score of Mahler Two is published by Universal Edition, copyright by the International Gustav Mahler Society. My understanding of the piece was aided greatly by the facsimile of the manuscript published, with additional material, by the Kaplan Foundation (New York: 1986). I also consulted other Mahler symphonic and vocal scores, the trumpet part from Scriabin's *Poem of Ecstasy* published in *Orchestral Excerpts*, Volume III (New York: International Music Company) and J. B. Arban's *Complete Conservatory Method for Trumpet* (Boston: Carl Fischer, 1936).

During my research, I listened to more than two dozen different recordings of Mahler Two, as well as numerous other recordings of other works, many by Mahler, and other recordings by

Sources and Acknowledgments

268

the BSO. *The Symphonies of Gustav Mahler: A Critical Discography* by Lewis M. Smoley (New York: Greenwood Press, 1986), though highly opinionated, was a useful volume to me.

The splendid BSO recording of Mahler Two was issued late in 1987 by Philips and is available on LP, cassette, and compact disc. The BSO's earlier recording of Mahler Eight is also available, as is a new recording of Mahler Four. Other recordings in the series are forthcoming.

Leonard Bernstein has also been recording the Mahler cycle—again—and his reading of Mahler Two with the New York Philharmonic (on Deutsche Grammophon) is illuminating for its tempo contrasts to the BSO's. Gilbert Kaplan has recently recorded the symphony with the London Symphony Orchestra, as has Simon Rattle with the City of Birmingham Symphony Orchestra. The classic recording remains Bruno Walter's, recently reissued on CD, with Maureen Forrester as the contralto.

The other three recordings the BSO made in 1986–87 have all been issued on Deutsche Grammophon. Especially good is the Prokofiev *Romeo and Juliet*. As the Boston Pops, the orchestra continues to produce several recordings a year for Philips, with John Williams conducting. New releases include *Bernstein by Boston* and *Swing, Swing, Swing*.

A 1981 Pro Arte release of Tchaikovsky's *Swan Lake* (Suite), Leonard Slatkin conducting the Minnesota Orchestra, features a gorgeous cornet solo by Charlie Schlueter in the "Neapolitan Dance." With three other BSO members and some players from the New York Philharmonic, Charlie appears on a new Canadian Brass recording issued by CBS.

Throughout my work on this book, my children, Christian and Anna, were a constant reminder of the joy that music also inspires. My wife, Bonnie, gave me her unwavering support and her editorial help. My brother, Nils, a composer, read the manuscript in draft. For an early reading and his counsel, I am grateful to Richard Todd. My thanks also to Susan Todd, to David and Sarah for bed and board, to Tracy for being there, to Bill Hart, and to my agent, John A. Ware.

James Landis at Morrow gave me his friendship and encouragement and introduced me to my editor, Jeanne F. Bernkopf. My thanks to them both for believing in me and in this book are immense, my gratitude to Jeanne for her guidance and care incalculable.

Also at Morrow, I wish to thank Christine Monroe, Lori Ames, Susan Halligan, Larry Norton, and Lisa Queen, and at the Hearst Corporation, Robert Hawley.

I began attending concerts by the Boston Symphony Orchestra at Tanglewood when I was a very young child. My father, Hans, an organist and choral director, had been a member of Tanglewood's first class for conductors in 1940, and my mother, Ruth, is a singer. I learned to love music through them, and this is their book, too.